THE NEW CAMBRIDGE SHAKESPEARE

GENERAL EDITOR
Brian Gibbons

ASSOCIATE GENERAL EDITOR
A. R. Braunmuller

From the publication of the first volumes in 1984 the General Editor of the New Cambridge Shakespeare was Philip Brockbank and the Associate General Editors were Brian Gibbons and Robin Hood. From 1990 to 1994 the General Editor was Brian Gibbons and the Associate General Editors were A. R. Braunmuller and Robin Hood.

TITUS ANDRONICUS

Titus Andronicus is still regarded by many as a bad play of dubious authorship. Its adversaries have abhorred the violence of the action and the apparent lapses in the quality of the verse. Since 1945, however, the play has been taken increasingly seriously in both the theatre and the study: the violence and cruelty it depicts were disconcertingly matched by the events of two World Wars. Alan Hughes joins those critics who take the play seriously, arguing for its unity of theme and its grim humour, and demonstrates that it is the work of a brilliant stage craftsman, confident in his mastery of space, movement and verse.

The text is based on the first quarto, supplemented by crucial additions and stage directions from the Folio. The critical account of the play's fortunes is integrated within a description of major modern productions, including those directed by Peter Brook, Brian Bedford and Deborah Warner. In addition there is a complete stage history which includes the eighteenth-century adaptation by Edward Ravenscroft and a reconstruction of the version performed by the nineteenth-century black American actor Ira Aldridge. For this updated edition, a new section is included on recent stage, film and critical interpretations by Sue Hall-Smith. There are also sections on text, authorship and the relevance of the famous Longleat drawing of the play. Appendices explore how the play might have been performed at the Rose playhouse in London, and how it could be adapted for a touring company of fourteen men and boys. An updated reading list completes the edition.

THE NEW CAMBRIDGE SHAKESPEARE

TITUS ANDRONICUS

Updated edition

Edited by

ALAN HUGHES

Emeritus Professor of Theatre,
University of Victoria

CAMBRIDGE UNIVERSITY PRESS
Cambridge, New York, Melbourne, Madrid, Cape Town, Singapore, São Paulo

Cambridge University Press
The Edinburgh Building, Cambridge CB2 2RU, UK

Published in the United States of America by Cambridge University Press, New York

www.cambridge.org
Information on this title: www.cambridge.org/9780521673822

© Cambridge University Press, 1994, 2006

First published 1994
Reprinted 2002, 2004
Updated edition 2006

Printed in the United Kingdom at the University Press, Cambridge

A catalogue record for this publication is available from the British Library

ISBN-13 978-0-251-85708-6 hardback
ISBN-10 0-521-85708-2 hardback
ISBN-13 978-0-521-67382-2 paperback
ISBN-10 0-521-67382-8 paperback

CONTENTS

ILLUSTRATIONS

PREFACE

Titus Andronicus is not everyone's favourite play. It 'reads badly'; but in comparatively recent years, theatre audiences have been learning that it frequently 'plays well'. Philip Brockbank, the Founding General Editor of this series, recognised that when he appointed a theatre historian to edit it. Much that is best in this edition must be attributed to his insight and wisdom. Its faults are all my own.

I owe Albert Braunmuller a similar debt. He has dedicated a large part of a busy life to painstaking editorial comment without which I do not think my work would ever have been finished. To him and to Clifford Leech I owe most of what I know about editing; and to F. D. Hoeniger, a large part of what I know about Shakespeare. I am grateful for the advice of Stanley Wells, who advised me to edit less conventionally than I fear I have done, and to Sarah Stanton for her patience.

If the reader finds in this volume some insights about why *Titus* plays well, I owe them to many actors and directors. Chief amongst these are Anthony Quayle, who invited me to tea and showed me how Aaron can be played, and Edward Atienza, the Clown in the same production, directed by Peter Brook.

The staffs of many libraries have been of invaluable assistance, particularly those of the University of Victoria Library, the British Library, and the long-suffering staff of its newspaper repository at Colindale.

Finally, I cannot adequately express my gratitude to my wife Mary, who has put up with *Titus* far too long; and to my children, who have no doubt come to regard it as an immutable part of their lives.

A.H.

University of Victoria

Titus Andronicus has enjoyed a vigorous revival in recent years, generated by successful productions which demonstrated how stageworthy the play can be. In this edition, Sue Hall-Smith very effectively brings its performance and critical history up to date.

A.H. 2006

ABBREVIATIONS AND CONVENTIONS

Shakespeare's plays, when cited in this edition, are abbreviated in a style modified slightly from that used in the *Harvard Concordance to Shakespeare*. Other editions of Shakespeare are abbreviated under the editor's surname (Dyce, Waith) unless they are the work of more than one editor. In such cases, an abbreviated series name is used (Cam.). When more than one edition by the same editor is cited, later editions are discriminated with a raised figure (Rowe [2]). All quotations from Shakespeare, except those from *Titus Andronicus*, use the text and lineation of *The Riverside Shakespeare*, under the textual editorship of G. Blakemore Evans.

1. Shakespeare's plays

Ado	*Much Ado About Nothing*
Ant.	*Antony and Cleopatra*
AWW	*All's Well That Ends Well*
AYLI	*As You Like It*
Cor.	*Coriolanus*
Cym.	*Cymbeline*
Err.	*The Comedy of Errors*
Ham.	*Hamlet*
1H4	*The First Part of King Henry the Fourth*
2H4	*The Second Part of King Henry the Fourth*
H5	*King Henry the Fifth*
1H6	*The First Part of King Henry the Sixth*
2H6	*The Second Part of King Henry the Sixth*
3H6	*The Third Part of King Henry the Sixth*
H8	*King Henry the Eighth*
JC	*Julius Caesar*
John	*King John*
LLL	*Love's Labour's Lost*
Lear	*King Lear*
Mac.	*Macbeth*
MM	*Measure for Measure*
MND	*A Midsummer Night's Dream*
MV	*The Merchant of Venice*
Oth.	*Othello*
Per.	*Pericles*
R2	*King Richard the Second*
R3	*King Richard the Third*
Rom.	*Romeo and Juliet*
Shr.	*The Taming of the Shrew*
STM	*Sir Thomas More*
Temp.	*The Tempest*
TGV	*The Two Gentlemen of Verona*
Tim.	*Timon of Athens*

Tit.	*Titus Andronicus*
TN	*Twelfth Night*
TNK	*The Two Noble Kinsmen*
Tro.	*Troilus and Cressida*
Wiv.	*The Merry Wives of Windsor*
WT	*The Winter's Tale*

2. Other works cited and general references

Adams	*Shakespeare's 'Titus Andronicus': The First Quarto, 1594*, introduction by J. Q. Adams, 1936
Alexander	*William Shakespeare: The Complete Works*, ed. Peter Alexander, 4 vols., 1951
Baldwin	T. W. Baldwin, *On the Literary Genetics of Shakespere's Plays 1592–1594*, 1959
Barnet	*The Tragedy of Titus Andronicus*, ed. Sylvan Barnet, 1964 (Signet Classic Shakespeare)
Bevington	*The Complete Works of Shakespeare*, ed. David Bevington, 3rd edn, 1980
Bolton	Joseph S. G. Bolton, 'The authentic text of *Titus Andronicus*', *PMLA* 44 (1929), 765–88
Bradbrook	M. C. Bradbrook, *Themes and Conventions in Elizabethan Tragedy*, 1933
Bullough	*Narrative and Dramatic Sources of Shakespeare*, ed. Geoffrey Bullough, 8 vols., 1957–75, VI
Cam.	*The Works of William Shakespeare*, ed. W. G. Clark, J. Glover and W. A. Wright, 9 vols., 1863–6 (The Cambridge Shakespeare)
Capell	*Mr William Shakespeare His Comedies, Histories, and Tragedies*, ed. Edward Capell, 10 vols., 1767–8
Chambers, *Shakespeare*	E. K. Chambers, *William Shakespeare: A Study of Facts and Problems*, 2 vols., 1930
Chambers, *Stage*	E. K. Chambers, *The Elizabethan Stage*, 4 vols., 1951
conj.	conjecture
corr.	correction
Cross	*Titus Andronicus*, ed. Gustav Cross, revised edn, 1977 (Pelican Shakespeare)
Delius	*Shakespere's Werke*, ed. Nicolaus Delius, 7 vols., 1854–60
Dent	R. W. Dent, *Shakespeare's Proverbial Language: An Index*, 1981 (references are to numbered proverbs)
Dessen	Alan C. Dessen, *Shakespeare in Performance: 'Titus Andronicus'*, 1989
Dyce	*The Works of William Shakespeare*, ed. Alexander Dyce, 6 vols., 1857
Dyce ²	*The Works of William Shakespeare*, ed. Alexander Dyce, 9 vols., 1864–7
EIC	*Essays in Criticism*
ELH	*ELH: A Journal of English Literary History*

ES	*English Studies*
F	*Mr William Shakespeares Comedies, Histories, and Tragedies,* 1623 (First Folio)
F2	*Mr William Shakespeares Comedies, Histories, and Tragedies,* 1632 (Second Folio)
F3	*Mr William Shakespear's Comedies, Histories, and Tragedies,* 1663 (Third Folio)
F4	*Mr William Shakespear's Comedies, Histories, and Tragedies,* 1685 (Fourth Folio)
Greg, *Folio*	W. W. Greg, *The Shakespeare First Folio: Its Bibliographical and Textual History,* 1955
Greg, *Problem*	W. W. Greg, *The Editorial Problem in Shakespeare,* 3rd edn, 1954
Hanmer	*The Works of Shakespear,* ed. Thomas Hanmer, 6 vols., 1743–4
Hinman	Charlton K. Hinman, *The Printing and Proof-reading of the First Folio of Shakespeare,* 2 vols., 1963
Hudson	*The Works of Shakespeare,* ed. Henry N. Hudson, 11 vols., 1851–6
JEGP	*Journal of English and Germanic Philology*
Johnson	*The Plays of William Shakespeare,* ed. Samuel Johnson, 8 vols., 1765
Kittredge	*The Complete Works of Shakespeare,* ed. George Lyman Kittredge, 1936
Kyd	Thomas Kyd, *The Spanish Tragedy; or, Hieronimo Is Mad Again,* in *The Spanish Comedy; or, the First Part of Hieronimo, and The Spanish Tragedy,* ed. Andrew S. Cairncross, 1967
Malone	*The Plays and Poems of William Shakespeare,* ed. Edmond Malone, 10 vols., 1790
Marlowe	Christopher Marlowe, *Tamburlaine the Great, Parts I and II,* ed. John D. Jump, 1967
Maxwell	*Titus Andronicus,* ed. J. C. Maxwell, 3rd edn, 1961 (Arden Shakespeare)
miscorr.	miscorrected
MLN	*Modern Language Notes*
MLR	*Modern Language Review*
N&Q	*Notes and Queries*
NCS	The New Cambridge Shakespeare
ODEP	*The Oxford Dictionary of English Proverbs,* 3rd edn, rev. F. P. Wilson, 1970
OED	*The Oxford English Dictionary,* 2nd edn, 1989
Onions	C. T. Onions, *A Shakespeare Glossary,* rev. Robert D. Eagleson, 1986
Ovid	P. Ovidius Naso, *Metamorphoses,* trans. A. D. Melville, 1987
Partridge	Eric Partridge, *Shakespeare's Bawdy,* 1968
PMLA	*Publications of the Modern Language Association of America*
Pope	*The Works of Shakespear,* ed. Alexander Pope, 6 vols., 1723–5
Q	*The Most Lamentable Romaine Tragedie of Titus Andronicus . . .* Printed by Iohn Danter, 1594

Q2	*The most lamentable Romaine Tragedie of Titus Andronicus . . .* Printed by I.R. for Edward White, 1600
Q3	*The Most Lamentable Tragedie of Titus Andronicus . . .* Printed for Eedward White, 1611
Qq	quarto editions
Ravenscroft	Edward Ravenscroft, *Titus Andronicus; or, The Rape of Lavinia*, 1687
Riverside	*The Riverside Shakespeare*, ed. G. Blakemore Evans, 1974
RNT	Royal National Theatre
Robertson	J. M. Robertson, *An Introduction to the Study of the Shakespeare Canon*, 1924
Rowe	*The Works of Mr William Shakespear*, ed. Nicholas Rowe, 6 vols., 1709
Rowe [2]	*The Works of Mr William Shakespear*, ed. Nicholas Rowe, 8 vols., 1714
RSC	Royal Shakespeare Company
Rubinstein	Frankie Rubinstein, *A Dictionary of Shakespeare's Sexual Puns and Their Significance*, 2nd edn, 1989
SD	stage direction
SH	speech heading
Sisson	*William Shakespeare: The Complete Works*, ed. C. J. Sisson, 1954
SNL	*Shakespeare Newsletter*
SP	*Studies in Philology*
SQ	*Shakespeare Quarterly*
S.St.	*Shakespeare Studies*
S.Sur.	*Shakespeare Survey*
Steevens	*The Plays of William Shakespeare*, notes by Samuel Johnson and George Steevens, 10 vols., 1773 (The Johnson–Steevens Variorum)
subst.	substantively
Theobald	*The Works of Shakespear*, ed. Lewis Theobald, 7 vols., 1733
Tilley	M. P. Tilley, *A Dictionary of the Proverbs in England in the Sixteenth and Seventeenth Centuries*, 1950 (references are to numbered proverbs)
TLS	*The Times Literary Supplement*
uncorr.	uncorrected
Virgil	*Aeneid* in *P. Vergili Maronis, Opera*, ed. F. A. Hirtzell, 1900
Waith	*Titus Andronicus*, ed. Eugene M. Waith, 1984 (Oxford Shakespeare)
Wells	Stanley Wells, *Re-editing Shakespeare for the Modern Reader*, 1984
Wilson	*Titus Andronicus*, ed. J. Dover Wilson, 1948 (New Shakespeare)
Witherspoon	*Titus Andronicus*, ed. A. M. Witherspoon, 1926 (Yale Shakespeare)

INTRODUCTION

Date

The earliest reliable reference to *Titus Andronicus* comes from the *Diary* of the Elizabethan entrepreneur Philip Henslowe, proprietor of the Rose playhouse on Bankside.
The *Diary* is really an account-book which records the share of the players' receipts
which was the 'rent' Henslowe charged companies performing in his playhouses.[1]
According to the *Diary*, the Earl of Sussex's Men played a season from 26 December
1593 to 6 February 1594, probably at the Rose. On 23 January the play was 'titus &
ondronicus'; in the margin Henslowe wrote 'ne', which is usually taken to mean 'new'[2].
Two more performances followed, on 28 January and 6 February, after which a new
outbreak of the plague moved the Privy Council to close the playhouses.[3] On the same
date, both 'a booke intituled a Noble Roman Historye of Tytus Andronicus' and 'the
ballad thereof' were entered for copyright in the Stationers' Register by John Danter,
who printed Q.[4] We cannot be certain whether Danter's 'booke' was Shakespeare's play,
or an early version of the prose *History of Titus Andronicus*.[5] If it was the former, this
was the first of Shakespeare's plays to be registered for publication. Amongst his works,
only *Venus and Adonis* was entered earlier, on 18 April 1593.

Henslowe's only reference to the suburban playhouse at Newington Butts records a
short season by 'my Lord Admeralle men & my Lorde Chamberlen men' from 3 June
to 13 June 1594. There were performances of 'andronicous' on 5 and 12 June.

These are the only specific records we have of performances of *Titus Andronicus* in
the public playhouses. Even if the Stationers' Register entry should refer to the prose
History, as Adams suggests,[6] there is no particular reason to suspect that the date of Q is
wrong. Accordingly, we may accept January 1594 as a pretty reliable *terminus ante quem*
for the composition of *Titus Andronicus*. The real problems arise when we seek a *terminus
post quem* which is rather more exact than, let us say, Shakespeare's twelfth birthday. By
early 1594 he had composed *Richard III* and was on the point of writing *Romeo and Juliet*:
detractors of *Titus* cannot believe that Shakespeare was still capable of perpetrating

---

[1] R. A. Foakes and R. T. Rickert (eds.), *Henslowe's Diary*, 1961, p. xxviii, agree with W. W. Greg (ed.),
Henslowe's Diary, 2 vols., 1904–8, II, 128–34, who argues that Henslowe's share represents half the gallery
receipts.

[2] Since we know that some of the plays Henslowe marked 'ne' were not new, he may have meant something
different: for instance, that the play was newly revised, as may have been the case with *Titus*. Interpretation
is controversial; see Foakes and Rickert, pp. xxvi–xxx.

[3] Chambers, *Stage*, II, 95.

[4] Of the eight plays known to have been published by Danter, only one is a really 'bad' quarto which he may
have printed illegitimately. Perhaps because this was *Romeo and Juliet*, his reputation amongst modern
scholars is worse than he deserves. See Harry R. Hoppe, *The Bad Quarto of 'Romeo and Juliet'*, 1948.

[5] See pp. 9–10 and 160 below.

[6] Adams, p. 9.

I

1 'My lord, I aim a mile beyond the moon': a possible staging of 4.3.66 by C. Walter Hodges, showing the Rose Theatre as reconstructed from its foundations, excavated in 1989

such a play by that date.[1] Some have suggested that it is not by Shakespeare at all, or that it is his incomplete revision of another man's play; others have suggested an earlier date. The evidence for the former is reviewed below (pp. 10–12); evidence for the latter is slight and circumstantial.

Since it was in Danter's commercial interest to present his Q edition as the authentic text of a playhouse success, we cannot be certain that the information printed on the title page is perfectly accurate. Nevertheless, it gives unique information about the play's history: 'The Most Lamentable Romaine Tragedie of Titus Andronicus: As it was Plaide by the Right Honourable the Earle of *Darbie*, Earle of *Pembrooke*, and Earle of *Sussex* their Seruants'. The reference to Sussex's Men tends to confirm that Henslowe's entries in January and February of that year refer to Shakespeare's play as published in Q. If the other companies really had performed the play, there is no guarantee that it was in the form that reached print. The Earl of Derby's Men were simply Lord Strange's under a new name, which they cannot have adopted before their patron succeeded to the title on 25 September 1593; however, the name used on the title page has more significance for the publication date of Q than for the alleged performances. Danter would naturally use the patron's new and more impressive title, but there is no real evidence that the performances referred to were recent. On the other hand, the reference to the Earl of Pembroke's Men may push the history of the play, or some form of it, back a little. We have no record of this company before the autumn of 1592, and the last we hear of them for several years is a vivid vignette of Elizabethan theatrical life. The London playhouses were closed because of the plague, and the companies were dispersed, most of them touring in the provinces. On 28 September 1593, Henslowe wrote to his son-in-law, Edward Alleyn: 'As for my lorde a Penbrookes w[ch] you desier to knowe whear they be they ar all at home and hausse ben this v or six weackes for they cane not saue ther carges wth trauell as I heare & weare fayne to pane ther parell for ther carge.'[2] Assuming that both Henslowe and the Q title page are accurate in all respects, that would mean that Pembroke's Men could not have played *Titus Andronicus* after the last week in August 1593. The fact that Derby's Men are named before Pembroke's may point to an even earlier performance, but speculation on this subject, while fascinating, is bound to be inconclusive: quite possibly it has no significance at all.[3]

Earlier still is an apparent reference to *Titus Andronicus* in an anonymous play called *A Knack to Know a Knave*, which Henslowe marked as 'ne' during a season in which Strange's Men acted something called 'tittus and vespasia' (February to June 1592). One character bids another welcome,

---

[1] See Chambers, *Shakespeare*, I, 317–18; and R. F. Hill, 'The composition of *Titus Andronicus*', S.Sur. 10 (1957), 68–9.

[2] Chambers, *Stage*, II, 128; Chambers, *Shakespeare*, I, 320; Wilson, pp.xl–xlviii; Waith, pp. 5, 8–9.

[3] Chambers, *Stage*, II, 129–32; David George, 'Shakespeare and Pembroke's Men', *SQ* 32 (1981), 305–23.

> As Titus was unto the Roman Senators,
> When he had made a conquest on the Goths:
> That in requital of his seruice done,
> Did offer him the imperial Diademe . . .[1]

While this is not precisely what happens in *Titus Andronicus*, it is difficult to agree with those who have tried to explain it away in order to support a later date.[2] It is possible, nevertheless, that it refers to Shakespeare's lost source, or even to 'tittus and vespasia'.

In the Induction to Ben Jonson's *Bartholomew Fair* (1614), a character speaks ironically of the spectator who is 'fixed and settled in his censure . . . He that will swear *Jeronimo* or *Andronicus* are the best plays yet, shall pass unexcepted at here as a man whose judgement shows it is constant, and hath stood still these five and twenty or thirty years.' A literal interpretation would date both *Titus* and *Jeronimo* (presumably *The Spanish Tragedy*) between 1584 and 1589. But Jonson (b. 1572) was a boy in the 1580s, and even if he knew or cared about the original dates, common sense suggests that he would have cared more about his joke and meant only that both were hopelessly old-fashioned plays which, maddeningly, the groundlings still preferred to such up-to-date flops as his own tragedy, *Catiline* (1611).[3] Jonson also implies, however, that they were *similar* old plays, as indeed they are.

Violence is commonplace in Elizabethan drama, but these plays are linked by a bizarre and sensational type of violence in which dismemberment is unusually conspicuous: Lavinia's tongue is cut out, Hieronimo bites his off and apparently spits it onto the stage. Both tragedies have grand old heroes driven mad by suffering and oppression, and the Senecan rhetoric of their madness enjoyed such an enduring vogue that additional mad scenes were commissioned to exploit it. Similar tastes are reflected in some of Marlowe's earlier plays. His 'mighty line' fairly wallows in rhetoric. The cannibal imagery of the banquet scene in *Tamburlaine the Great, Part 1* (*c.* 1587) parallels the physical horrors of the climactic banquet in *Titus Andronicus*: Marlowe even refers to Procne's revenge, a conspicuous theme in Shakespeare's play.[4] Compare the style of violence in *Titus* with the suicides of Bajazeth and Zenocrate, who brain themselves onstage, and, at the climax of *The Jew of Malta* (*c.* 1590), the death of Barabas, who falls into a boiling cauldron. Like Aaron, Barabas revels in evil: John Dover Wilson has demonstrated the resemblance.[5] J. C. Maxwell notes a close parallel between part of Aaron's defiant confession and a speech in *The Troublesome Raigne of John King of England*, published in 1591 but probably performed several years earlier:

---

[1] G. R. Proudfoot (ed.), *A Knack to Know a Knave*, Malone Society Reprints, 1963, sig. F2 ᵛ.
[2] Paul Bennett, 'An apparent allusion to *Titus Andronicus*', *N&Q* 200 (1955), 422–4; and 'The word "Goths" in *A Knack to Know a Knave*', *N&Q* 200 (1955), 462–3; Wilson, pp. xli–xliv.
[3] Chambers, *Shakespeare*, I, 319–29. Wilson, p. xl, and Waith, p. 4, give Jonson's evidence little credit; Maxwell, p.xxii, thinks it suggests a date earlier than 1594, at least; Hill, 'Composition', p. 69, is convinced by it; see also G. Harold Metz, 'The date of composition of *Titus Andronicus*', *N&Q* 223 (1978), 116–17.
[4] Christopher Marlowe, *Tamburlaine the Great*, ed. John D. Jump, 1967, Part I, 4.4; *Tit.* 5.3; see note on 2.3.43.
[5] Wilson, p. lxii.

How, what, when, and where, have I bestowd a day
That tended not to some notorious ill.[1]

Compare Aaron:

Even now I curse the day – and yet I think
Few come within the compass of my curse –
Wherein I did not some notorious ill . . .   (5.1.125–7)

Apparently, then, *Titus Andronicus* has much in common with a type of play which was being written before 1590. If it was written much after that date, it was a belated specimen of the type.

   Passing from even such circumstantial evidence to internal evidence is like entering a carnival fun-house with its distorting mirrors. 'The game of verbal parallels', as Wilson calls it, is a fascinating but unreliable way of establishing dates. In the light of that remark, it is surprising to find him playing it himself. In the first place, one person's 'indisputable echo' is another's far-fetched nonsense. Coincidences and common sources are both difficult to rule out, the latter especially when we recall how much Elizabethan literature we have lost. Even when a parallel is as clear as such things may be, we often cannot know which author wrote first, or how much time separated first writing from imitation. Let us take the example of the coined word 'palliament', which is used twice in extant Renaissance literature: at *Titus* 1.1.182 and in George Peele's poem, *The Honour of the Garter* (line 92), which can be dated with precision to May–June 1593. Wilson uses this coincidence to argue that Peele not only wrote both passages, but did so at very nearly the same time, and that the play must be slightly the earlier of the two because he thinks the word is better suited to its context there than in the poem.[2] With respect to Aaron's speech, quoted above, Maxwell warns us that we cannot know who is the borrower, but leans towards the author of *The Troublesome Raigne* on the grounds that he is 'a shameless borrower' and because Aaron uses it more felicitously than King John.[3] Since this is the same argument Wilson uses to attribute *Titus Andronicus* to the author of *The Honour of the Garter*, the evidence – such as it is – cancels itself out. Furthermore, since the play shows signs of revision, a parallel may belong to either a first draft or a revised version. The same hazards attend any hope of using recent archaeology to date the stagecraft in *Titus Andronicus*. For example, Aaron buries gold under a 'tree' (2.3.2), perhaps one of the stage columns which may have been a novel feature of the Rose after its renovation (*c.* 1592). Like a verbal parallel, however, this stage business could as easily date from a revision as from the original draft.

   The only real evidence for the date of the play, then, is external, but it is scanty and not beyond question: Henslowe might have been mistaken, perhaps Danter lied. With these *caveats*, we can say that *Titus Andronicus* was probably established on the stage by mid 1593, and possibly earlier. Circumstantial evidence suggests that it might have

[1] J. W. Sider (ed.), *The Troublesome Raigne of John, King of England*, 1979, 5.85–6.
[2] Wilson, pp. xlv–xlvi.
[3] Maxwell, p. xxi.

been first written several years before: the style of its violence and language seems to link it to *The Spanish Tragedy, Tamburlaine* and *The Troublesome Raigne*. In the end, we can only conjecture or despair. Thus, discarding all pretence of objective proof, I shall base a conjecture upon my subjective assessment of style.

As I have shown, *Titus Andronicus* resembles several sensational plays which were all written somewhat earlier than 1592. Moreover, the writing seems stylistically uneven. Some of it is Ovidian, formal and mannered, as in Marcus's speech to the ravished Lavinia (2.4.11–57); some is crude, particularly in Act 1. These passages feel like the work of a young poet. Other portions more closely resemble Shakespeare's mature style: see for example Aaron's defence of his child (4.2.65–111). The stagecraft, on the other hand, is as dexterous as anything Shakespeare ever accomplished, which suggests a working familiarity with the theatre.

From these observations I conjecture that the young Shakespeare wrote a crude draft of *Titus Andronicus* before he turned dramatist – even as early as 1588, when he may still have been living in Stratford; that it accompanied him to London, where nobody would produce it; and that having established himself to Robert Greene's dissatisfaction in 1592,[1] he revised it and offered it either to Strange's or Pembroke's Men. They may have played it in the provinces. But by the summer of 1593 the latter company, being bankrupt and currently in possession of the play, sold it to Sussex's Men, who played it at the Rose in early 1594, and subsequently sold the copy to Danter when plague closed the playhouses. The scene of Titus's mad banquet, which appears only in the First Folio, was added later. This complicated hypothesis must await the discovery of new, *reliable* evidence to be tested. It may wait long.

Sources

It is uncertain whether Shakespeare's major source for *Titus Andronicus* has survived. The context of the story is the decline of the Roman Empire, but the events are fictional: thus, the source was also fiction. Shakespeare is unlikely to have invented the story; his only original plots are found in comedy: *A Midsummer Night's Dream, Love's Labour's Lost, The Merry Wives of Windsor*, the Beatrice and Benedick plot in *Much Ado About Nothing*. For tragedy and history plays, he and his fellow dramatists turned to historians such as Livy, Plutarch and Holinshed; to old plays like *King Leir* or *The Troublesome Raigne of John King of England*; or to the Italian *novella*, which the Titus story resembles.

In 1936 J. Q. Adams announced his discovery, in the Folger Shakespeare Library, of a volume containing a short prose *History of Titus Andronicus* and a 120-line ballad, *Titus Andronicus' Complaint*.[2] Since it was published between 1736 and 1764, this little chapbook seems an unlikely place in which to seek Shakespeare's source. Nevertheless, some scholars believe they have found it in either the ballad or the *History*.

---

[1] *Greene's Groats-Worth of Witte bought with a Million of Repentance* refers to 'an upstart Crow, beautified with our feathers, that with his *Tygers hart wrapt in a Players hyde*, supposes he is as well able to bombast out a blanke verse as the best of you: and beeing an absolute *Iohannes fac totum*, is in his owne conceit the onely Shake-scene in a countrey' (Scolar Press facsimile (n.d.), F1 ᵛ).

[2] Adams, pp. 7–9.

The publisher, C. Dicey, is known to have reprinted old works on other occasions. The ballad was certainly old; it had been published in 1620, in Richard Johnson's *The Golden Garland of Princely Pleasures and Delicate Delights*. It is possible that Johnson merely reprinted a ballad that was old enough to be Shakespeare's source. No early edition of the *History* is known, but while spelling and punctuation follow eighteenth-century practice, the diction is archaic. This suggests that the claim printed on the title page, that it was 'Newly Translated from the Italian Copy printed at Rome', was false at the time of publication.

The ballad and the *History* are linked by an identical couplet, which Lavinia writes with her staff to identify her assailants:

> The lustful sons of the proud Empress
> Are doers of this hateful wickedness.[1]

The *History* is unlikely to have been the source of the ballad. The latter narrates the incident (5.2) in which the empress and her sons appear to Titus disguised as Revenge, Rape and Murder. This is not in the *History*. Since the ballad is original in no other respect, this incident may be drawn from a lost source, or from the play. The latter seems more likely. Marco Mincoff[2] argues that the ballad is the source of the *History*, but his case has been exploded by G. Harold Metz.[3] G. K. Hunter suggests that the ballad was written to capitalise on the popularity of Shakespeare's play.[4]

The *History* is essentially different from the play. Sargent points out that it 'presents a whole which has a consistency of its own, a consistency which is not the same as the play's'.[5] It tells the same story, with some different names and details of plot, but neither Shakespeare's concern with evil and justice nor the serious political theme which requires a Lucius to restore order is present in the bald narrative. Nevertheless, there must be some link. Since the entire story is fiction, all versions must be related to each other. Sargent also notes that there is little quoted speech in the *History*, and that 'A careful search reveals no verbal resemblance between the history and the play; the spoken lines of the drama owe nothing to the language of this prose version.'[6] This is true, if the search is confined to dialogue; but there are several close parallels between the narrative phrasing of the *History* and Shakespeare's dialogue. Compare the following:

> Hark, wretches, how I mean to marty you;
> This one hand yet is left to cut your throats
> Whiles that Lavinia 'tween her stumps doth hold
> The basin that receives your guilty blood.   (5.2.180–3)

[1] Ralph M. Sargent, 'The source of *Titus Andronicus*', *SP* 46 (1949), 170.
[2] Marco Mincoff, 'The source of *Titus Andronicus*', *N&Q* 216 (April 1971), 131–4.
[3] G. Harold Metz, '*The History of Titus Andronicus* and Shakespeare's play', *N&Q* 220 (April 1975), 163–6.
[4] G. K. Hunter, 'Sources and meanings in *Titus Andronicus*', in J. C. Gray (ed.), *Mirror up to Shakespeare: Essays in Honour of G. R. Hibbard*, 1984, pp. 179–85.
[5] Sargent, 'Source', p. 169.
[6] *Ibid.*, p. 171.

Andronicus cut their throats whilst Lavinia, by his command, held a bowl between her stumps
to receive the blood.   (*History*, p. 43)[1]

> Hark, villains, I will grind your bones to dust,
> And with your blood and it I'll make a paste,
> And of the paste a coffin I will rear,
> And make two pasties of your shameful heads . . .   (5.2.186–9)

Then conveying the bodies home to his own house privately, he cut the flesh into fit pieces and
ground the bones to powder, and made of them two mighty pasties . . .   (*History*, p. 43)

If this is enough to show that there was a direct link between the play and the *History*,
what is its nature?

If we rule out the ballad as a source, only three possibilities remain: the play and the
History have a common source, which might be an Italian *novella*, or a translation in
either French or English; the play is the source of the *History*; or an early edition of the
History is Shakespeare's source.

Shakespeare preferred English sources, but he may have been able to read Italian
and could certainly read French. A *novella* by Cinthio, either in the original Italian
or a French translation by Gabriel Chappuys, is the chief source of *Othello*;[2] some
critics believe he turned to Boccaccio for the wager theme in *Cymbeline*;[3] *The Merchant
of Venice* draws upon Ser Giovanni's *Il Pecorone* (1558), probably in Italian;[4] either
Bandello's *Novelle* or Belleforest's French translation is a probable source of *Much Ado
About Nothing*.[5] Thus, a *novella* in Italian or French is not an impossible source. No
such work is known, however.

Hunter argues that some details of the *History* seem to be drawn from ancient sources
which were not available in English in the sixteenth century. 'One must assume either
that the chap-book author was a learned man or that a learned intermediary (learned,
perhaps, in "the Italian copy printed at Rome" cited in the heading) had already digested
the sources into a form which could be applied to the Titus Andronicus story.'[6] On the
other hand, the *History* might have been written as late as the eighteenth century, when
its author would have needed only Shakespeare's play and Gibbon or other sources that
were readily available by that time. If that was the case, however, he amalgamated his
historical sources with the play in an imaginative and creative manner which appears to
be inconsistent with his modest literary abilities. It is easier to believe that Shakespeare
worked up a dry tale like the *History* into drama. If we consider the creative changes he
frequently made, for dramatic effect, in the narrative of his sources, it seems probable
that the *History* or a common source came first.

---

[1] The *History* is quoted from Bullough.
[2] Norman Sanders (ed.), *Oth.*, 1984, pp. 2–3.
[3] J. M. Nosworthy (ed.), *Cym.*, 1955, pp. xx–xxii, who thinks 'There is little evidence that he could read
     Italian.'
[4] M. M. Mahood (ed.), *MV*, 1987, pp. 2–5.
[5] F. H. Mares (ed.), *Ado*, 1988, p. 1.
[6] Hunter, 'Sources and meanings', p. 178.

Besides, there is external evidence to consider. On 6 February 1594, the date of the third and last recorded performance of *Titus Andronicus* by Sussex's Men, John Danter entered 'a booke intituled a Noble Roman Historye of Tytus Andronicus' and 'the ballad thereof' in the Stationers' Register. This gave him the sole right to publish the book named in the entry, much in the manner of modern copyright. It does not prove that he exercised that right.

Danter published the first quarto (Q), which is dated 1594 on the title page. There is no reason to doubt the date. Had his Stationers' Register entry clearly referred to the book of Shakespeare's play, the case would be simple. But his wording appears to refer to the *History*, and since the ballad is mentioned as well, it looks as though he meant to print something rather like the eighteenth-century chapbook. If this was so, the *History* had evidently existed long enough to permit the ballad to be written. If *Titus Andronicus* was really new when it was first performed on 23 January, less than a fortnight elapsed before Danter's entry in the Register.

If the *History* was based on the play, several people had been incredibly busy. We would have to suppose that the author of the *History* saw the 23 January performance and adapted the play, with major changes; that the author of the ballad then somehow saw the *History*, and adapted it too; and that both subsequently took their works to Danter and persuaded him to publish, all in a few days. It is easier to believe that the *History* was based on an earlier version of the play, or completely preceded it.

More probably, Danter took the initiative. *Titus Andronicus* was a playhouse success, and he intended to capitalise on it by publishing the *History* and the ballad. We cannot be certain that he never did so; his edition is not extant, but to argue from absence of evidence will not do. Nevertheless, he published his quarto of *Titus Andronicus* in the same year, without making any further entry in the Stationers' Register. W. W. Greg says 'it would be quite in keeping with Danter's character to make one entrance serve for two separate publications',[1] but it is possible that Danter saw his chance when the playhouses were closed by plague (immediately after the 6 February performance), bought the play from Sussex's Men, and used the rights he had established for the *History* and ballad to publish the play instead. The principal flaw in this suggestion is that Danter entered his copy on the very day of the play's last performance. This is a difficult coincidence to swallow, but no other explanation readily presents itself.

We are left with the probability that the *History* had existed for some time before 1594, and that it, or its Italian original, was Shakespeare's source. Unless we suppose that not only he but Danter and the author of the ballad read the *History* in manuscript, in Italian, or both, there must have been an earlier printed English edition which Danter proposed to reprint. There is no way of knowing how old it was in 1594, but if it was still in print Danter was surely risking trouble with its publisher. It follows that this lost edition must have been several years old.

The archaic diction of the chapbook *History* casts doubt upon the claim of the title page that it was 'Newly Translated from the Italian Copy printed at Rome'. More probably, the publisher simply reprinted that line along with the rest of the text. In that

---

[1] W. W. Greg, *A Bibliography of English Printed Drama to the Restoration*, 4 vols., 1939, I, xxv.

case, the old edition was probably the *first* in English, but adapted or translated from an Italian source. Since an English version was available, Shakespeare is likely to have used it instead of the original, a suspicion which the verbal parallels quoted above tend to confirm.

The *History* may not have been Shakespeare's only source, but if it was the major one, there is no reason to argue that he went elsewhere for details that could be found in the book that lay open before him. Possible secondary sources might be the story of Philomel in Ovid's *Metamorphoses*, and Seneca's *Thyestes*; but since a copy of the former actually figures in the action of *Titus Andronicus* (4.1) and Lavinia's story closely resembles Philomel's, Ovid was probably more important. Perhaps Shakespeare knew both works so well that he did not need to open either as he wrote; but Ovid was fresher in his memory.

Authorship

The external evidence that Shakespeare wrote *Titus Andronicus* rests upon two solid facts. (1) It was included in the First Folio (1623), published by John Heminge and Henry Condell as a memorial to their friend and colleague. They would hardly have included a play they believed to be spurious, and as senior partners in the same company of players as Shakespeare they were in a position to know. (2) Comparing ancient and contemporary poets in *Palladis Tamia: Wit's Treasury* (1598), Francis Meres counts *Titus Andronicus* with Shakespeare's early tragedies. Meres may have lacked inside knowledge, but he was an educated man who was living in London by 1587.[1]

The only evidence that the play might be spurious comes from Edward Ravenscroft, who was born almost 25 years after Shakespeare's death. The address to the reader published with his adaptation of *Titus Andronicus* (1687) excuses Ravenscroft of plagiarism, claiming

I have been told by some anciently conversant with the Stage, that it was not Originally his, but brought by a private Author to be Acted, and he only gave some Master-touches to one or two of the Principal Parts or Characters; this I am apt to believe, because 'tis the most incorrect and indigested piece in all his Works; It seems rather a heap of Rubbish than a Structure.

In view of the relative authority of the evidence, it seems odd that so many scholars have agreed with Ravenscroft. In the eighteenth century Theobald, Johnson, Steevens and Malone all declared against Shakespeare's authorship, with Capell the only significant dissenter. The nineteenth century followed suit, with the exception of the Germans (apart from Gervinus). Those who doubted the tragedy's authenticity had no evidence, but flinched from the 'horrors', found the characters shallow and unsympathetic, and the language inferior to Shakespeare's usual standard. In fact, *Titus Andronicus* simply offended their literary taste, and they wished to absolve Shakespeare of the responsibility for perpetrating it.

---

[1] E. A. J. Honigmann believes Meres was 'not up-to-date in theatre affairs', but this view is disputed. See A. R. Braunmuller (ed.), *John*, 1989, p. 2.

Scholars in the twentieth century have turned to internal evidence. In *Did Shake-speare Write 'Titus Andronicus'?* (1905), J. M. Robertson used verbal parallels to propose George Peele as principal author. Despite the demolition of Robertson's reputation by E. K. Chambers in *The Disintegration of Shakespeare* (1924),[1] some still find Shake-speare's sole authorship a difficult proposition to accept. Dover Wilson mustered an impressive list of parallels which he believed show Shakespeare's hand in every act except the first. He proposed a complicated hypothesis in which Peele wrote an early version for a touring company and was subsequently commissioned by Sussex's Men to expand it for performance in London, with aid from a reluctant Shakespeare. In his scheme, Act 1 is entirely by Peele.[2] Even J. C. Maxwell, after arguing persuasively for Shakespeare's exclusive authorship, concluded, 'I can never quite believe it while reading Act 1.'[3] His literary taste rebelled against the evidence.

There have been several attempts to apply objective tests to the text. T. M. Parrott used statistics on feminine line-endings to argue for Shakespeare as reviser.[4] A recent computer analysis of works by Shakespeare and Peele indicates that *Titus Andronicus* is authentically by Shakespeare.[5] In the face of the contradictory results of these appar-ently scientific studies, it is difficult to avoid concluding, with R. F. Hill, that the tests 'were either insufficiently thoroughgoing or else pressed to conclusions beyond their legitimate scope'. He argues that the search for parallel phrases is equally ineffective, because the results simply tend to confirm the literary taste of the scholar who seeks them. It will not do, Hill urges, 'to gather together a few clichés from a play of known authorship and then to look for those specifics in the disputed or anonymous play' where, inevitably, the sleuth will find what he seeks.[6]

The search for internal evidence has concentrated upon language because that is the source of doubt about Shakespeare's authorship. While methods are questionable and results inconclusive, many good scholars intuitively feel that much of the verse is too clichéd and monotonous to be Shakespeare's, particularly in Act 1. These doubts tend to evaporate, however, when we recall that he was a dramatist and theatrical craftsman as well as a poet. Indeed, it is conceivable that his theatrical talents matured first.[7] Perhaps when he first drafted *Titus Andronicus*, at the beginning of his career, Peele's literary influence stifled his embryonic style. Revising later, possibly in 1593, he may have left Act 1 substantially unchanged. That would explain why its poetry seems inferior to that of the remainder of the play. But if we turn from language to dramaturgy and stagecraft, his signature is everywhere.

While Hill points to flaws in the plot, A. M. Sampley argues that Kyd was the only other dramatist writing at the time who was capable of plotting of this order –

---

[1] See also Robertson, *An Introduction to the Study of the Shakespeare Canon*, 1924.
[2] Wilson, pp. xix–xxxvii.
[3] Maxwell, p. xxvii.
[4] T. M. Parrott, 'Shakespeare's revision of *Titus Andronicus*', *MLR* 14 (1919), 16–37.
[5] G. Harold Metz, 'A stylometric comparison of Shakespeare's *Titus Andronicus*, *Pericles*, and *Julius Caesar*', *SNL* 29 (1979), 42.
[6] Hill, 'Composition', p. 61.
[7] See Appendix 1, p. 167 below.

and Kyd cannot have written it.[1] Bertram Evans's unique approach to practice and practisers shows that the plot follows Shakespearean methods,[2] and Derek Traversi argues that the play's unity of theme and imagery suggests unity of authorship.[3] To this I would add that the stagecraft is beyond the powers of any of Shakespeare's early contemporaries. In *Titus Andronicus* a master stage craftsman commands the resources of an Elizabethan playhouse and its company with an authority which neither Peele nor Kyd could match.[4] This instinct for stagecraft is characteristic of Shakespeare, yet it is particularly apparent in the disputed first act and links it firmly to the rest of the play.

If Act I is accepted as authentic, only one doubtful scene remains. There are signs that the 'family banquet' (3.2) may be an afterthought. It was printed in the First Folio, but not in the earlier quartos. It adds nothing to the plot, and the transition to the next scene is awkward and uncharacteristic of Shakespeare's normal practice. The opening stage direction is the only one in F where Titus is called 'Andronicus', and the use of other names also varies from the rest of the play.[5] Mad scenes for Hieronimo were added to *The Spanish Tragedy*, and comic scenes to *Doctor Faustus*, no doubt to exploit public taste. The motive here was probably the same, but there is no strong evidence to identify Shakespeare or another as the author. If it really is an addition, all we can say is that it was written between the completion of the copy-text for Q (1593) and the publication of F (1623).

Early stage history

In the summer of 1594 the players were in difficulties. A particularly virulent and tenacious outbreak of plague in London had dictated the almost continuous closure of the playhouses since June 1592. Most of the companies had taken to the road, touring the provinces to pick up a more or less precarious living. Pembroke's company collapsed. Sussex's vanished in April, after playing an eight-day joint engagement with the Queen's Men for Henslowe. On 16 April Derby's (previously Strange's) Men lost their patron. By June they had found a new one, and as the Lord Chamberlain's Men they played a few days with the Lord Admiral's Men at Newington Butts. This was the end of a long amalgamation of the Admiral's company, led by Edward Alleyn, with Lord Strange's, which included William Kempe, Thomas Pope, John Heminge, Augustine Phillips and George Bryan. Now Alleyn took the lead in an independent Admiral's company, which played for his father-in-law, Henslowe, probably at the Rose.

Important new sharers had joined the Lord Chamberlain's Men by the time they had played at court in December: Richard Burbage and William Shakespeare. Soon the company would take up residence at the Theatre, which was the property of Burbage's father. We do not know where either Burbage or Shakespeare was before joining the

---

[1] A. M. Sampley, 'Plot-structure in Peele's plays as a test of authorship', *PMLA* 51 (1936), 689–70.
[2] Bertram Evans, *Shakespeare's Tragic Practice*, 1979, pp. 1–21.
[3] Derek Traversi, *An Approach to Shakespeare*, 1: *'Henry VI' to 'Twelfth Night'*, 3rd edn, 1968, pp. 62–7.
[4] See Appendix 1, p. 167 below.
[5] See Note on the Text, p. 61 below, and Textual Analysis, p. 164.

Lord Chamberlain's Men, but henceforth they were to be prominent as star and resident dramatist, and as sharers.[1]

This is the period of the first recorded performances of *Titus Andronicus*. According to Henslowe, Sussex's Men played it three times towards the end of a brief season, probably at the Rose, on 23 and 28 January and 6 February 1594. It was played twice more, on 5 and 12 June, by the combined Admiral's and Chamberlain's (formerly Strange's) companies during an even shorter season at Newington Butts.

The housekeeper's share of receipts for the first performance on 23 January was 68 shillings; only the opening of *Buckingham* (*Richard III*?) and of *Huon of Bordeaux* yielded Henslowe a bigger profit (70 shillings each), in a season consisting of thirty performances of twelve plays. Each subsequent performance of *Titus Andronicus* paid £2, which compared so well with second and subsequent performances of the rest of the repertoire that it made average daily receipts for *Titus* by far the highest of the season. The play was popular, perhaps because it suited public taste that season particularly well, or possibly because it was new: that may be what Henslowe meant when he wrote 'ne' beside the title in his *Diary*. But if it was an attractive novelty at the Rose in January and February, why did it pay Henslowe only 12 shillings and 7 shillings at Newington Butts in June? None of the other plays did very well either; only a piece Henslowe calls 'belendon' earned him more.[2] Two performances of *The Jew of Malta*, for instance, made a total of 14 shillings, while a *Hamlet* brought in only 8 shillings. Since this is Henslowe's only reference to Newington Butts, we cannot know whether these were typical receipts for that playhouse. Henslowe's share may have been calculated on a different basis there; but it is possible that the audience had seen too many touring productions of the plays in the Admiral's and Chamberlain's repertoire. Perhaps it rained all week. The point is that the relatively poor receipts need not necessarily mean that *Titus Andronicus* failed there.

The only other early performance of which we have any record took place at Burley-on-the-Hill in Rutland, the country seat of Sir John Harington, on 1 January 1596. Gustav Ungerer, who discovered a letter in which Anthony Bacon's French servant Jacques Petit told his master about the performance, shows that while any of the companies we have discussed could have been 'Les commediens de Londres' who played it, the Lord Chamberlain's is the most probable.[3] *Titus Andronicus* remained their property, and probably a popular item in their repertory, for twenty years or more. In *Palladis Tamia* (1598), Francis Meres listed it amongst the tragedies which he thought proved Shakespeare England's 'most excellent' writer in both traditional genres. Second and third quarto editions, published in 1600 and 1611, indicate that the play was still popular enough on the stage to attract readers. The title page of Q2 claims that it 'hath sundry times been playde by the Right Honourable the Earle of Pembrooke, the Earle of Darbie, the Earle of Sussex, and the Lorde Chamberlaine theyr

---

[1] Chambers, *Stage*, II, 92–6, 118–26, 128–49, 192–202; see also George, 'Shakespeare and Pembroke's Men', pp. 305–23.

[2] Chambers (*Stage*, II, 145) identifies this as *The true tragicall historie of Kinge Rufus the first with the life and deathe of Belyn Dun the first thief that ever was hanged in England*.

[3] Gustav Ungerer, 'An unrecorded Elizabethan performance of *Titus Andronicus*', *S.Sur.* 14 (1961), 106.

Seruants';[1] Q3 mentions only Shakespeare's company, 'the King's Maiesties Seruants', the title they had enjoyed since 1603.

An apparent reference by Thomas Middleton in 1604 would have been pointless if Titus had not still been a familiar figure, though the reference might conceivably be to the ballad or prose history rather than to the play. The speaker has lost an arm and a leg in battle: 'Nevertheless, for all my lamentable action of one arm, like old Titus Andronicus, I could purchase no more than one month's pay.'[2] Jonson's satire in *Bartholomew Fair* shows that *Titus Andronicus* was still popular, and hence still performed, in 1614. A German *Tragoedia von Tito Andronico* was published in *Engelische Comedien und Tragedien* (1620), which suggests that it was played on the Continent in some form, possibly by some of the English actors who are known to have worked there,[3] and that it was successful enough for German actors to want a translation (however garbled) for their own use. The similar Dutch version by Jan Vos, *Aran en Titus* (1641), suggests that it may have held the stage in Holland until quite a late date.[4]

There is no further evidence of performance before the Restoration, except for the 'Longleat manuscript' (see illustration 2).

The Longleat manuscript

E. K. Chambers calls this document 'The first illustration to "Shakespeare"'.[5] It certainly seems to be an illustration of a scene from *Titus Andronicus*. The drawing is quite well executed in pen-and-ink. It is captioned, in Secretary hand, 'Enter Tamora pleadinge for her sonnes going to execution'; this is followed by 40 lines of dialogue attributed to Tamora, Titus and Aaron. It ends with a speech heading for Alarbus, but there is no speech. Tamora's lines are a good transcription of her plea for her son's life (1.1.104–20), the only substantive variation from Qq and F being the substitution of 'sonnes' for 'sonne' at 107. But Titus replies,

> Patient your selfe madame for dy hee must
> Aaron do you likewise prepare your selfe
> And now at last repent your wicked life

The first line condenses the equivalent speech in the play:

> Patient yourself, madam, and pardon me . . .
> To this your son is marked, and die he must . . . (1.1.121–5)

---

[1] Q2 was printed from Q, but the order in which the companies were listed on the title pages was changed: this is probably not significant.

[2] Thomas Middleton, *Father Hubbard's Tubs; or, The Ant and the Nightengale*, in A. H. Bullen (ed.), *The Works of Thomas Middleton*, 8 vols., 1885–6, VIII, 94–5. Bullen compares *Tit.* 5.2.17–18.

[3] See Chambers, *Stage*, II, 270–94. This collection of translated English plays was published in Leipzig. It seems to be linked to the repertoire of an English company that applied to perform in Gdansk in 1619: Jerzy Limon, *Gentlemen of a Company: English Players in Central and Eastern Europe, 1590–1660*, 1985, pp. 50–1.

[4] Chambers, *Shakespeare*, I, 314.

[5] See E. K. Chambers, 'The first illustration to "Shakespeare"', *Shakespearean Gleanings*, 1944, pp. 57–60.

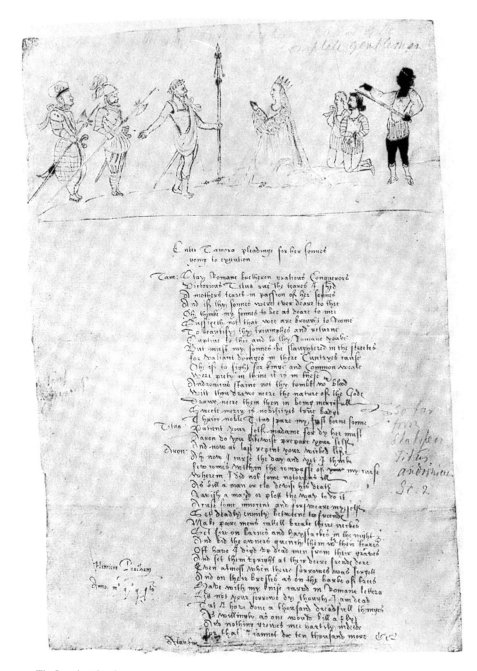

2   The Longleat drawing

The rest is invented in order to justify an immediate transition to Aaron's vindictive boast in Act 5:

LUCIUS Art thou not sorry for these heinous deeds?

AARON Ay, that I had not done a thousand more.
Even now I curse the day – and yet I think
Few come within the compass of my curse –
Wherein I did not some notorious ill . . .   (5.1.123–7)

The first two lines of his speech are slightly altered to disguise the join.

Since the text can have no authority, the manuscript's chief significance lies in its value as a document in the history of theatre: is it an accurate representation of an actual performance? Its value depends upon its relationship to the playhouse. If we admit that work of this quality can hardly have been done during a performance, might it be based upon a playhouse sketch? Or was it drawn from memory of a performance, and, if so, how long afterwards? Might it depict nothing more than an imaginary performance, or could it be a 'fantasy picture', a representation of someone's conception of the 'real' events which the play also dramatises?

If the artist meant to represent a performance, it is hard to see why he telescoped two moments at opposite ends of the play. John Munro interprets it as a picture in the archaic manner he calls 'comprehensive', in which separate incidents in an action are depicted in a single composition. Eugene Waith supports Munro with several examples:[1] woodcut frontispieces from *The Witch of Edmonton* (1658 edition) and William Sampson's *The Vow Breaker* (1636) show several scenes in the same frame, but the composition and the arrangement of speech 'balloons' clearly divide the picture into separate vignettes. Waith's best example is the title page of *The Spanish Tragedy* (1615 edition), which shows Lorenzo silencing Bel-imperia while, in the same frame, Hieronimo discovers Horatio's corpse (see illustration 3). Frontispieces from *Philaster* (1620), *Friar Bacon and Friar Bungay* (1630) and *The Second Part of the Iron Age* (1632) may also be interpreted as 'comprehensive' illustrations.[2] But these are woodcuts, for the most part crude and naïve, while the Longleat sketch is the work of a comparatively sophisticated realist who gives the viewer no clue that the picture is to be regarded as anything but a literal representation of a single scene: there are no 'balloons' here.

If the Longleat drawing is intended to be 'comprehensive', Tamora's sons participate in both scenes at once: they support their mother's plea for Alarbus, as in Act 1, while Aaron gestures at them in his capacity as their adviser in villainy, as he does in Act 5. None of the pictures named above uses this convention, although one woodcut shows two Friar Bacons at different moments in the play, and an illustration of the murder scene in *Arden of Faversham* (1633) may also be read in this way. But I can find an undeniably

---

[1] John Munro, *TLS* 10 June 1949, p. 385; Waith, p. 22.
[2] These frontispieces are all reproduced and discussed in R. A. Foakes, *Illustrations of the English Stage, 1580–1642*, 1985.

The Spanish Tragedie

OR,

Hieronimo is mad againe.

Containing the lamentable end of *Don Horatio*, and
Belimperia; with the pittifull death of *Hieronimo*.

Newly corrected, amended, and enlarged with new
Additions of the *Painters* part, and others, as
it hath of late been diuers times acted.

LONDON,

Printed by W. White, and are to be sold by I. White
and *T. Langley* at their Shop ouer against the
Sarazens head without New-gate. 1615.

3   Title page of *The Spanish Tragedy*, 1615 edition

comprehensive convention in only two dramatic illustrations: the crude woodcut from *The Spanish Tragedy*, and an engraved title page for Middleton's *A Game at Chess* (1625) (see illustration 4). Here, the Fat Bishop receives a letter from the Black Knight, with dialogue from Act 3, while the White Knight's words, also spoken to the Black Knight, are from Act 5.[1] This is the work of an accomplished craftsman; it is as realistic as the Longleat drawing, save for the 'balloons'. If this were not such a lonely, late example it might be possible to accept Munro's thesis.[2] But while recognising that there is cause for doubt, I believe we must still take the Longleat drawing literally. In that case, the artist has misrepresented the play's action. Unless we can arrive at a plausible hypothesis to explain why he would have done so deliberately, we must conclude that he did it by mistake. That can only mean that if he had ever seen a performance of *Titus Andronicus*, he remembered it inaccurately.

If that is true, how did the text get there? Wilson has suggested that it was added later, and adapted to explain the eccentricities of the picture.[3] To this, several obvious objections must be raised. There is no visible sign that drawing and text are by different hands or of different periods. And it is difficult to explain why an artist with a whole sheet of paper before him would draw his picture across the top and leave the rest blank, unless he meant to fill the space with something else – such as dialogue.

But there is evidence we have not yet examined. Near the bottom of the page, someone has written 'Henricus Peacham, Anno m °q °[q?]q tᵒ'. It is generally agreed that the enigmatic signs should be interpreted as a date, either 1594 or 1595, and 'Henricus' identified with Henry Peacham, author of *The Compleat Gentleman* (1622).[4] Is this a dated signature? Or is it an addition by a scribe, who added the dialogue and attributed the picture, but was not the artist? If it is the latter, attribution and date could both be wrong; if the former, Peacham was both artist and scribe. Later in life he was certainly both artist and author. In 1606 he published *The Art of Drawing with the Pen* for the instruction of 'the young learner' in 'an accomplishment required in a Schollar or Gentleman'.[5] Such of his precepts as relate to a drawing of this kind – the proper position of a nose, techniques for rendering eyes, profiles, 'the paps of a man', drapery – all agree with our artist's practice, with the exception of certain points related to shading. This last technique occupies a good deal of space in *The Art of Drawing*, and is used extensively in the engraved illustrations, but it is almost absent from the drawing. Perhaps the artist had not yet learned its proper use: born in 1576, Peacham was only 18 or 19 in 1594 or 1595.[6]

If the shading were removed from a Roman profile illustrating *The Art of Drawing*, its other techniques would be seen to resemble those of the Longleat drawing (see illustration 5). There is a striking similarity between the eyes of the bust and the figure

---

[1] C. F. Tucker Brook and N. B. Paradise (eds.), *English Drama, 1580–1642*, 1933, 3.1.24–7; 5.3.159–60.
[2] Madeleine Doran, in *Endeavors of Art: A Study of Form in Elizabethan Drama*, 1954, pp. 174–5, discusses 'comprehensive' illustrations in a Strasburg edition of Terence published in 1496, but points out that these are medieval in style, and narrative rather than dramatic in character.
[3] J. Dover Wilson, '*Titus Andronicus* on the stage in 1595', *S.Sur.* 1 (1948), 19–20.
[4] Chambers, 'First illustration', p. 57; Waith, p. 23; Adams, p. 3.
[5] 'To the Reader', in *The Art of Drawing with the Pen*.
[6] Alan R. Young, *Henry Peacham*, 1979, p. 18.

4   Title page of *A Game at Chess*, 1625 edition

5   Roman profile by Henry Peacham, from *The Art of Drawing with the Pen* (1606)

of Titus, and their scarves are treated in much the same manner. Waith notes that it is difficult to compare the Secretary hand in the drawing with the italic style Peacham uses in other surviving manuscripts, but perhaps it is noteworthy that the Foreword of his MS. *Emblemata Varia* (*c.* 1621) is signed 'Henricus Peacham'. Accordingly, I agree with Waith that Peacham was probably both artist and scribe,[1] and that the date must hence be right. But why would he draw the scene inaccurately?

I can only conjecture that he drew from memory, without consulting the text. Indeed, a fresh look at the picture suggests that his memory may have been worse than we first supposed. Aaron's drawn sword could be interpreted as a threat to Tamora's kneeling sons, and if we recall that Peacham's text refers to '. . . Tamora pleadinge for her *sonnes* going to execution' (my italics) we may suspect that Peacham remembered Aaron as the instrument of Titus's rough justice. Having finished his drawing, perhaps the artist turned to the script – he had left space to transcribe some suitable dialogue – and discovering his error, doctored the text rather than scrap his picture. In any case, the likelihood is that we have a picture based on playhouse observation, but at a considerable distance.

[1] Waith, p. 24.

As an undergraduate at Cambridge whose home was in London, Peacham could have seen one of Henslowe's summer tours (1594) or an otherwise unrecorded performance of *Titus Andronicus*. His inaccuracy with respect to story, however, casts doubt upon the value of his evidence in other matters: might this be a fantasy picture after all? I think not. The anachronisms suggest theatrical costume: the attendant soldiers at left wear contemporary armour; Titus, Aaron, Chiron and Demetrius wear something like the *habit à la romaine* which became commonplace in French tragedy at the time of Racine, and Tamora's gown is of the theatre, not of any real place or time. A fantasy picture would depict Tamora as a woman, but in the playhouse the part would have been played by a man. This figure, I believe, is a man: the nose is large, the mouth is thin, and if Tamora were to stand, 'she' would tower over both Titus and Aaron. If we compare the way Peacham renders female figures in his published emblems, we shall note that there ought to be some sign, if this is a woman, of the beginning of breasts just above the left arm.[1] Nevertheless, Peacham is more likely to have drawn upon normal Elizabethan stage practices than details observed at a particular performance. Aside from the pitch blackness of Aaron, I think we must accept that the Longleat drawing can tell us more about general theatrical practice than it does about the specific staging of *Titus Andronicus*.

Several other features of the picture invite comment. Peacham's later style favours the three-quarter face, but all seven actors in the Longleat drawing are depicted in profile. In fact, the stage grouping is entirely lateral, an awkward arrangement on the thrust stage of the public playhouses, but appropriate enough on an improvised stage in the great hall of a manor or college, where the players would probably use the dais at one end of the room or the screens at the other. Perhaps Peacham's experience of theatre was obtained at touring performances in spaces of this kind. The picture shows that while the actors' torsos are 'cheated' towards the audience, their faces are turned inward towards each other. This implies that they did not follow the convention of tragic acting used in French classical and Restoration theatres, in which each speaker in turn stepped out and delivered a *tirade* straight to the audience.

Gestures are large, but the actors (or is the artist responsible?) seem oblivious of the classically-based principles of *contrapposto* which baroque actors, like baroque painters, considered essential to grace of action and attitude. By those standards, both Titus and Aaron are gesturing with the wrong arm; and while the positions of their feet exhibit some contrast, the attitudes of the other figures are awkwardly symmetrical from the feet up.[2] Indeed, it might be argued that the awkwardness of the soldiers has been subtly emphasised. The bearded man trails his halberd as though to trip his colleague, who holds his upside down. The exaggerated military bearing of the former soldier puts the viewer in mind of Dogberry, while the slight slouch and ludicrous costume of the latter draw attention to their lack of uniformity: their swords do not match.[3] With

---

[1] See Peacham's *Minerva Britanna; or, A Garden of Heroical Devices*, 1612, pp. 35, 47, 69, 119, 151.

[2] See Alan Hughes, 'Art and eighteenth-century acting style. Part I: aesthetics; part II: attitudes; part III: passions', *Theatre Notebook* XLI (1987), 24–31, 79–89, 128–39.

[3] The weapons and armour in Peacham's drawing are discussed by Charles Edelman, *Brawl Ridiculous: Swordfighting in Shakespeare's Plays*, 1992, pp. 31–2.

this scruffy 'army' Titus entered in triumph. Here are the 'four or five most vile and ragged foils' that embarrassed the name of Agincourt.

From the Restoration to the nineteenth century

There is no trace of any performance of *Titus Andronicus* between Jonson's joke in 1614 and the closing of the playhouses in 1642. This does not mean, of course, that none took place. After 1642, few new plays were written, but old ones seem to have been eagerly read, and when playing resumed in 1660, these were the players' only stock until some new plays could be written. The right to perform the old repertoire was vital, and Sir William Davenant of the new Duke's Company found himself at a great disadvantage because practically the entire stock had been inherited by Thomas Killigrew, who held the patent of the King's Company. In December, the Lord Chamberlain transferred to Davenant the right to perform nine of Shakespeare's plays, on condition of his 'reforming' and 'makeing them fitt' for his company.[1] The balance of the Shakespeare canon, including *Titus Andronicus*, remained with the King's Company: in January 1668 the Lord Chamberlain listed it amongst 21 Shakespeare plays in 'A Catalogue of part of His Ma[tes] Servants Playes as they were formerly acted at the Blackfryers & now allowed of to his Ma[tes] Servants at y[e] New Theatre'.[2] Ownership did not necessarily imply performance, however. Listing 36 plays in the company's active repertoire at this period, John Downes names only five by Shakespeare; last of all is *Titus Andronicus*.[3]

In 1687, Edward Ravenscroft published his adaptation, *Titus Andronicus; or, the Rape of Lavinia*.[4] The King's Company had evidently performed it at the Theatre Royal in Drury Lane some nine years earlier: the dramatist says, 'it first appeared upon the stage at the beginning of the pretended Popish Plot' (August 1678), a period when theatrical receipts were low,[5] but it prospered 'and is confirm'd a Stock-Play'. In the absence of other evidence we must cautiously take his word for it, but exaggerated claims to originality elsewhere in Ravenscroft's preface cast doubt upon his claim to popular success: after all, this is a 'puff'. 'Compare the Old Play with this', Ravenscroft boasts, 'you'l finde that none in all that Authors Works ever receiv'd greater Alterations or Additions, the Language not only refin'd, but many Scenes entirely New: Besides

---

[1] See Allardyce Nicoll, *A History of English Drama, 1660–1900*, 4th edn, 1961, I, 352–3; and Robert D. Hume, *The Development of English Drama in the Late Seventeenth Century*, 1976, pp. 235–6.

[2] Nicoll, *English Drama*, I, 353–4; William Van Lennep (ed.), *The London Stage 1660–1900, Part I, 1660–1700*, 1965, pp. 151–2.

[3] John Downes, *Roscius Anglicanus*, 1708, pp. 3–9.

[4] The date is confirmed by the Term Catalogue, 28 February 1687, and an advertisement in *The Observator*, 2 March 1687: see Sybil Rosenfeld, 'Dramatic advertisements in the Burney newspapers, 1660–1700', *PMLA* 51 (1936), 134.

[5] Hume, *Development of English Drama*, pp. 318–20; internal evidence dates the Prologues: 1 to the Lent following the Popish Plot, i.e. 1679; 2 to later that summer, when Joseph Haines was in Scotland; and 3 to early autumn, 1682, 1683 or 1684, between his sojourns in Paris and Rome. The Epilogue refers to the Popish Plot. But nothing links any of these occasional pieces with *Titus Andronicus*. Ravenscroft says the originals are lost, and these were 'Written by me to other Persons Labours', i.e. for performances of *other* plays, and printed here to give the reader his money's worth.

most of the principal Characters heighten'd, and the Plot much encreas'd.' Compared to Nahum Tate's recent operations on *King Lear* (1681), Ravenscroft's version of *Titus* was conservative. Even if it were not, there would be little point in waxing facetious at his expense, as though *Titus Andronicus* were beyond the reach of improvement; its most ardent admirers would scarcely claim that much, and we cannot blame the man for trying.

To understand is to pardon, and Restoration adaptations of Shakespeare are too often ridiculed without understanding. Conditions had changed since Shakespeare's youth. Audiences were smaller, differently composed, and had acquired new tastes. Shakespeare's was a playwright's theatre, but after the Restoration old plays began to emerge as classics, and when there are classics, there is an actor's theatre, and an actress's. Ravenscroft altered *Titus Andronicus* to suit the theatre of his day: if he had not, it would never have been performed at all. Such stage vitality as the tragedy enjoyed between 1678 and our century, it chiefly owed to him. None of this is to say that the adaptation does not contain many ill-conceived things, not the least of which is Ravenscroft's verse – but there is not much of that before Act 5; most of it is Shakespeare, cut and rearranged.

The Restoration playhouse had a proscenium arch and pictorial scenery which imposed entirely new conventions. Scenic neutrality in the Elizabethan manner was impossible; every scene had to be clearly and specifically located. Shakespeare's Act 1 contains no scene changes, but the action takes place both before the 'Capitol' and the tomb of the Andronici. Their physical juxtaposition would have been incongruous. Accordingly, Ravenscroft's version begins before the Capitol; then, when Saturninus and Bassianus exit (Shakespeare's 1.1.63), the scene changes to the exterior of a temple which subsequently opens to discover 'A Glorious Tomb' (1.1.89). It closes when Titus has buried his sons (1.1.156), then the scene changes back to the Capitol (1.1.179) where Marcus offers him the symbolic 'palliament'. Perhaps because scenery was expensive and changes could be awkward, Ravenscroft cuts several scenes entirely. Amongst these are the 'fly' scene (3.2), which is acknowledged to be an addition, and the 'archery' scene (4.3): the players may have been able to shoot arrows right out of the open Rose or, rather appropriately, the playhouse at Newington Butts, but they certainly could not do that at Drury Lane.

Under the fluid stage conventions which prevailed in the Elizabethan playhouse, actors in a new scene probably entered before their predecessors were fairly off the stage. Thus, entrances were much more important than exits. But in a scenic theatre the stage must be cleared before the set can be changed. Before turning his attention to the arrival of actors in a new scene, the spectator watches the old ones depart. As a result, actors insist on 'strong' exists, particularly at the end of an act, because now there will be an interval during which a dramatic exit will have time to make a lasting impression. Ravenscroft cut and rearranged to provide what was needed. Act 1 ends as Bassianus abducts Lavinia and Titus pursues, Act 2 as Chiron and Demetrius set out to rape Lavinia, Act 3 as Marcus leads the mutilated girl away to show her father, and Act 4 with Lucius's exile. In each case the audience asks, 'What will happen next?' and is left in suspense through the interval. That question usually concerns Lavinia: she is in the new subtitle, and is generally more prominent than in Shakespeare. After all, this theatre had actresses.

Ravenscroft promises that the reader will find 'most of the principal Characters heighten'd', as one would expect in an actor's theatre. The most striking change is in Aaron's role. Apparently Ravenscroft anticipated the dissatisfaction of some modern critics with a major character who is present throughout Act 1, but has nothing to say: in the adaptation he is given enough lines to attract attention. More important, his captivity and torture are made a prominent feature of the climactic banquet. A screen is withdrawn and Tamora is shown her paramour on the rack, where he remains to the end, when flames engulf him. By surviving to the end he becomes the arch-villain, because he gets the last word, and his enemies settle with him last. In fact, Aaron becomes the star part.

Reversing Elizabethan practice, Lucius's young son was worked up to make the part suitable for an actress, and re-named 'Junius'. Junius takes a more active part in the plot. He uses a bold stratagem to tempt Chiron and Demetrius to enter Titus's garden, where they will be murdered; and this change is part of a consistent effort to eliminate the implausibilities and confusions that sometimes distress modern critics. Aaron lures Titus's sons to the fatal pit with a forged *billet-doux*, an ironic echo of the trap Junius lays for the sons of Tamora. Aaron's child is not born during the action of the play, but brought to him by a Gothic woman, whom he murders. It is her husband's revenge to capture the Moor and bring him to justice: it all makes simple, direct sense.

Restoration audiences liked their good and evil characters to be unalloyed. Bassianus and Lavinia enter in time to catch Aaron kissing Tamora: there is no guesswork. Nevertheless, Lavinia is too ladylike to join her husband in calling them names. Shakespeare's Titus barbarously permits Lucius to sacrifice Alarbus to the spirits of his dead brothers, but Ravenscroft humanises his motive. Titus's sons have made him swear revenge because Tamora once murdered their captive brother:

> LUCIUS Deaf like the Gods when Thunder fills the Air,
> Were you to all our Suppliant *Romans* then;
> Unmov'd beheld him made a Sacrifice
> T'appease your Angry Gods; what Gods are they
> Are pleas'd with Humane Blood and Cruelty?[1]

The Clown is cut because Restoration audiences were unaccustomed to comic scenes in tragedy: Nahum Tate's excision of Lear's Fool is notorious. But Ravenscroft was no slave to the French 'rules' of tragedy. Titus's hand is chopped off on-stage in defiance of classical precepts, and there is no shrinking from violence in Act 5. The last scene uses the resources of the new scenery and machines for sensation. Fire and the rack are not the only embellishments: a curtain is drawn aside to show Tamora '*the heads and hands of* Dem. *and* Chir. *hanging up against the wall. Their bodys in Chairs in bloody Linnen*'. At the end, Tamora stabs the baby: 'She has out-done me in my own Art', Aaron cries; 'Kill'd her own Child.' And then, sublimely evil, supremely funny: 'Give it me – I'le eat it.'

---

[1] Edward Ravenscroft, *Titus Andronicus; or, the Rape of Lavinia* (1687), 1.3, p. 4.

It seems likely that *Titus*, in one version or another, was never very long off the stage between the Restoration and the first datable performance in the eighteenth century, when the playhouses began to advertise in London's new daily newspapers. These advertisements often provide our only documentation of performances. The first reference to *Titus Andronicus* implies at least one performance about 1698: on 23 August 1704 the *Daily Courant* announced: 'Not Acted these Six Years. At the Theatre Royal in Drury Lane . . . will be reviv'd a Play call'd Titus Andronicus; or, the Rape of Lavinia . . . It being the last time of acting this season.' Similar notices appeared twice in the next season, on 16 September and 17 November 1704, but since advertising at this time was sporadic, we cannot be sure that other performances did not take place at Drury Lane in the summer of 1704–5. Then there is a gap; the next time *Titus Andronicus* was presented, the Theatre Royal had long advertised virtually all of its bills in the *Courant*. The paper announced a revival on 17 August 1717 and added, inaccurately, 'Not Acted these Fifteen Years'. The Aaron was a young actor by the name of James Quin. After two repetitions 'At the particular Desire of several Persons of Quality', *Titus* again closed the season. It is a curious fact that ever since its performance at the Rose in 1594, *Titus* had been given at the end of a season. Drury Lane trotted it out three more times, just before the playhouses closed for Bartholomew Fair.[1] After 1721, it was dropped from the repertoire; meanwhile, the competition had tasted modest success with it.

In 1720–1, despite poor facilities, the rival company at the old converted tennis court in Lincoln's Inn Fields embarked upon a vigorous season of Shakespeare revivals. In rapid succession they presented *King Lear*, 'never acted there before', *The Merry Wives of Windsor*, 'not acted these sixteen years', Dryden's adaptation of *Troilus and Cressida*, *Measure for Measure*, *Titus Andronicus*, 'Never Acted There', and *Much Ado About Nothing*, not acted there for thirty years, as well as nine revivals of plays from the company's Shakespeare repertoire: the proportion of Shakespeare in the season was unprecedented.[2] The lessee was no Shakespearean: under the stage name of 'Lun', John Rich was already appearing as Harlequin in the short entertainments which were to develop into English Pantomime. His motive was not idealism; rather, it is to be found in the defection from Drury Lane of three ambitious young actors: James Quin in January 1718, his friend Lacy Ryan in February, and Mrs Seymour at the end of the season.[3] At Drury Lane they had been overshadowed by Barton Booth, Colley Cibber, John Mills, and Anne Oldfield, but few of Rich's company had Shakespearean pretensions and the newcomers were free to take the leading parts if they could attract the public. No doubt they urged Rich to let them try, and gradually he agreed.

Titus Andronicus was presented twice that season, with the obvious purpose of letting Quin shine as Aaron. By 1720–1 the young star's other parts included Othello, Brutus, Hector, Hotspur, Macbeth, and Falstaff in *Merry Wives*. Ryan's included Hamlet, Edgar, Iago, Cassius, Troilus, Claudio in *Measure for Measure* and Lucius; he probably played Benedick, too. Mrs Seymour played Cordelia, Desdemona, Mrs Page, Cressida,

---

[1] 13, 16, 20, 23 August 1717, with Quin as Aaron; 8 July 1718, 28 July 1719, 27 June 1721, without him.
[2] Emmett L. Avery (ed.), *The London Stage 1660–1900, Part 2, 1700–29*, 2 vols., 1960, II, 461–2.
[3] Quin played Aaron at Lincoln's Inn Fields on 21 and 30 December 1720, 7 February 1721, 18 March 1724 (his Benefit), and 25 April 1724. On 27 June 1721 and 1 August 1722, Walker played Aaron there.

Isabella and, no doubt, Beatrice. She did not appear in *Titus* until 1722, when she played Tamora.

As it happens, we know the receipts for the 1720–1 season, which give us a tangible measure of the popularity of *Titus* compared to other Shakespeare plays in the bill.[1] *Merry Wives* was the success of the year, earning more than £1000 in fifteen performances; six performances of *Measure for Measure* made an average of almost £36 each. But *Titus* is best compared with *Troilus* and *Much Ado*, which had, respectively, four performances averaging £44 and three averaging £20; the three representations of *Titus* grossed an average of £27. Amongst the revivals, *Othello* and *Macbeth* were comparably attractive.

Drury Lane evidently abandoned *Titus Andronicus* because of the defections. John Bickerstaff, who replaced Quin as Aaron in 1718, was promptly disabled by gout,[2] and Thomas Walker, who replaced him in 1721, defected soon afterwards.

Aaron was the star part. Neither John Mills, who played Titus at Drury Lane, nor Anthony Boheme, the Titus at Lincoln's Inn Fields, ever advanced beyond the second rank, but Quin chose to play the Moor at the very time when he was on the point of standing at the head of his profession. We do not know how he played Aaron, but I think his performance would surprise his twentieth-century detractors. Today, he is known almost entirely from an unfortunate engraving as Thomson's Coriolanus (1749), a satirical rear-view in William Hogarth's *Analysis of Beauty*,[3] and scurrilous descriptions by enemies like Tobias Smollett (in *Peregrine Pickle*, 1751) and Charles Churchill (in *The Rosciad*, 1760). It is noteworthy that the earliest of these portraits and attacks is dated almost thirty years after Quin played Aaron. By 1749 his career had outlasted his style, and he was called a ranter. His baroque style had been superseded by the rococo of which Garrick was the most celebrated exponent. But in 1717 he was twenty-four years old. If he had wanted to rant, Titus was his part; Ravenscroft's text did not change that. Aaron calls for a different quality. That part of society which attended the theatre seems to have been passing through one of those periods when people delight in what we might call 'gallows humour'. Like Richard III, Iago, Edmund – and indeed Harlequin – Aaron revels in mayhem, and he expects the audience to share his zest for crime, to laugh and gloat with him. When they are prepared to do that, Aaron becomes the star part. What we know about Quin's style and the parts in which he excelled suggests the contours of his interpretation; youth and energy tempered with dignity, but with humour close to the heart, irrepressible like Falstaff's, but overshadowed with cruel irony. It should come as no surprise that as the age of sensibility advanced, a new audience that could applaud Steele's *Conscious Lovers* (1722) soon banished Aaron from the stage.

After Quin's last appearance as Aaron in 1724, *Titus Andronicus* disappeared from the repertoire for over a century. Only once more before the Second World War would the English-speaking theatre meet with audiences whose attitudes equipped them to

---

[1] Receipts exclude Benefit performances.
[2] Philip H. Highfill, Jr, Kalman A. Burnim, Edward Langhans, *A Biographical Dictionary of Actors . . . 1660–1800*, 16 vols., 1973–93, II, 111.
[3] William Hogarth, *The Analysis of Beauty*, 1753, Plate I, No. 19.

appreciate its ironies: the crowds who rejoiced in Joe Grimaldi's anarchic Clown in
Regency Pantomime would have understood the Aaron Edmund Kean could have
played. But he never played it. There is just one footnote. In 1776 an engraving of
Priscilla Hopkins as Lavinia was published in Bell's edition of Shakespeare. There is no
record that she ever played the part, and she had only joined the Drury Lane company
as a full-time actress in 1775. Conceivably, she may have appeared in a provincial
production.

Two nineteenth-century productions serve chiefly to show how alien the old tragedy
was to the sensibilities of that period. Nathaniel Bannister played Titus four times
at the Walnut Street Theatre in Philadelphia in 1839[1] in a 'clever alteration' which
seems to have been at least partly his own: 'He excluded the horrors with infinite skill,
yet preserved all the interest of the drama.'[2] The cast included the Clown and Young
Lucius, suggesting that Shakespeare's text rather than Ravenscroft's was the basis of
the adaptation. However, the emperor's name is spelled 'Saturnius' as in the *Daily
Courant* advertisements of 1717 to 1721, which may imply that the text derived from
Ravenscroft or an early-eighteenth-century adaptation.

More successful was the radical adaptation of Ira Aldridge. This black actor from
America was a naturalised Englishman who toured the British provinces and Europe
between 1825 and 1865 as 'the African Roscius'. While his favourite parts included
Shylock and Macbeth, Aldridge naturally sought roles in which his colour would be
an advantage: after Othello, what could he do? He played Aaron for his Benefit at the
Adelphi, Edinburgh, on 24 July 1850.[3] Despite negative reviews, Aldridge kept the
play in his repertoire, performing it occasionally for the next decade (see illustration
6).[4]

Aldridge claimed in his advertisements that 'while the horrifying incidents have been
expunged, the gems of the immortal author have been retained'.[5] The adaptation, by
C.A. Somerset, was so thorough that the result can scarcely be said to have been *Titus
Andronicus* at all, except in name and *dramatis personae*. It was really a new melodrama
'of intense interest' which critics found 'really powerful' or 'the weak invention of the
modern dramatic cobbler' according to taste.[6] Piecing together the plot from hints in
reviews, it seems that the story went something like this: Aaron is the hero, 'a noble and
lofty character' whose relationship with Tamora, 'a chaste but decidedly strong-minded

[1] 30 and 31 January, 1 and 2 February.
[2] Charles Durang, *History of the Philadelphia Stage*, arr. by Thompson Westcott, 4 vols., 1868, IV, 157. See
  also Arthur Herman Wilson, *A History of the Philadelphia Theatre, 1835 to 1855*, 1968, p. 202.
[3] Advertisement, *The Scotsman*, 24 July 1850. Herbert Marshall and Mildred Stock, *Ira Aldridge*, 1968,
  p. 171, refer to 'traces' of performances in Paisley the previous November and in Belfast on 13 May 1850,
  but I cannot confirm these.
[4] His provincial engagements seldom included *Titus Andronicus*. I do not know whether he ever played it on
  the Continent. I have traced a total of sixteen performances: Edinburgh, 24 July 1850; Britannia, Hoxton,
  17 March 1852, 20–5 and 30 April, 1–2 and 4–5 May 1857; Brighton, 3, 5 and 11 October 1860. I cannot
  confirm a statement by G. Harold Metz that Aldridge's 'last recorded performance' as Aaron took place
  in Glasgow on 7 November 1860: Metz, 'Stage history of *Titus Andronicus*,' *SQ* 28, 2 (Spring 1977), 159.
[5] *Brighton Examiner*, 9 October 1860.
[6] *Brighton Herald*, 6 October 1860; *Sunday Times*, 26 April 1857 and 21 March 1852.

6   Ira Aldridge as Aaron

female', is 'of a legitimate description'. Indeed, their marriage has been consummated before the play, and they have a child. The Goths have been captured and brought to Rome, where Alarbus is 'murdered', presumably by Saturnius, 'the only person whose sanguinary character is not much toned down'. Titus marries Lavinia to Bassianus, who is murdered too. Chiron and Demetrius 'vie with each other for her hand' and seize her, 'but she is honourably treated, and subsequently liberated by Aaron the Moor, who has been chosen King of the Goths'. There is a sensation scene: Saturnius orders Aaron's child thrown into the Tiber (at least one audience applauded the moonlit set), while the father is obliged to watch, chained to a tree. But the Moor breaks free, leaps into the river and saves his son, evidently with expressions of tenderness adapted from the original. In revenge, the emperor contrives to poison Titus, Tamora and Aaron at a banquet. Lavinia (who has been neither raped nor mutilated) rescues the child again, and 'promises the dying Moor that she will be a parent to it while she lives.'[1] One report gives the scenes which were entirely cut: 'the fifth scene of the second act' (?), all of Act 3, Act 4, Scenes 1 to 4, and Act 5, Scenes 2 and 3.[2] J. J. Sheahan claims that one 'great scene' was borrowed from *Zareffa, the Slave King*, 'written in Dublin for Mr. A'.[3] It was generally agreed that Aldridge's performance was 'remarkable for energy, tempered by dignity and discretion' and that 'there is as little "fustian" about him as in any one on the stage'.[4]

Twentieth-century performance and criticism

Reviewing this century's first production of *Titus Andronicus* in 1923, Herbert Farjeon remarked, 'Its horribilism has got the old Blue Books on War Atrocities beaten hollow.'[5] Its violence and cruelty, in other words, seemed unrealistic, exaggerated. Of course, Farjeon was writing before the twentieth century had shown what it could really achieve in the way of atrocities, but the Great War ought to have stretched his ability to believe in the human potential for unpleasantness. Gerald Freedman, who directed *Titus* in New York in 1967, finds it 'a particularly modern play for today – with its flawed hero, its existence in violence and yet its inevitable compassion'.[6] Harold Hobson thinks it 'comes disconcertingly near to the current standards of political behaviour'.[7] Since the Second World War, *Titus Andronicus* has been accepted in both the theatre and the study as a play to be taken seriously: it no longer seems so far-fetched and alien as it did in 1923.

Robert Atkins produced the play because he and Lilian Baylis wanted the Old Vic to be the first theatre to 'complete the set', and after *Titus* only *Troilus and Cressida* was left.

---

[1] *Brighton Gazette*, 4 October 1860; *Sunday Times*, 26 April 1857; *Brighton Herald*, 6 October 1860; *Brighton Examiner*, 9 October 1860; *The Edinburgh News and Literary Chronicle*, 27 July 1850; *Sunday Times*, 21 March 1852; *The Era*, 26 April 1857.

[2] *Brighton Examiner*, 9 October 1860.

[3] J. J. Sheahan, '*Titus Andronicus*: Ira Aldridge', *N&Q* 82, 17 August 1872, p. 132.

[4] *The Era*, 25 April 1857.

[5] Herbert Farjeon, *The Shakespearean Scene*, 1949, p. 114.

[6] Gerald Freedman (ed.), *Tit.*, 1970, p. 5.

[7] *Sunday Times*, 21 August 1955.

Duty was their motive, and in that spirit their faithful audience resigned themselves to sit through it. The production was careful to avoid giving offence: Lavinia turned her back when she took her father's severed hand between her teeth, and Tamora pecked daintily at the pie. Aaron's wickedness was of the delicious-thrill variety. George Hayes (the star) 'wallowed in a kind of Hoodoo villainy' that was 'most picturesque'; after his exit in 3.1, he returned to fill the stage with diabolical laughter.[1] The audience could not believe in such wickedness, so they felt free to respond warmly to the Moor's defence of his child. 'That redeeming stroke keeps him within the pale of humanity', said J. T. Grein; and to another critic the moment 'shone with unexpected splendours upon the sombre background of a character so evil'.[2] In the same spirit, everyone was delighted by Hay Petrie as the Clown: scarcely one critic connected the comic 'relief' with the rest of the play or even with his sticky end. With evil reduced to thrills, the play became a melodrama. Farjeon complained:

It does not make you vomit in your stall, a liberty to which, as a sensitive product of the twentieth century, I, personally, feel myself entitled. *Titus Andronicus* is, in many respects, an admirably managed piece of work, but since, emphatically, I abominate it, when I see it on the stage I claim the right to be allowed to abominate it to the top of my bent.[3]

In short, he considered this tasteful production a falsification of an offensive play.

There were no more productions until 1951, when a half-hour digest – part of an 'Evening of Grand Guignol' that transferred from the Irving Theatre Club to the Embassy – led J. C. Trewin to hope for 'one responsible full-length production of this First Executioner among Elizabethan shockers'.[4] John Barton doubled it with *Friar Bacon and Friar Bungay* for the Cambridge Marlowe Society in 1953. But it was Peter Brook who made *Titus Andronicus* a theatrical triumph in 1955, at Stratford-upon-Avon.

On opening night the Festival Theatre audience stood and cheered the curtain calls. After an initial run when crowds queued for seats and critics called it 'the most satisfactory and exciting production to be seen at Stratford-on-Avon this season',[5] it was revived in 1957 for a Continental tour, concluding with a London engagement at the 2,500-seat Stoll Theatre: a total of ninety performances. Sir Laurence Olivier (Titus) observed that 'after generations of neglect, it looks like becoming one of Shakespeare's most popular efforts, turning *Hamlet* green with envy'.[6] Did the credit belong to Shakespeare or to Peter Brook?

Some critics who were delighted with the production nevertheless thought it illegitimate. The play was 'twaddle', they said – a crude Elizabethan pot-boiler, a 'horror comic' without 'poetic characterization', a 'preposterous melodrama' and a 'bloody

[1] Farjeon, *Shakespearean Scene*, p. 115; *Evening Standard*, 9 October 1923; *The Era*, 10 October 1923; Gordon Crosse, *Fifty Years of Shakespearean Playgoing*, 1941, p. 79; *The Stage*, 11 October 1923.
[2] *The Sketch*, 24 October 1923; *The Times*, 9 October 1923.
[3] Farjeon, *Shakespearean Scene*, pp. 114–15.
[4] *Observer*, 11 November 1951.
[5] Milton Shulman, *Evening Standard*, 17 August 1955.
[6] *The Stage*, 4 July 1957.

awful play'[1]. One critic called the production a 'benevolent dishonesty' that disguised 'the raw nonsense of [Shakespeare's] nonage'[2]. Bernard Levin remarked that 'Mr Brook has committed upon the text a butchery scarcely less severe than that suffered by most of the people in the play. Mr Brook's play is a far better one than Shakespeare's.'[3] Where Farjeon thought the Old Vic production a travesty because it was not offensive, critics now found Brook's production equally false because it simply was not bad.

Titus Andronicus is still widely regarded as a bad play, notwithstanding the evidence to the contrary of a number of successful productions and a growing body of literary apology. Exactly what is wrong with Shakespeare's first tragedy? Until quite recently it was so unanimously disliked that few troubled to define its badness. Those who made the attempt often found it difficult to uncouple the question of quality from that of authorship. Edward Ravenscroft (1687) set the standard by echoing the language in which Nahum Tate justified his adaptation of King Lear: he found Titus 'the most incorrect and indigested piece' in the Folio.[4] This supported his belief that Shakespeare 'only gave some Master-touches to one or two of the Principal Parts or Characters'. In short, the play was badly constructed, according to the neo-classical standards of the day, and therefore could not be Shakespeare's. Ravenscroft's reasoning was unshaken by the fact that only the undoubted authenticity of King Lear prohibited Tate from drawing the same conclusion from similar evidence.

Most criticism has centred upon the notorious horrors, an issue which remained entangled with the question of authorship. From Theobald to Dowden, practically everyone accepted Johnson's proposition that since 'the barbarity of the spectacles'[5] was offensive, Shakespeare could not have perpetrated them. The minority who accepted his authorship, like Capell and Schlegel, thought Shakespeare could not have been serious: the play was a youthful attempt to thrill the injudicious groundlings by outdoing the sensations of Kyd and Marlowe. In short, if he wrote it at all, Shakespeare could not have meant anything so nasty as Titus Andronicus.

After E. K. Chambers and others discredited the disintegrator J. M. Robertson,[6] more sophisticated explanations became necessary. Some critics argued, in effect, that since Titus Andronicus is a youthful play, it was written before Shakespeare was fully himself; that his artistic judgement had been disarmed by the influence of the 'tragedy of blood', the cult of Seneca, or the cult of Ovid, which he had been unable to assimilate.[7]

---

[1] Richard David, 'Drams of eale', S.Sur. 10 (1957), 128; W. A. Darlington, Daily Telegraph, 17 August 1955; Harold Mathews, Theatre World 51, 368 (1955), 33; Philip Hope-Wallace, Manchester Guardian, 18 August 1955; Milton Shulman, Evening Standard, 2 July 1957; Ivor Brown, Plays and Players, December 1955; Bernard Levin, Truth, 26 August 1955.

[2] Ivor Brown, Drama, ns 38 (Autumn 1955), 37.

[3] Truth, 26 August 1955.

[4] See pp. 23–4 above. Tate found Lear 'a Heap of Jewels, unstrung and unpolish'd; yet so dazling in their Disorder, that I soon perceiv'd I had seiz'd a Treasure'. He set out 'to rectifie what was wanting in the Regularity and Probability of the Tale' (dedication, The History of King Lear, 1681).

[5] From Johnson's commentary, 1765 edn.

[6] For a brief account of this debate, see Wilson, p. xv.

[7] A summary of these viewpoints is to be found in A. C. Hamilton, 'Titus Andronicus: the form of Shakespearean tragedy', SQ 14 (1963), 201–13.

Thus, to Clemen, the play shows us the young poet challenging Greene's mastery of classical allusion, experimenting with the fashion for involved conceits, and imitating Marlowe's innovations in imagery, untempered by the discretion he would develop later.[1] Dover Wilson fell back on a variant of Capell's position: if this is Shakespeare, he didn't mean it. Shakespeare 'was called in to help Peele' to pad an old touring play for a London run; 'having undertaken it against the grain he took out compensation for himself in kind. Once catch the trick of it, you can see him laughing behind his hand through most of the scenes he rehandled.'[2] In his review of Brook's production, Evelyn Waugh was so convinced that the performance misrepresented a bad play that he detected a subtle mockery in Olivier's pronunciation of 'receptàcle'.[3] Wilson's view has not commended itself to posterity. Much recent criticism recognises ironic humour in the play, particularly in Aaron's scenes; but most commentators assume that Shakespeare was in full possession of his genius when he wrote *Titus Andronicus* and was consequently doing something subtle. Accordingly, it is for us to study the play and work out what that is. For example, Richard F. Brucher has argued that Shakespeare 'deliberately made some violence comic in order to thwart conventional moral expectations'.[4] With that, the critical wheel has come full circle.

The horrors remain the chief issue. There is a widespread feeling that the violence is peculiarly offensive. Elizabethan and Jacobean drama abounds in violence, ingenious, varied, and bizarre: there is little in *Titus Andronicus* which is not matched or exceeded in some other play of the period. Nevertheless, if some objective means were devised to measure a play's 'coefficient of violence' I suspect *Titus* would lead the drama of the English Renaissance by a short nose, but trail behind many a Hollywood film by several lengths. Johnson's objection to 'the barbarity of the spectacles' might be attributed to the fashionable squeamishness of the age of sensibility, and Farjeon's remarks about its 'horribilism' might be set down to lingering Edwardian hypocrisy. Justifying his early plays, Harold Pinter points out that the world is a violent place; technology has served merely to put within our grasp the means to commit and suffer violence on an unprecedented scale; modern art does not flinch from depicting violence, because it is real and must be faced. Very well. Why, then, do so many people continue to find *Titus Andronicus* excessively violent?

The answer lies, I think, not so much in excess of violence as in its apparent gratuitousness.[5] Pornography cases frequently hinge on whether the subject matter is essential to some artistic purpose; in the same way, violence that serves no artistic purpose is offensive. This is what T. S. Eliot meant when he condemned *Titus Andronicus* as 'one of the stupidest and most uninspired plays ever written . . . There is a wantonness, an irrelevance, about the crimes of which Seneca would never have been guilty.'[6] Thus,

---

[1] Wolfgang Clemen, *The Development of Shakespeare's Imagery*, 1951, pp. 21–9.

[2] Wilson, pp. xxxvii, li.

[3] *The Spectator*, 2 September 1955, p. 300.

[4] Richard F. Brucher, '"Tragedy, laugh on": comic violence in *Titus Andronicus*', *Renaissance Drama* 10 ns (1979), 73.

[5] Hamilton, 'Form of Shakespearean tragedy', p. 201.

[6] T. S. Eliot, 'Seneca in Elizabethan translation', *Selected Essays*, 2nd edn, 1934, p. 23; Waith, p. 67.

unless *Titus Andronicus* is a serious play the violence is gratuitous and offensive: those who see it as a joke or a pot-boiler must condemn it, while those who merely think it inept cannot excuse it.

Like Brucher, several commentators have explored a variety of serious artistic purposes which the play's violence might serve. As Waith puts it, 'The most satisfying comments on the atrocities have come from those who have explored their relationship to the patterns of ideas and images which dominate the play.'[1] The images 'create a thematic matrix . . . which governs the imagistic structure of the play, [and] culminates in a dialectic contrast between the play's predatory animal images and its cardinal emblem of the enduring but mutilated garden. Through these central image patterns, the play reveals the tragic efforts of the Andronici to preserve a world of civilized virtues from the onslaught of a demonic barbarism.'[2] Raped and mutilated, Lavinia is an emblem of the Roman body politic disordered by barbarians.[3] Derek Traversi finds 'a continuity of purpose' linking the visual and verbal images of human bodies 'lopp'd and hew'd' like trees, with the 'woods and natural surroundings which have already been so variously evoked in their relation to human passions and desires' in the woodland scenes of Act 2.[4] Nicholas Brooke shows that Shakespeare uses his violent incidents, as well as ceremonies and stage groupings, as visual images in the manner of Elizabethan emblems:

Titus grovelling on the floor while the State of Rome passes by in 3.1; or leaving the stage at the end of the same scene, headed for Revenge's cave, bearing the heads of his dead sons while Lavinia carries his own hand in her teeth; or in 4.3 shooting arrows at the stars – all these, and many more, are visual images of a kind that may be more familiar in descriptive verse than actually *seen* on the stage; but they are powerfully effective in establishing emblems of the play's significance.[5]

Titus Andronicus is the work of a brilliant stage craftsman, exploring the resources of his trade: the visual potentialities of human form and movement, the spatial dynamics and mechanical resources of the playhouse. Sometimes, perhaps, he is too ambitious; but while critics have traditionally pointed to the occasions when he has failed to synthesise language with visual imagery, there is a growing body of criticism which attempts to explain just what it is he tries to achieve, and frequently maintains that he has got it right.

For most critics, the attempted synthesis is at its most difficult and ambitious when Marcus confronts the raped and mutilated Lavinia.

> Who is this? My niece, that flies away so fast? . . .
> Speak, gentle niece, what stern ungentle hands
> Hath lopped and hewed and made thy body bare
> Of her two branches, those sweet ornaments
> Whose circling shadows kings have sought to sleep in,

---

[1] Waith, p. 67.
[2] Albert H. Tricomi, 'The mutilated garden in *Titus Andronicus*', *S.St.* 9 (1976), 89.
[3] Eugene M. Waith, 'The metamorphosis of violence in *Titus Andronicus*', *S.Sur.* 10 (1957), 39–49.
[4] Traversi, *Approach to Shakespeare*, I, 66–9.
[5] Nicholas Brooke, *Shakespeare's Early Tragedies*, 1968, p. 20.

And might not gain so great a happiness
As half thy love? Why dost not speak to me?
Alas, a crimson river of warm blood,
Like to a bubbling fountain stirred with wind,
Doth rise and fall between thy rosèd lips,
Coming and going with thy honey breath.
But sure some Tereus hath deflowered thee,
And, lest thou shouldst detect him, cut thy tongue.
Ah, now thou turn'st away thy face for shame,
And notwithstanding all this loss of blood,
As from a conduit with three issuing spouts,
Yet do thy cheeks look red as Titan's face,
Blushing to be encountered with a cloud.   (2.4.11–32)

There is much more: the speech is 47 lines long. The situation is unnatural, of course: while the shocked and mutilated girl stands bleeding before him, her uncle expounds upon her condition in exquisite Ovidian conceits without lifting a finger to help. Any rational modern spectator would react as G. R. Hibbard is tempted to do, yelling 'For God's sake, man, get her to a doctor before she bleeds to death instead of standing there talking.'[1] The juxtaposition of physical atrocity and artificial language is so incongruous that it neutralises the ordinary spectator's capacity to accept the unrealistic conventions of Elizabethan verse drama. The bleeding Lavinia is an image of Senecan violence, while the language is Ovidian – narrative rather than dramatic in style.[2] The result sounds insincere: 'The tone is cool and cultured in its effect', M. C. Bradbrook notes, and Clemen objects to 'the unconcerned nature of these images, as it were, their almost wanton playfulness'.[3]

If Shakespeare was pandering to the literary smart set with precious language, it was really no better than trying to please the groundlings with gratuitous violence. What he has given us is still what A.C. Hamilton characterises as excess: excessive artifice of language.[4] But is it gratuitous artifice? What was Shakespeare really trying to achieve? Many critics believe he was sincerely trying, as Sylvan Barnet puts it, 'to make art out of violence'.[5] The scene may be justified as the most ambitious of the young poet-dramatist's experiments. Perhaps he was trying to adapt the narrative techniques of *The Rape of Lucrece* to the stage.[6] Perhaps he was experimenting with what Rudolf Stamm calls his 'mirror technique' in which actions and visual images are described in order to make Lavinia more dramatic: by preventing her from becoming 'a purely visual theatrical element . . . a passive image of horror', it gives her 'sparks of an active

[1] G. R. Hibbard, 'The forced gait of a shuffling nag', read at the World Shakespeare Congress at Vancouver, quoted by Rudolf Stamm, 'The alphabet of speechless complaint: a study of the mangled daughter in *Titus Andronicus*', *ES* 55 (1974), 327.

[2] Waith, 'Metamorphosis', pp. 46–9.

[3] M. C. Bradbrook, *Themes and Conventions of Elizabethan Tragedy*, 1935, pp. 98–9; Clemen, *Development of Shakespeare's Imagery*, p. 26.

[4] Hamilton, 'Form of Shakespearean tragedy', p. 201.

[5] Barnet, p. xxxiii.

[6] Brooke, *Shakespeare's Early Tragedies*, p. 18.

life and touches of individuality'. Thus Shakespeare was able to create a scene with 'a greater theatrical potential than is usually conceded'.[1]

Some critics argue that it 'has a heightening effect rather than a reductive one'[2] and that 'Far from being divorced from the action as many critics claim, the figurative language points continually toward the lurid events that govern the tragedy.' Shakespeare's metaphor strives 'to unite language and action in an endeavour to render the events of the tragedy more real and painful'. Marcus 'forces us to see, detail by descriptive detail, the spectacle we are already beholding'. Indeed, the play is rich in witty, ironic wordplay: 'Come hither, Aaron . . . Lend me thy hand, and I will give thee mine' (3.1.185–6); thus for example 'hands become powerful dramatic symbols, not simply because they are mentioned sixty times in the text, but because they become *images in action*'.[3] Perhaps in *Titus* Shakespeare 'tests how much reality a tragedy can contain'.[4]

Others maintain that the language distances the horror,[5] 'prettifies' the situation and distracts our attention from its dreadful realities.[6] Waith has argued that Marcus abstracts and generalises Lavinia; Shakespeare borrowed from Ovid not only his pathos but also his theme of metamorphosis, the 'transforming power of intense states of emotion'. By portraying 'the extraordinary pitch of emotion to which a person can be raised by the most violent outrage', the poet transforms the character into pure emotion.[7]

Some commentators find themes of Pinteresque modernity in *Titus Andronicus*: the failure of language, 'an attempt to find dramatic expression for the unbearably horrible and tragic experience . . . The structural turning point of the play is unique in Shakespeare because it is marked by the failure of words, Titus's groan of "Ha, ha, ha!"'[8] Grace Starry West notes that not only Marcus's speech but the whole play contains far more classical allusions than contemporary taste can tolerate, but then goes on to show how even this can be explained as an example of Shakespeare's art rather than artifice. We must distinguish the poet from his characters; it is they who 'speak beautifully, wittily and learnedly'; yet they act brutally. They are steeped in their Roman literary tradition, but 'the moral excellence which one would expect to be the fruit of such study is missing' because they have become effete. Marcus cannot turn words into effective action; his obsession with beautiful speech has made him silly and ineffectual. These are Romans of the decadent late Empire, steeped in a tradition of

---

[1] Stamm, 'Alphabet', pp. 325–31.

[2] Ann Thompson, 'Philomel in *Titus Andronicus* and *Cymbeline*', *S.Sur.* 31 (1978), 30.

[3] Tricomi, 'Mutilated garden', pp. 11–19.

[4] Hamilton, 'Form of Shakespearean tragedy', p. 204.

[5] Waith, pp. 60–2.

[6] Kenneth Muir, *Shakespeare's Tragic Sequence*, 1972, p. 2. See also John R. Velz, 'The ancient world in Shakespeare: authenticity or anachronism? A retrospect', *S.Sur.* 31 (1978), 1–10.

[7] Waith, 'Metamorphosis', pp. 41, 46.

[8] J. L. Simmons, 'Shakespearean rhetoric and realism', *The Georgia Review* 24, 4 (Winter 1970), 458–9. See also Andrew V. Ettin, 'Shakespeare's first Roman tragedy', *ELH* 37, 3 (September 1970), 325–41; David Bevington, *Action is Eloquence: Shakespeare's Language of Gesture*, 1984, p. 29; and S. Clark Hulse, 'Wresting the alphabet: oratory and action in *Titus Andronicus*', *Criticism* 21 (1979), 106–18.

which their literature is a part.[1] A. C. Hamilton also shows how allusions support the intricate web of ironies which establish the fallen, tragic world of the play.[2]

It is difficult, however, to imagine how actors could convey these subtleties quickly and clearly enough to avert a modern audience's resentment of classical allusions. If the audience is not to react with laughter or indignation at Marcus's rhetoric, they must be shown that Shakespeare was trying to do something which makes sense in our time. 'Shakespeare is like the world, or life itself', Jan Kott says. 'Every historical period finds in him what it is looking for and what it wants to see.'[3] Indeed, a director might conclude that some of these critical apologies are a little too ingenious to be credible. Classical allusion, for example, was fashionable amongst the young literati early in Shakespeare's career; like *Titus, Lucrece* is full of them, but nobody could claim that its early Roman characters are steeped in a literary tradition that had not yet been invented. A director might nevertheless be grateful for an interpretation which presents Titus as a hero flawed by excessive devotion to tradition: that would help his production to function as tragedy.

A. W. Schlegel complained that *Titus Andronicus* was 'framed according to a false idea of the tragic, which by an accumulation of cruelties and enormities, degenerated into the horrible and yet leaves no deep impression behind'.[4] But if Titus is a man whose greatness is flawed by excessive devotion to tradition, he can be seen as a tragic character. In the first act he makes errors of heroic proportions. He has Alarbus brutally sacrificed, turning Tamora into an implacable foe; he names Saturninus emperor, although Bassianus is obviously the better man; and he kills Mutius in 'wrongful quarrel'. Each of these acts is attributable to his conservative principles.[5] The sacrifice is carried out according to 'our Roman rites', Saturninus succeeds because he is 'our emperor's eldest son', and Mutius dies like the sons of the archaic hero Lucius Junius Brutus, at the will of a stern *paterfamilias*.

This interpretation would work very well, if only all the disasters which the Andronici subsequently suffer were direct results of the errors of Act 1, but that is simply not the case. Tamora and Saturninus are rather ineffective enemies. Despite repeated references to

> her sacred wit
> To villainy and vengeance consecrate,   (2.1.120–1)

and her vaunt,

> I'll find a day to massacre them all
> And raze their faction and their family,   (1.1.450–1)

---

[1] Grace Starry West, 'Going by the book: classical allusions in Shakespeare's *Titus Andronicus*', *SP* 79, 1 (Winter 1982), 62–77.

[2] Hamilton, 'Form of Shakespearean tragedy', pp. 204–8.

[3] Jan Kott, *Shakespeare Our Contemporary*, 1965, p. 5.

[4] A. W. Schlegel, *Lectures on Dramatic Art and Literature*, trans. John Black, 1879, p. 442.

[5] See Ronald Broude, 'Roman and Goth in *Titus Andronicus*', *S.St.* 6 (1970),227–34; H. T. Price, 'The authorship of *Titus Andronicus*', JEGP 42 (1943), 55–81.

she initiates no action against the Andronici until Act 4, when her inept disguise-plot leads to the death of her remaining sons but does Titus no harm at all. And while Saturninus orders the execution of Quintus and Martius, he acts in the belief that they are guilty of Bassianus's murder. In this he is as much the victim of practice as Titus and his sons. The practiser, of course, is Aaron, the only effective villain and unquestionably the best character in the play, anticipating Richard III, Edmund and Iago. Indeed, he is such an interesting character that he threatens to take the play away from Titus, and it has been suggested that he 'takes on much of the character of one kind of tragic hero himself'.[1] If *Titus Andronicus* fails as tragedy, the fault is Aaron's. Titus might have fallen as the result of his own errors, either as they provoked the revenge of a really 'high-witted Tamora' and a mad emperor he chose himself, or because he loosed upon himself the mysterious forces of an ironic universe. But in fact he is the victim of a villain whose wickedness is neither cosmic nor explicable, but essentially melodramatic.[2]

This is not to say that *Titus Andronicus* is not tragic at all. Nicholas Brooke has effectively argued that there is no single kind of 'true tragedy'.[3] The play can be interpreted, not as Aristotelian or Bradleyan tragedy, but as a tragedy in the medieval tradition, *de casibus virorum illustrium*. Seen in that light, the tragedy of Titus is complete by the end of the first act. Offending against the bonds of family, the laws of society, the state and heaven, he has driven from the earth Astraea, goddess of Justice, who symbolises Order, Degree, and Ceremony: '*Terras Astraea reliquit*' (4.3.4). For the rest of the play he seeks her in an ironic world of original chaos[4] where anarchic villains like Aaron are free to do their dirty work. Even if it is agreed that the play lacks 'any human or moral frame of reference',[5] that the characters lack humanity or that suffering fails to bring Titus to self-knowledge, but transforms him instead into a 'sub-human revenger' at the end,[6] it cannot be denied that in the theatre *Titus Andronicus* is fully capable of delivering a tragic experience.[7] At least three modern productions have done that: Peter Brook's (1955), Brian Bedford's (1978 and 1980) and Deborah Warner's (1987 and 1988).

Literary apologies for Shakespeare's play frequently fail because they do not take into account its theatrical values. The key to its failure at the Old Vic, and to Brook's success, is, in part, sincerity. That is to say, *Titus Andronicus* works in the theatre only when the actors and director believe in the reality of the characters and the truth of the action. Robert Atkins never believed in the play, and his production was consequently

---

[1] Nicholas Brooke, 'Marlowe as provocative agent in Shakespeare's early plays', *S.Sur.* 14 (1961), 37.

[2] If civilisation versus barbarism is the theme, Titus and Aaron function well as antagonists: see Waith, pp. 64–5.

[3] Brooke, *Shakespeare's Early Tragedies*, pp. 1–11.

[4] Hamilton, 'Form of Shakespearean tragedy', pp. 204–8.

[5] Hill, 'Composition', p. 63.

[6] Brooke, 'Marlowe', p. 36.

[7] See Alan Sommers, '"Wilderness of tigers": structure and symbolism in *Titus Andronicus*', *EIC* 10 (1960), 275–89, and Ruth Nevo, 'Tragic form in *Titus Andronicus*', in A. A. Mendilow (ed.), *Further Studies in English Language and Literature*, Jerusalem, 1973, pp. 1–18, who defend the play's structure and argue that it is tragic in conception and, according to Nevo, 'a kind of blueprint of Shakespearean tragedy over which all of his subsequent essays in the tragic kind were palimpsestically to be laid'.

insincere. But if we can believe that the horrors are not gratuitous, and that the rhetoric serves an honest dramatic purpose, Shakespeare's sincerity is vindicated and we shall be ready to take *Titus Andronicus* seriously. That is what Peter Brook did. In praising the 'conviction and fervour of the playing and direction',[1] one observer put a finger on the means Brook had used. From the first cast meeting, Anthony Quayle recalled, Brook strove to impart fervour: 'Actors can catch that, and it will be transmitted to the audience. It came early this time, not during the rehearsal period as sometimes happens. Brook generated intensity.'[2]

It is true that he tinkered with the text, and that his production was very much an interpretation. Brook was accused of making a travesty by cutting extensively, ritualising the violence and making *Titus Andronicus* seem a better play than it really is. Critics pointed to the deletion of the last five words of Titus's notorious line about Chiron and Demetrius, 'Why there they are, *both bakèd in this pie*' (5.3.59). Perhaps it is our changed sense of humour which makes this a predestinate 'bad laugh', but Brook had no practical alternative to cutting it. Again, custom had rendered audiences in the 1950s almost incapable of accepting any convention other than proscenium-arch naturalism. They could not be expected to tolerate Marcus's Ovidian apostrophe to Lavinia. Brook cut it, in the way any modern director cuts outdated topical allusions. Critics lamented the loss of some of the play's 'best' poetry, but like any good production, Brook's found new poetic moments. Anthony Quayle brought tears to many eyes with 'Sweet blowse, you are a beauteous blossom, sure' and Olivier's 'When will this fearful slumber have an end?' was deeply evocative, a line that 'echoes down endless corridors of departed splendour'. Perhaps only those who remember the production could explain what made 'two words, "Ah, Rome!" something that will long haunt the mind'.[3]

There are always dreamers who ask why directors 'can't do Shakespeare straight'. The answer is that Shakespeare is never straight: his plays are full of complexities, choices that cannot be ducked. To direct *Titus Andronicus* passively would be to court failure. 'If you just let the play speak, it may not make a sound', Brook wrote. 'If what you want is for the play to be heard, then you must conjure its sound from it.' He believed that we long for a theatre that will make visible the 'invisible currents that rule our lives'. If the theatre could find new rituals, fresh and true; 'if the theatre were the only place one could go to experience certain things that you know correspond profoundly to life . . . then the theatre would indeed be necessary'. But post-war man's vision is 'locked to the dark end of the spectrum'; that is why Brook turned to *Titus Andronicus*. It appealed to everyone because 'it was obviously for everyone in the audience about the most modern of emotions – about violence, hatred, cruelty, pain'. Brook's production 'tapped . . . a ritual of bloodshed which was recognized as true'.[4] Whether we accept Brook's approach or not, it is difficult to deny that in this production *Titus Andronicus* emerged as a thoroughly modern play: consider the strong

---

[1] J. B. Boothroyd, *Punch*, 24 August 1955, p. 226.
[2] Interview with Anthony Quayle, 17 March 1983.
[3] J. C. Trewin, *The Sketch*, 24 August 1955.
[4] Peter Brook, *The Empty Space*, 1972, pp. 43–53; 'Search for a hunger', *Encore* 8, 4 (July–August 1961), 16–17.

emotions it demonstrably aroused. The horrors no longer seemed far-fetched: this was an audience to whom the memory of Buchenwald was fresh. 'The play does come up astonishingly in performance', J. C. Trewin said. 'Brook has had the right vision.'[1]

The young director was fortunate in his cast. Olivier made Titus 'one of the great things in his career'. He entered, 'not as a beaming hero but as a battered veteran, stubborn and shambling, long past caring about the people's cheers'. He showed the audience 'not strength itself, but the vast exhaustion which is strength's aftermath. No little man could be so weary . . .' It did not seem incongruous when this weary conqueror killed his son. 'A hundred campaigns have tanned his heart to leather.' But he was still vulnerable. He could be touched through Lavinia, and when he was, he suffered on a superhuman scale: 'Sir Laurence doesn't *play* this part, he hews it out of solid rock with the hammer of Thor.' Yet he somehow managed to move the audience to pity, despite the titanic scale of the characterisation; and he avoided monotony with the 'astonishing variety of his reactions to disaster'. With 'the crowning frenzy of "I am the sea" Olivier seemed to break through the illusion and become, not old Hieronymo run mad again, but madness itself'.[2]

Next to the violence, the greatest problem *Titus Andronicus* presents to a modern director is what to do with Aaron: how significant is he? Aldridge and Quin made him the star's role, but neither played Shakespeare's text. Robert Atkins cast his leading man, George Hayes, as the Moor in the first modern production of the original text. But in several post-war productions, Titus has been preferred. This was the case at Stratford: in a cast of stars, Olivier was unquestionably the brightest. Aaron has no lines in the first act. He may be inconspicuous, or prominent: it is the director's choice. But Aaron has a way of taking over later in the play. Even in Brook's production, some critics thought Anthony Quayle took command in the later acts. Quayle was a superb actor, but to take the focus from Olivier, he would need a very remarkable part. Interviewing him at his home, I felt like a regimental historian (a Lieutenant) meeting the legendary wartime Colonel: he projected that sort of respect and normality. He had felt miscast, he said; Aaron was grotesque, exaggerated, huge, not his sort of part at all. But Brook had pushed him to reach out and find a character who was more and more unlike himself, and in a week or ten days 'it was all right'.

History shows it was more than all right. Aaron was like a big, black athlete. Describing his characterisation, Quayle began to quote, and then to act; and in a moment, there was Aaron, striding across the British India rug. His voice was rich, African, almost accented. His eyes were round and prominent, his arms and legs long, his gait subtly black, joints loose, hands enormous: the palms and nails seemed pink. This was no white man in blackface: blackness was the centre of the man, alone in the white man's world. Two remarkable traits made this Aaron work brilliantly: his humour, and his innocence. He was very funny, Quayle said, 'a demon of humour' laughing a big

[1] *The Sketch*, 24 August 1955.
[2] *The Times*, 2 July 1957; Kenneth Tynan, *A View of the English Stage, 1944–63*, 1975, p. 163; *Sunday Times*, 7 July 1957; David, 'Drams of eale', p. 127; Levin, *Truth*, 26 August 1955; Quayle interview, 17 March 1983.

7 Anthony Quayle as Aaron in Peter Brook's production, 1955

black laugh with his great pink mouth. Even chopping off a hand, he maintained an open-eyed innocence which made it easy for him to behave in public as though he were innocent indeed; he had no sense of wrongdoing, which made him doubly evil. This was how Quayle contrived to eschew 'easy pantomime golliwoggery' without going to the opposite extreme of teasing a sympathetic tear from the eye by his defence of his

8   Act 2, Scene 4: 'Enter . . . Lavinia, her hands cut off, and her tongue cut out, and ravished': Vivien Leigh
in Peter Brook's production, 1955

child. The result was 'alarmingly credible', a 'walking principle of evil' whose ignoble
but 'superbly corrupt flamboyance' won reluctant admiration.[1]

Much of the play's violence was left to the imagination. Chiron and Demetrius were
slain off-stage, Lavinia 'did not hold that dreadful bowl between her stumps', Titus
swiftly wrapped his lopped arm in his cloak.[2] Lavinia's wounds were ritualised; long
crimson scarves hung from her sleeves, symbolising blood (see illustration 8). This
transfigured her suffering rather than disguising it. Brook's rejection of realism kept
the audience from distancing the violence by ridiculing an inadequate illusion. They
could not escape from imagination.

The hand-cutting action was concealed. Titus put his wrist on a block; he cried
out, Aaron grunted and stamped, and from off-stage came 'a nice scrunch of bone.
That's when most people faint', explained a theatre official. 'At least three people pass
out nightly. Twenty fainted at one performance. Ten swooned on Friday.' Bernard

---

[1] Quayle interview. Levin, *Truth*, 26 August 1955; *Birmingham Evening Despatch*, 17 August 1955; *The Times*,
17 August 1955; *Drama* 46 (Autumn 1957), 22; Tynan, *View of the English Stage*, p. 163; *The Stage*, 18
August 1955.
[2] Waugh, *The Spectator*, 2 September 1955; J. C. Trewin, *Shakespeare on the English Stage, 1900–1964*, 1964,
p. 236; David, 'Drams of eale', p. 128.

Levin heard 'what sounded remarkably like someone on the left-hand side of the stalls being violently sick'.[1] Surely the objection that the production shrank from the play's 'horrors' cannot be sustained. Shakespeare probably wanted to shock his audience. But for an audience in 1955, Brook knew that the methods of 1594 would produce the opposite of the desired effect. So he used means which would have the corresponding effect in *his* time.

The most serious charge, however, was that the production somehow misrepresented the play. Richard David concluded: 'this piece on which so much labour and ingenuity had been lavished was – twaddle'. Kenneth Tynan thought that 'the director has imposed on a bloodstained, uneven play a unifying conception of his own'.[2] In short, critics preferred their own evaluation of *Titus Andronicus* to the evidence of performance. But surely this will not do. Unless we are inflexibly committed to L. C. Knights's assertion that we ought to take Shakespeare's plays as 'so many lines of verse on a printed page which we read as we should read any other poem',[3] we must be prepared to admit that a play cannot be finally judged until it is performed. *Titus Andronicus* 'does come up astonishingly in performance'. Brook said 'it begins to yield its secrets the moment one ceases to regard it as a string of gratuitous strokes of melodrama and begins to look for its completeness'.[4]

Is *Titus Andronicus* a bad play, or a good one whose merit became clear in performance? Asking that question, we find ourselves in a rare and intimidating position. Established literary tradition found it bad, as the same tradition found *Hamlet* good. But whereas a long and lively stage history confirms the critical assessment of *Hamlet*, *Titus Andronicus* has enjoyed no similar history. In 1955, most readers still held the traditional view. Then Brook confronted them with a production so successful that the consensus was called into question. Scholars began to return to the text. Many found unexpected excellences there, but the real test lay with the theatre. If Brook's success can be repeated, perhaps *Titus Andronicus* really is a good play for the theatre. Thus modern productions are important new evidence, and more is coming in every year as *Titus Andronicus* takes its place in the performing repertoire. In the end, we shall have to make our own judgement.

A factor in the success of Brian Bedford's production at Stratford, Ontario, in 1978 and 1980 was the relative intimacy of the thrust stage. The horrors were neither gratuitous nor half-hearted, and their impact was no laughing matter. Chiron and Demetrius were trussed with their heads bent backwards over the edge of the stage; a realistic line of blood followed Titus's knife as he cut each throat. Bedford shied away from some of the most difficult moments. He cut Marcus's speech to Lavinia, the squabbling over whose hand was to be cut off in 3.1, and everything after the death of Saturninus. As the play ended, the focus narrowed to Aaron standing alone on the upper level while the voice of the Sibyl predicted Rome's fall, an alteration which changed the meaning: for affirmation and healing under Lucius the production substituted a sceptical modern

---

[1] Quayle interview; *Daily Express*, 24 October 1955; Levin, *Truth*, 26 August 1955.
[2] David, 'Drams of eale', p. 128; Tynan, *View of the English Stage*, p. 265.
[3] L. C. Knights, 'How many children had Lady Macbeth?', in *Explorations*, 1964, p. 28.
[4] Brook, *Empty Space*, p. 106.

9   Stephen Russell as Demetrius, Pat Galloway as Tamora and Rodger Barton as Chiron in Brian Bedford's
production at Stratford, Ontario, 1980

theme of evil triumphant and Rome's decadence. The Goths' barbaric dress and the
way they hunkered on their heels with their hands on their knees, like nomads (see
illustration 9), stressed the contrast between Rome and barbarism.

The heart of the production was human tragedy, 'the strange, sad, paradoxical,
terrible, exalted forms into which Titus' humanity is forced as the "tigers" savage
him'. Even when he was plotting his dreadful revenge, William Hutt's Titus seemed

to *The Nation* 'always comprehensible, always sympathetic, always somehow like us. When he folds his ravished daughter in his arms and stabs her . . . what we feel is the lovely tenderness with which he does it. He leads the play to a transcendence of its own horrors; he makes it a magnificent affirmation of the persistence with which human beings can remain human.'[1] Perhaps the strongest moment was in 3.1, when Titus pleaded for his sons while a silent procession of tribunes and senators crossed the stage and filed down the vomitorium into a cold, eerie light.[2]

Jane Howell's BBC-TV production (1985) made few alterations in the text, but used the camera's power to direct attention away from awkward subjects such as Lavinia with her father's hand in her mouth. It emphasised the appalling experience of Young Lucius as he lives his family's tragedy. At the end, while his father addresses the Romans off-camera, the focus is on the boy. He stares horrified at a small coffin containing the corpse of Aaron's child, killed despite Lucius's oath in the name of his gods. The new emperor emerges as a hypocritical opportunist.

Deborah Warner's production at the Swan in Stratford-upon-Avon (1987) was remounted at the Barbican's Pit in 1988. Both are intimate spaces, which gave moments previously regarded as risky sufficient impact to play successfully. The play was uncut. Warner's watchword was trust: 'trust in the script, in the audience, in the Swan (a major component in the success of this show), in each other'.[3] Blood was used sparingly. During Marcus's long speech to Lavinia (2.4.11–57), 'Lavinia's plight was therefore signalled not by visible blood or by silken streamers but by a coating of clay or mud, by what appeared to be hastily-applied wrappings on her stumps, and by the abject posture of Sonia Ritter's shamed, half-crazed figure.'[4] The image of the fountain of blood, then, was created both by Marcus's speech and by the imagination of the audience. At the most difficult lines,

> Why dost not speak to me?
> Alas, a crimson river of warm blood,
> Like to a bubbling fountain stirred with wind,
> Doth rise and fall between thy rosèd lips . . .

a trickle of blood from her mouth 'elicited shocked gasps from the audience'.[5]

As in Bedford's production, the play worked because the emotions were real, rooted in honest characterisation and genuine human relationships. Alan Dessen correctly points out that by playing the full text, Warner allowed the characters to develop more fully and at the right pace, rather than an accelerated one.[6] Brian Cox 'established Titus as a credible, human character by making him a bit of a card – an odd, shambling

---

[1] *The Nation*, 16–23 August 1980.
[2] The vomitorium is the entrance leading to a thrust stage from beneath the audience; at Stratford, Ontario, there are two of them, on opposite sides of the stage.
[3] Alan Dessen, *Shakespeare in Performance: Titus Andronicus*, 1989, p. 57.
[4] *Ibid.*, p. 59.
[5] *Ibid.*, p. 60.
[6] *Ibid.*, pp. 60–6.

hero, very much a law unto himself'.[1] Thus he could remove the danger of unwanted humour in scenes like 3.2 by tragicomic playing that invited laughter.

The evidence of successful productions suggests that readers dissatisfied with the quality of *Titus Andronicus* as literature should remember that it was written for the theatre, where it does very well if certain conditions prevail. First, the director and actors must trust the script. If they do that truly, there is no need to cut. Real emotion based on honest characterisation will carry them through even those moments which have been considered too risky to play. Second, it does not seem to matter whether the violence is stylised or realistic, so long as it is not gratuitous: it must be seen to reinforce a serious theme. Typically modern themes like the loss of innocence in the face of the inevitable corruption bred by power (Howell), the power of evil (Bedford) or the consequences of violence (Warner) can be found in *Titus Andronicus*. But modern ideas require a modern tone, and the play must be allowed to generate its own grim humour; if it does not, audiences will find humour for themselves. Finally, the play seems to function best in intimate theatres where audience and players share the same aesthetic space: the barrier of a proscenium arch insulates an audience from its assault, and allows them to seek refuge in laughter.

Recent stage, film and critical interpretations by Sue Hall-Smith

PERFORMANCE HISTORY

'Our virtues lie in th' interpretation of the time'[2]

The last fifty years have seen a renewed interest in the production of *Titus Andronicus*. Historically, the work has been generally regarded, as Hughes notes (p. 30 ff. above), as a tasteless spectacle of gratuitous violence, practically unplayable and a somewhat dubious member of the Shakespearian canon. The seminal 1955 production directed by Peter Brook at the Shakespeare Memorial Theatre, Stratford-upon-Avon, however, conferred an element of respectability on the work and ensured that it received a more prominent place in the theatrical repertoire. At the same time, the violence enacted in the play has increasingly found an echo in political events, which has given particular immediacy to its portrayal of the human condition *in extremis*. Furthermore, audiences who have access to unflinching twenty-four-hour news coverage of horrific scenes and are familiar with the work of film directors such as Quentin Tarantino are less daunted by the graphic violence and black humour of one of Shakespeare's grimmest works.

The frequency with which the play is now performed across the globe demonstrates its relevance to contemporary concerns. Over two hundred productions have been mounted in the course of the last fifty years in spaces as widely separated as the Royal Shakespeare Theatre at Stratford-upon-Avon and the 'Boggo Road' prison in Brisbane,

---

[1] Stanley Wells, 'Shakespeare performances in London and Stratford-upon-Avon, 1986–87', *S.Sur.* 41 (1988), 179.
[2] *Cor.* 4.7.49–50. Quoted from Lee Bliss (ed.), NCS, 2000.

10　Ozana Oancea as Lavinia in Silviu Pucarete's production, 1997.

and in styles ranging from the conceptual to the overtly political, and from full-text[1] to radically shortened, and even musical versions.[2] The text (both Folio and adapted) has been translated into and performed in a huge number of languages including Afrikaans, Catalonian, Chinese, Croatian, Dutch, French, German, Greek, Hungarian, Italian, Japanese, Norwegian, Polish, Romanian, Russian, Serbian, Slovac, Spanish, Swedish, and British Sign Language.

A number of theatre practitioners have demonstrated the political relevance of the play. The Romanian director, Silviu Pucarete,[3] resisted attempts to associate his interpretation with the collapse of the Ceausescu regime, but, as Michael Billington observed, it was 'impossible to divorce the production from Ceausescu's Romania, as it brings out the arbitrariness, cruelty and absurdity of tyranny'.[4] The staging was simple but effective, with a variety of visual signifiers enforcing the play's modernity, including a hospital trolley and white operating-theatre gowns, television sets and microphones. In addition Pucarete used silhouettes and shadows in combination with white, clinical drapes to create a claustrophobic box-like structure enclosing the stage. Jonathan Bate observed the way in which 'the fragile figure of Lavinia is backed up against a huge white drop; she is grabbed from behind and pinned against it like a butterfly on a card before being dragged under and raped'[5] (see illustration 10). The same image was created for Chiron and Demetrius when Titus captured them, trapping them in the curtain before dragging them underneath to exact his revenge. The audience were thus drawn into a disturbing world where people disappeared quickly and silently. The final Thyestean banquet was enacted to Mozart's last piano concerto, the E flat Larghetto, bringing the action 'to a close on an aesthetic harmonisation, but with no illusions of political restoration'.[6] This final fusion of aesthetic beauty with the physical horror of the action became a metaphor for the fall of the Ceausescu regime but also carried more

[1] In 1987 Deborah Warner's groundbreaking full-text production for the Royal Shakespeare Company demonstrated that the play could be successfully performed in its entirety but paradoxically contributed to its absence from the Stratford stages until September 2003, as subsequent directors were apprehensive about matching her achievement. According to Bill Alexander, the director of the 2003 *Titus Andronicus*, the resounding success of Warner's production 'cast a long shadow' for later RSC producers (interview with Bill Alexander, 14 August 2003). Nevertheless, Warner's deconceptualised interpretation demonstrated the possibilities of an uncut text, and undoubtedly played its part in the renaissance of the work.

[2] Conceptual productions include those by French director Daniel Mesguich (1989–92), who staged the action in a set resembling an inverted library acting as a metaphor for the history of culture, and Johan Doesburg (1997, Netherlands), who saw the work as an exercise in delivering rhetoric. Overtly political productions include Nenni Delmestre's 1992 version (itd Theatre, Zagreb) that focused on the plight of the Croatian people. Ruthlessly cut productions include those by Stefan Bachmann (1992, Theater Gruppe Affekt, Berlin) and Silviu Pucarete (1992–7). Musical versions include the 2002 *Titus Andronicus! The Musical!* by Brian Colonna, Erik Edborg, Erin Rollman, Hannah Duggan and Muni Kulasinghe (Buntport Theater, Denver, Colorado).

[3] With the National Theatre of Craiova. The premiere in Bucharest in Romania in 1992 was followed by tours in 1993, 1995 and 1997, which included venues in Japan, Canada, Germany, Belgium, Australia, Brazil, Singapore, France, Italy, the former Yugoslavia and the UK.

[4] *The Guardian*, 'Theatre review: *Titus Andronicus*', 22 May 1997.

[5] 'Conquering despair', *TLS*, 28 July 1995, pp. 18–19. Lavinia, on her first entrance, wore a simple peasant dress and headscarf, allowing her eventual rape to be constructed as a metaphor for the degradation of the Romanian people.

[6] *Ibid.*, p. 18.

distant reminders, specifically of Holocaust victims being taken to the gas chambers to the accompaniment of classical music. The director's vision was acclaimed in Romania by critics and audiences alike, and theatregoers regularly returned to the production, describing it as an 'utterly mesmerising' experience, during which they imagined they had 'walked in the shadow of evil'.[1]

Peter Stein used the play as a means of offering a broader commentary on corrupt political ideologies.[2] Stein resisted anchoring his vision in any one recognisable period, or overtly aligning it with a specific historical event, choosing to present the play in an eclectic mix of visual styles as a more generalised reflection of contemporary society: 'one in which monolithic Empire-building civilisations dwindle into chaos'.[3] Nevertheless, the references to a particular culture – if not one specific regime – were palpable throughout, as Italian audiences were quick to note.

The staging of the production evoked both ancient and twentieth-century Rome. The stage was bordered on three sides with marble-coloured walls, 'with hints of the neo-imperial style of Piacentini (Mussolini's favourite architect)'.[4] Culturally specific signifiers were insistently employed: for example, Titus's hand and the heads of his sons were returned to him in transparent plastic bags, 'a technological torture characteristic of a post-*Godfather* era'.[5] Costumes were similarly designed 'to imply past centuries while anchoring the play in our own time'.[6] Titus wore a laurel wreath and a short red Roman military cloak on his triumphal return to Rome, while his sons had 'the rounded helmets of Mussolini acolytes'.[7] Twentieth-century allusions continued during the hunt scene when the characters lined up on-stage wearing feathered hats and carrying guns, evoking a Fascist shooting party.

Stein's conflation of a violent contemporary society and its equally corrupt Roman past received mixed reactions from Italian audiences, resulting in dissention between the director, the actors and the media. Raf Vallone (Marcus), for example, objected to his character participating in the play's denouement as the did not want to alienate his fans, and expressed his dissatisfaction with Stein (in the French press) when the production reached Paris.[8] Stein's was a world the Italian public recognised, but the general consensus was one of resentment towards 'a barbarian descended from the North to tell us about another descent of barbarians'.[9] The representation of their

[1] Lyn Gardner, untitled article, *The Guardian*, *G2*, 19 May 1997.
[2] Stein's venture grew from a collaboration between the Teatro di Stabile Genova and the Centro Teatro Ateneo at the Università di Roma 'La Sapienza', and marked Stein's first work outside his native Germany. The play toured Italy (Bari, Bologna, Perugia, Ferrara, Modena, Rome, Milan and Genoa), and visited Spain, France and Germany between 1989 and 1990.
[3] Michael Billington, 'Connoisseur of cruelty', *The Guardian*, 28 November 1989.
[4] *Ibid.*
[5] Fabiola Gulino, 'Peter Stein's *Titus* at the Teatro Genova, 1990', in Philip C. Kolin (ed.), *Titus Andronicus: Critical Essays*, 1995, p. 478.
[6] Billington, 28 November 1989.
[7] *Ibid.*
[8] Marion Thébaud, 'Les curiosités de Raf Vallone', *Le Figaro* (4 May 1990), quoted in Dominique Goy-Blanquet, 'Titus resartus: Deborah Warner, Peter Stein and Daniel Mesguich have a cut at Titus Andronicus', in Dennis Kennedy (ed.), *Foreign Shakespeare: Contemporary Performance*, 1993, p. 54n.
[9] Quadri, 'Tito Andronico in doppio petto', quoted in Kennedy (ed.), *Foreign Shakespeare*, p. 49.

own history and evocation of twentieth-century Fascism combined to project an image that resonated deeply and 'hit too close to home'.[1] Nevertheless, despite its lukewarm reception by Italian audiences, the production was revived to tour Europe during 1990. By this time, however, a number of the original cast shared Raf Vallone's frustrations with the work and refused to work with Stein on the revival.

Contemporary political tensions also informed Gregory Doran's staging of *Titus Andronicus* for the UK's Royal National Theatre and the Market Theatre of Johannesburg in 1995.[2] Doran publicly disavowed a political reading of the text but in his production diary, *Woza Shakespeare!*, which he co-wrote with Antony Sher, he reflected: 'surely, to be relevant, theatre must have an umbilical connection to the lives of the people watching it.'[3] Doran achieved this connection by overtly locating the action in an African context, and presenting it, according to Michael Billington, 'as a mirror of modern South Africa'.[4] Though Doran repudiated the suggestion that the piece was politically motivated, the production inevitably became embroiled in issues related to the ongoing ethnic conflict. His decision to use indigenous accents, for example, rather than traditional Received Pronunciation, challenged the preconceptions of the mainstream, predominantly white, South African audiences. One woman wrote a private letter to Sher explaining that she could not see the production because 'she could not abide the excruciating experience of the ugly accents of southern Africa abusing some of the most beautiful language ever written'.[5] Doran's production touched deeply rooted cultural sensitivities and divisions and, according to Robert Lloyd Parry: 'The questions raised by "Titus" went far beyond the play itself [to] many of the tensions that exist in the new South Africa: the gulf of mistrust that still exists between blacks and whites . . . *Titus Andronicus* has proved itself to be political theatre in the truest sense.'[6]

The Croatian director Nenni Delmestre, who staged a controversial version of the drama at the itd Theatre in Zagreb in 1992, was more overt in her emphasis on ethnic conflict. Delmestre explicitly linked her choice of play to the Croatian situation, where 'massacres and bloodshed had become our tragic everyday reality'.[7] Though the war between Croatia and Yugoslavia had formally come to an end when the play was staged, and Croatia had received recognition as an independent state, Croatian and Serbian forces were still fighting in Bosnia–Herzegovina, giving the play a terrible immediacy. Events in Bosnia (together with those in Beirut and Belfast) also informed British director Ron Daniels's production at the Saison Theatre in Tokyo in 1992. With a

---

[1] Kolin (ed.), *Titus Andronicus: Critical Essays*, p. 477.
[2] The production, which brought together British and South African actors, starred Antony Sher as Titus. It premiered in South Africa before touring to the West Yorkshire Playhouse in Leeds, the Cottesloe Theatre (RNT, London), and the Almagro Festival, Spain.
[3] Antony Sher and Gregory Doran, *Woza Shakespeare!*, 1996, p. 34.
[4] *The Guardian*, 'A brutal sort of interrogation', 14 July 1995.
[5] Quoted in Doran, *Woza Shakespeare!*, p. 226.
[6] *Plays International* (August 1995), p. 11.
[7] Janja Ciglar-Zanic, 'Recruiting the Bard: onstage and offstage glimpses of recent Shakespeare productions in Croatia', in Michael Hattaway, Boika Sokolova and Derek Roper (eds.), *Shakespeare in the New Europe*, 1994, p. 267.

Japanese translation by Yushi Odashima, Daniels used these contemporary conflicts to contextualise *Titus Andronicus* for a modern Japanese audience. Jeff Love (who directed the play for Point of You Productions at the Trilogy Theatre in New York in September 2000) used by-play in a similar manner to explore the tensions in American society. His production focused upon current racial tensions in New York and depicted the play's two factions as the city police (Romans) and the ethnic minorities (Goths). In the same way Qiping Xu's 1986 Chinese production[1] was fuelled by images of his own cultural history. Qiping Xu intended his audience to perceive parallels between the character of Titus, 'famous for his loyalty',[2] and figures from Mao Zedong's Cultural Revolution, when students (the Red Guard) were encouraged to demonstrate against government and party officials and to take direct action against their own teachers as an expression of revenge, contempt and class hatred.

Bill Alexander by contrast, in his 2003 production for the RSC at the Royal Shakespeare Theatre, Stratford-upon-Avon, while acknowledging that *Titus Andronicus* 'seems so contemporary[3] decided against presenting the play in modern dress to shift the focus away from one specific event or political ideology. He argued that '*Titus Andronicus* poses the question of revenge, so it can't not be relevant . . . If [its] society is portrayed truthfully, the issues will be relevant. The plays must be relevant if they're done in the right way because Shakespeare was writing about what mattered to human beings.'[4] Inspired partly by the Peacham drawing (see above, pp. 14–22) Alexander decided to acknowledge the broader relevance of the play, and to create a world 'that drew from and brought together the classical Roman of the story and the late Renaissance of the author.'[5] What was fundamental to Alexander was the *story* and the timeless examination of revenge and its aftermath presented straightforwardly by focusing upon the text.

Alexander decided that the Folio text itself presented a challenge, particularly in Act 1, which seemed to him to have a different rhythm and construction from the rest of the work. He suspected that the first act was the work of George Peele, not Shakespeare, a view supported by his reading of Brian Vickers, *Shakespeare, Co-Author*, and the continuing academic debate regarding the authorship issue. Confident that Act 1 was by Peele, Alexander felt that he would not alter the shape of Shakespeare's design if he radically edited the exposition of the work. Consequently he re-shaped the whole of Act 1 to make it possible for Saturninus and Tamora to remain on-stage throughout, following their initial entrance. He dispensed with the 'above' and 'below' of the Folio text and, most radically, cut Mutius and the plea for his honourable burial. In total approximately one hundred lines were omitted (largely from Act 1) but Alexander was

---

[1] At the First China Shakespeare Festival, held in Shanghai. Qiping Xu was a professor at the Shanghai Drama Institute.

[2] Qiping Xu, 'Directing *Titus Andronicus* in China, 1986', translated by Jianqing Zheng, in Kolin (ed.), *Titus Andronicus: Critical Essays*, p. 445.

[3] Bill Alexander, 'The Director Bill Alexander talks about Titus Andronicus and the question of Revenge', RSC website. Internet search date 11 June 2005.

[4] *Ibid.*

[5] Bill Alexander, unpublished *Titus Andronicus* production journal. No page numbers.

11   Ian Gelder (Marcus), Eve Myles (Lavinia) and David Bradley (Titus) in Bill Alexander's 2003 production for the RSC.

emphatic about remaining faithful in the remainder of the play to the language of the Folio text.

Michael Billington observed that although 'less voluptuous than Peter Brook's Stratford production, Alexander's version makes a strong case for *Titus* as the raw essence of tragedy'.[1] Similarly Patrick Carnegy noted that:

Bill Alexander's production is in the unflinchingly serious mode . . . The emphasis is on the sorrows of Titus, not his anger. His stoicism and that of the sorry remnant of his family is set against the manic excitability of his enemies. It's a strategy that casts the play in a compelling new light.[2]

Mindful of the success of the previous RSC production, by Deborah Warner (1987), staged in the intimacy of the Swan Theatre, and the cool reception accorded to the previous production of *Titus Andronicus* on the vast main stage at Stratford by John Barton in 1981, Alexander elected to present much of the action of the play at the front of the playing space, between the audience and the proscenium arch. The wooden stage, common to all the main-house productions of the 2003 season, extended approximately ten feet into the auditorium, enabling Alexander to bring the action forwards towards the audience, breaking down the physical barriers between play and spectator enforced

[1]   '*Titus Andronicus*', *The Guardian*, 24 September 2003.
[2]   'Seriously bloody', *The Spectator*, 4 October 2003.

by the size of the venue itself, thus creating 'a pitiless apocalyptic atmosphere that commands rapt, appalled attention'.[1]

Other directors have chosen to stage the work in more unconventional venues yet further removed from the 'traditional' theatrical space with proscenium arch and inflexible seating and have thus contributed to the growing sense of the contemporary applicability of the play. These productions have largely concentrated on the intensity of the atmosphere created in a confined playing-space and the flexible actor–audience relationship generated by 'new venues, companies, and performance methods'.[2] Stefan Bachmann, for example, created a memorable theatrical event in 1992, for Theater Gruppe Affekt at the Theater Zerbrochene Fenster in Krenzberg, Berlin. The 'theatre' was an old warehouse on the top floor of a building at some considerable distance from the centre of the city. In his review for *The Stage* Patrick Martyn wrote:

It's difficult to fake things when performing in such close proximity to a packed audience of just over a hundred . . . There are many times when I thought the actors would really hurt themselves the way they tackled their roles with such realism. And when the actors believe in what they're doing, so does the audience.[3]

In an even more extreme rejection of conventional performance conditions, Pierre Peyrou with Théâtre Présent in Paris (1983) staged a production of the play in a converted abattoir. For those members of the audience familiar with the play the implications evoked by the choice of the venue must have been horrifying. For the 'innocent' spectator the notion of visiting a converted abattoir for an evening of 'entertainment' may well have heightened any latent sense of unease at watching an unfamiliar, and reputedly violent work. The review in *Cahiers Elisabéthains* commented that 'seeing *Titus Andronicus* is a rare treat at all times, seeing it in a modified abattoir adds an ironic though harmonious touch'.[4]

Coupled with the knowledge of the previous history of an unconventional playing-space, the process of entering and leaving a venue has particular relevance for an audience in relation to a play generally regarded as being disturbing or unsettling. Richard Schechner noted the significance of the way in which an audience negotiates a venue, suggesting that 'how the audience gets to, and into, the performance place, and how they go from that place'[5] is a vital component of the total experience. The promotion of a sense of discomfort in relation to the arena of the action was particularly evident with John Longenbaugh's 1993 production of *Titus Andronicus* for Big Space Theatre at the Hornsea Road Swimming Baths in North London. The swimming-bath complex was completely derelict, with broken windows, rubbish, rubble and corrugated iron suggesting a working building-site rather than a theatre. The audience entered the complex through an extended labyrinth of open-topped tunnels daubed with graffiti,

[1] Charles Spencer, 'The horror, the humour', *The Weekly Telegraph*, 8 October 2003.
[2] Susan Bennett, *Theatre Audiences: A Theory of Production and Reception*, 1997, p. 19.
[3] Patrick Martyn, *The Stage*, 17 December 1992 (no page numbers).
[4] J. Fuzier, F. Laroque, J. M. Maguin, '*Titus Andronicus*', *Cahiers Elisabéthains*, April 1984, no. 25, p. 119.
[5] *Essays on Performance Theory 1970–1976*, New York: Drama Book Specialists, 1977, p. 122, quoted by Bennett, *Theatre Audiences*, p. 11.

and were seated extremely close to the action, 'like spectators in an amphitheatre'.[1] The pool lights remained on at all times, so the audience members could clearly see one another, and were conscious that the actors could see them.

A similar sense of unease was created by Silviu Pucarete who engineered his production in such a way that the audience left the venue after the performance to be confronted by Aaron, 'buried' waist-deep in tarpaulin in the foyer. As Jeremy Kingston noted in his review in *The Times*,[2] 'he waits for us on the stairs outside, snarling yet'. Mariangela Tempera described the effect of this final action on the audience at the 1996 Parma theatre festival:

Even those who did wonder why 'Aaron' was not taking his curtain call were unprepared for the sight that greeted them in the foyer . . . From his place of torment he hurled his curses at an audience made more vulnerable by the fact that the play was officially over.[3]

An equally thought-provoking and disturbing production was mounted outdoors by Brett Heath in 1995 in a former prison (nicknamed 'Boggo Road') in Brisbane, Australia. In Heath's production, the plot of *Titus Andronicus* was loosely framed with a device involving actors playing prisoners engaged in staging the play for a visiting audience. Critics applauded the choice of venue: Richard Waller, writing in Brisbane's *Sunday Mail*, noted that spaces such as this instilled productions with 'an energy and immediacy that might not surface if the same production were to be played out upon a conventional stage'.[4] Similarly, Alison Cotes in *The Brisbane Review* observed that 'the stroke of genius was to set it in Boggo Road jail, where the resonances of brutality and pain give the play an extra dimension'.[5]

The resonances evoked by Brett Heath's production were heightened in Curt Tofteland's staging of the drama at Luther Luckett Correctional Complex, LaGrange, Kentucky in 2001. Where Heath's actors pretended to be prisoners staging a performance for an audience of visitors, Tofteland's actors were serving prisoners taking part in a Shakespeare Behind Bars prison project. Mary Wiltenburg noted the way in which the play acquired a new dynamic as a result of the environment in which it was performed: 'In a place like this [and] spoken by a man with a life sentence for killing a police officer, the words "right", "justice", and "arms" [in Saturninus's opening speech] sound different than they would on a high school or professional stage.'[6]

Just as the play's political resonances and amenability to challenging playing conditions have contributed to the foregrounding of *Titus Andronicus* as a work of particular relevance to modern society, so its filmic qualities have heightened the emerging sense of its contemporaneity. According to Jan Kott, the success of Peter Brook's stage production lay in his ability to inhabit Shakespeare's own 'cinematic' imagination and to unite it with his own modernity of vision. Brook, Kott claimed, created a quasi-film

---

[1] Reviewer not recorded, '*Titus Andronicus*', *TLS*, 24 September 1993.
[2] 'Curtains for Shakespeare's worst', 22 May 1997.
[3] Mariangela Tempera, *Feasting with Centaurs: 'Titus Andronicus' from Stage to Text*, 1999, p. 32.
[4] Richard Waller, 'Daring staging lends grisly reality to play', *The Sunday Mail*, 9 June 1995.
[5] Alison Cotes, '*Titus Andronicus*: blood curdling saga', *The Brisbane Review*, June 1995.
[6] Mary Wiltenburg, 'Shakespeare behind bars', *Christian Science Monitor*, csmonitor.com, December 2001.

world on-stage, in that the scenes were 'composed like film shots and follow[ed] each other like film sequences'.[1] To Kott, Brook's cinematic staging enabled spectators to find an immediate connection between their own experience and an Elizabethan tragedy, conceived as both a 'newsreel, and an historical chronicle' and incorporating 'everyday events, tales of crime, bits of history, legends, politics and philosophy'.[2] Similarly Mark Kermode, commenting upon Bill Alexander's 2003 Stratford production (interestingly, performed in the same venue as Brook's) felt that a pivotal moment in the play was cinematic in its effect: 'When Lavinia having had her hands and tongue off, comes out from the back of the stage . . . it's a marvellously cinematic, expressionistic moment.'[3] Deborah Cartmell has described *Titus Andronicus* as the most filmic of Shakespeare's plays 'which resembled Quentin Tarantino's *Reservoir Dogs* (1992) or *Pulp Fiction* (1994) in its unnerving blend of violence and humour'.[4] Unsurprisingly, therefore, a host of theatre directors have sought to forge associations between the play and the world of film. Bryan Clarkson chose to stage the play because of its similarity to the popular contemporary Hammer Horror films (Denbigh School, Milton Keynes, 1970); Joel G. Fink gained inspiration for his Colorado Shakespeare Festival production (1988) from George A. Romero's 1968 horror film *The Night of the Living Dead*; Trevor Nunn (1972, RSC), Bill Alexander (2003, RSC) and Richard Risso (1990, Utah Shakespearian Festival) all acknowledged the influence of Federico Fellini's 1969 *Satyricon* on their work; while Terrence O'Brien's 1999 Hudson Valley production owed much to George Miller's *Mad Max* (1979). Lawrence Till described his Bolton Octagon British Sign Language production (1993) as '*Terminator*' Shakespeare, drawing parallels between his work and James Cameron's 1984 film, and its 1991 sequel (*Terminator 2: Judgment Day*). Phil Willmott (at the Battersea Arts Centre, 2001) and Ian Gledhill (of Sheffield University Drama Society, 2001) both credited Quentin Tarantino's 1994 *Pulp Fiction* as a major influence on their productions, while Rob Conkie based his stage production in 1999[5] directly on *Pulp Fiction* and *Reservoir Dogs* (1992).

In addition to making overt references to Tarantino's film, Conkie's production also involved a critique of the contemporary preoccupation with voyeurism, echoing the uneasy audience–action dynamic created by Silviu Pucarete and John Longenbaugh in the productions noted above. Conkie's version of the play was framed by the characters of Demetrius (Dan Winter) and Chiron (Gary Cicinskas) situated in the audience watching a video at home – that video being of *Titus Andronicus*. At the appropriate points in the action the actors left the audience to enter the world on-stage and assume the roles assigned to them in the Folio text. When Lucius left to join the Goths, the interval was signalled by Demetrius, sitting in the audience again, asking Chiron to get some food, seemingly unmoved by the horrors he had watched. Artifice and reality were thus deliberately blurred, inviting members of the audience to consider their own

---

[1] Kott, *Shakespeare our Contemporary*, p. 283.
[2] *Ibid.*, p. 284.
[3] Newsnight Review, BBC-TV, 26 September 2003.
[4] Deborah Cartmell, *Interpreting Shakespeare on Screen*, 2000, p. 11.
[5] With the King Alfred's Performing Arts Company (King Alfred's College, Winchester).

voyeuristic roles and exploring the notion that modern society was so saturated with images of violence that people were anaesthetised to its effects.

The blurring of the boundaries between art and reality as a means of commenting upon contemporary society was also evident in Julie Taymor's film, *Titus*, which, according to Lisa Starks, offered a challenge to the audience to consider the 'act of viewing horror'.[1] Taymor, who adapted her 1994 off-Broadway production of the play[2] into a film version released in 1999, starring Anthony Hopkins, commented on its relevance to a modern audience, who read daily of 'tabloid sex scandals, teenage gang rape, high school gun sprees and the private details of a celebrity murder trial', and who themselves lived at a politically unstable time when 'racism, ethnic cleansing and genocide have almost ceased to shock by being so commonplace and seemingly inevitable'.[3] In Taymor's film, as in Peter Stein's stage production, political undertones manifested themselves in the analogy between ancient Rome and Fascist Italy, particularly Benito Mussolini's Rome.[4]

To create the world of *Titus* Taymor juxtaposed the expectations of a ready-made cinemagoing audience against a framing commentary on contemporary voyeurism. This was primarily achieved through casting, particularly the choice of Anthony Hopkins as Titus:

Because most audiences read backward from film to Shakespeare . . . given that Titus serves human flesh at his banquet [it] inevitably call[ed] to the minds of many reviewers and other audiences the serial-killer cannibal, Hannibal Lecter. The connection between Titus and Lecter [was] underlined by Hopkins' quotation of his role in *Silence of the Lambs* when he suck[ed] in his spit before slitting Chiron and Demetrius' throats.[5]

Many members of the audience would therefore have entered the screening of *Titus* with a prior knowledge of Hopkins's work and his capacity for playing dark complex characters from nightmare worlds. As a result, they came with expectations based upon past cinemagoing experiences which, in turn, informed their experience of the film. Osheen Jones, who played Young Lucius, might also have sparked significant intertextual associations for a well-informed cinemagoing audience. In Taymor's interpretation, the role of Young Lucius was expanded to position him as an on-screen audience to the action,[6] a role similar to that the same young actor had played in Adrian Noble's film version of *A Midsummer Night's Dream* (1996). In Noble's film, the experience of a little boy also functioned as a framing device, in that the action of the comedy was his dream. This positive dream in Noble's film became, in Taymor's, the same actor's

[1] Lisa S. Starks, 'Cinema of cruelty: powers of horror in Julie Taymor's *Titus*', in Lisa S. Starks and Courtney Lehmann (eds.), *The Reel Shakespeare. Alternative Cinema and Theory*, 2002, p. 122.
[2] With Theatre For A New Audience at St Clement's Church, New York.
[3] Julie Taymor, *'Titus': The Illustrated Screenplay*, 2000, p. 174.
[4] Much of the action was filmed in Mussolini's EUR government centre, modelled on the Roman Colosseum (nicknamed 'The Square Colosseum') and Cinecittà, the film studio founded by Mussolini.
[5] Richard Burt, 'Shakespeare and the Holocaust: Julie Taymor's *Titus* is beautiful, or Shakesploi meets (the) camp', in Richard Burt (ed.), *Shakespeare after Mass Media*, p. 308.
[6] A framing perspective similar to that used by Jane Howell in her 1985 BBC-TV version, see p. 44 above.

nightmare.[1] Similarly, the casting of Geraldine McEwan as the Nurse in Taymor's *Titus* would have carried particular resonances for audiences familiar with Kenneth Branagh's film versions of Shakespeare's plays, in Branagh's *Henry V* (1989) McEwan played Alice, the lady-in-waiting present during the courting of Katherine by Henry. There, she was pleased at what she witnessed and encouraged the union, celebrating the events taking place around her. Again, as with the reversal in the perspective of the child played by Osheen Jones, the attendant's attitude in Taymor's work shifts to disgust, and she 'pay[s] for that disgust with her life'.[2] In each case, inter-textual casting choices informed audience perception and, arguably, invited cinemagoers to reflect on their own roles as observers of horror.

In addition to the inversion of the on-screen spectator's role, further associations between Taymor's *Titus* and Kenneth Branagh's Shakespeare films have been noted. Stephen Buhler argued that the sequence in which Titus and his soldiers wash off the mud of battle echoed and confronted the 'ideological revisions of Shakespeare'[3] at work in Branagh's *Henry V* and *Much Ado About Nothing* (1993). According to Buhler

Titus and his soldiers return from the war against the Goths covered in mud, but find no justification in hardship as Branagh's Henry does. They grimly wash off the mud under huge conduits, a visual echo not only of Roman 'civilization' (the aqueducts) but also of the exuberant bathing – by both sexes – that marks the return of men from battle at the start of Branagh's *Much Ado*.[4]

Other references to the world of film evoked by Taymor include Peter Greenaway's *The Cook, The Thief, His Wife and Her Lover* (1989), which incorporated acts of extreme violence culminating in a cannibalistic feast, and the works of Fellini, particularly the corrupt and depraved Rome of the Emperor Nero (*Satyricon*), and brutish circus strong-man, Zampanò (Anthony Quinn) in *La Strada* (1954).[5]

As noted above, Taymor used Mussolini's Rome to suggest an analogy between the classical world and modern times. Film references underlining this political parallel included Visconti's film about Nazi Germany, *The Damned* (1969), and the work of Leni Riefenstahl, the German Third Reich filmmaker (cf. Taymor's scene depicting soldiers marching at night into the Coliseum). An even more overt political commentary was offered by Richard Griffin in his 2000 version of the play, filmed on location in Rhode Island. Griffin drew explicit parallels between the work and American society (cf. Jeff Love's stage production noted above) grounding the comparison in the view that 'you

---

[1] Dreams and nightmares were key production concepts for Tony Nicholls's 1983 production for WAIT Theatre in Perth, Australia and for Kevin Ewert's 1985 Trinity College Drama Society production at the University of Toronto with Alexander Leggatt as Titus. Silviu Pucarete's production, in tandem with the contemporary resonance, also endowed his version with a dream-like/nightmare quality through the use of shadows, hypnotic swirling lights and dissonant sound effects such as howling and roaring.

[2] Stephen M. Buhler, *Shakespeare in the Cinema, Ocular Proof*, 2002, p. 191.

[3] *Ibid.*

[4] *Ibid.*

[5] Significantly, Taymor's production designer, Dante Ferretti, had worked with Fellini five times, between 1978 and 1990.

don't know what political corruption is until you've lived . . . in Rhode Island. For such a small state, we are surrounded by little Neros and Cæsars.'[1]

A variety of less politically charged cinematic versions of *Titus Andronicus* were made in the latter part of the last century, aimed, unsurprisingly, at the horror market. Seattle-based Lorn Richey directed a low-budget horror film of the play in 1997 using blue-screen technology to recreate ancient Rome. His advertisement promised filmgoers that low budget would meet 'High Art in this 'Shakes-ploitation' extravaganza! . . . Roman Generals and outlaw Goths clash in a drama of love, intrigue, brutality, adultery, murder, dismemberment, decapitation and cannibalism!'[2] and Christopher Dunne designed his 1998 version, filmed in Tampa, Florida, for a similar market. Advertising the work on the Internet, the production company (Joe Redner Film and Production) announced: 'Twenty-seven varied murders and mutilations, featuring severed limbs, evisceration, unglamorized brutality, swordplay and cruel torture place TITUS firmly in the "Horror" feature genre.'[3] Douglas Hickox's classic *Theater of Blood* (1973)[4] exploited, for similar effect, the casting of Vincent Price in the leading role. In Hickox's film, Edward Lionheart (Price), a disillusioned Shakespearian actor, kills various London drama critics who had denied him the Best Actor Award, each death being based on a killing in one of Shakespeare's plays. One of the victims, Meredith Merridew (Robert Morley) is forced, in a clear allusion to *Titus Andronicus*, to eat the heads of his two pet poodles, baked in a pie, until he himself chokes to death. Here, as with Taymor, the director's casting decision created a ready-made market for the film through the audience's knowledge of the actor's previous work – notably Roger Corman's series of Edgar Allan Poe adaptations, with Price in the principal roles.

CRITICAL HISTORY

The wealth of productions of *Titus Andronicus* staged in recent years has been paralleled by an upsurge of critical interest in the play across the spectrum of current Shakespearian studies, affording new insights into a once marginalised text.[5] The last twenty years have produced a variety of books devoted entirely to the work, indicating the new prominence now enjoyed by the play. Mariangela Tempera's *Feasting with Centaurs: 'Titus Andronicus' from Stage to Text* (1999), for example, explores the relationship set up in the drama between culture and violence, arguing that the explosion of productions of the work since the 1980s is largely attributable to a 'change in

---

[1] Phil Hall, 'Richard Griffin: brushing up his Shakespeare', *Film Threat*, 12/12/2000 (Internet search 15 July 2003).

[2] Burt (ed.), *Shakespeare after Mass Media*, p. 302.

[3] Christopher Dunne, 'TITUS ANDRONICUS is a killer! (In more ways than one)', home1.gte.net/titus98 (Internet search date 13 September 1998).

[4] Video release produced by United Artists/Cineman. UK/USA. Certificate 18. Interestingly, the National Theatre in London produced an extremely successful stage version of the film in the summer of 2005 with Jim Broadbent starring as Edward Lionheart and Rachael Stirling as his daughter (the role played by her mother Diana Rigg in the film).

[5] For a broader overview than is possible here of recent studies of all aspects of the play, see the annual surveys of Shakespeare criticism in *Shakespeare Survey* and *Shakespeare Quarterly* (*World Bibliography*), which offer a useful starting point for further research.

cultural climate' which has turned 'some of the play's liabilities into assets.'[1] Whereas Tempera's study investigates a number of European productions from the perspective of audience response, Alan Dessen's invaluable *Shakespeare in Performance: 'Titus Andronicus'* (1989) focuses exclusively on the performance history of the play, offering detailed analyses of the main issues facing directors, and exploring a number of major productions in the UK and North America, including those of Brian Bedford (1978, Stratford, Ontario), Jane Howell (1985, BBC-TV), Deborah Warner (1987, Stratford-upon-Avon), and Mark Rucker (1988, Santa Cruz, California).[2] The mid-1990s saw the publication of two particularly helpful works drawing together a huge range of critical studies. The first, *'Titus Andronicus': Critical Essays* edited by Philip C. Kolin (1995), reprints essays on all aspects of the work: authorship, structure, symbolism, sexual violence and revenge including, among other significant items, Eugene Waith's seminal 'The metamorphosis of violence in *Titus Andronicus*' (1957), Emily C. Bartels's 'Making more of the Moor: Othello and Renaissance refashionings of race' (1990) and Heather James's 'Cultural disintegration in *Titus Andronicus*: mutilating Titus, Virgil and Rome' (1991). In addition to the critical material, the collection also includes a selection of essays devoted exclusively to the staging of the play, ranging from Edward Ravenscroft's *'To the Reader'* (1687) to accounts of a number of early twentieth-century productions. The second useful work, *Shakespeare's Earliest Tragedy: Studies in 'Titus Andronicus'* by G. Harold Metz (1996), explores a spectrum of criticism on the much-debated issues associated with the drama, including its text, sources and date of composition and includes important material on its performance history from 1970 to 1994.

   Thought-provoking reassessments of *Titus Andronicus* may also be found in works engaging more broadly with the Shakespearian corpus. Francis Barker's *The Culture of Violence: Essays on Tragedy and History* (1993), for example, includes a chapter on *Titus Andronicus* ('A wilderness of tigers') which locates the violence of the play in its wider cultural framework. Barker notes that the representations of violence in *Titus Andronicus*, and the wider world of Renaissance drama, question the degree to which the early modern stage endorses the 'signifying practices of the dominant culture' or 'alternatively unsettles such structures and institutions by . . . contesting or making "dysfunctional" the categories and representations they support'.[3] By contrast, Alexander Leggatt's *Shakespeare's Tragedies Violation and Identity* (2005) explores how physical abuse triggers questions about identity both for the victim and the perpetrator and how such acts resonate beyond the individual. The book opens with the assault on Lavinia, an event central to an essay by Deborah Willis, ' "The gnawing vulture": revenge, trauma theory, and *Titus Andronicus*',[4] which considers violence and revenge in the context of recent psychoanalytical trauma theory. In addition to offering a thought-provoking account of the play as a whole, the essay directs the reader to a spectrum of feminist studies of the drama (including discussions of its womb, tomb and pit imagery,

[1] Tempera, *Feasting with Centaurs*, p. 9.
[2] This work is currently being revised and updated and is expected to appear in 2007.
[3] Barker, *The Culture of Violence*, pp. 194–5.
[4] *SQ* 53 (2002), 21–52.

its treatment of rape, and the handling of the female characters), together with a range
of other critical approaches.

Trauma theory also figures in David McCandless's study: 'A tale of two *Titus*es: Julie
Taymor's vision on stage and screen'.[1] McCandless examines Taymor's invitation to her
audience to assess their reaction to watching traumatic events (see the contemporary
interest in voyeurism discussed above) arguing that Taymor's stage version of the
play was more successful in deconstructing its violence than her film due, in part, to
the latter's more optimistic ending with Young Lucius holding Aaron's child. Carol
Chillington Rutter also looks at the role of children in Taymor's film in 'Looking like a
child – or – *Titus*: the comedy'.[2] Rutter notes that across the canon the lines between
tragedy and comedy are frequently blurred and at 'points where, generically, the play
could go either way' Shakespeare 'puts a child on stage to look, to be looked at, to focus
what's at stake'.[3] Examining two productions from this perspective, Adrian Noble's
A Midsummer Night's Dream and Julie Taymor's *Titus*, she concludes that Taymor
'translates *Titus* into something *like* comedy'.[4] A different aspect of film studies is
considered by Courtney Lehmann in her essay: 'Crouching tiger, hidden agenda: how
Shakespeare and the Renaissance are taking the rage out of feminism'.[5] Lehmann
focuses upon four late twentieth-century films looking back in some way to the early
modern period, including Julie Taymor's *Titus* and Shekar Kapur's *Elizabeth* (1998),
and considers whether the portrayal of the female protagonists in these works may be
seen as part of an anti-feminist reaction in contemporary film.

Not surprisingly, as much of the previous discussion indicates, the play has attracted
the notice of numerous feminist critics. Coppélia Kahn in *Roman Shakespeare: Warriors, Wounds and Women* (1997) explores the gender ideologies underpinning the notion
of Roman 'virtue', devoting a chapter to *Titus Andronicus* entitled 'The daughter's
seduction in *Titus Andronicus*, or, writing is the best revenge'. Marion Wynne-Davis,
in her influential '"The swallowing womb": consumed and consuming women in
Titus Andronicus'[6] locates the play's female roles in the context of Elizabethan attitudes towards rape while Nancy J. Vickers reflects on violence against women, the
'Petrarchan' treatment of Lavinia by Marcus, dismemberment and voyeurism in her
'Diana described: scattered woman and scattered rhyme'.[7] Mary Laughlin Fawcett in
'Arms/words/tears: language and the body in *Titus Andronicus*'[8] considers the play's
concern with words and body parts, while Katherine A. Rowe discusses the significance
of hands in her 'Dismembering and forgetting in *Titus Andronicus*'[9] and *Dead Hands:
Fictions of Agency, Renaissance to Modern* (1999). Gillian Murray Kendall's '"Lend me

[1] *Ibid.*, 487–511.
[2] *S. Sur.* 56 (2003), 1–26.
[3] *Ibid.*, 2.
[4] *Ibid.*, 26.
[5] *SQ* 53 (2002), 260–79.
[6] In Valerie Wayne (ed.), *The Matter of Difference: Materialist Feminist Criticism of Shakespeare*, 1991, pp.
129–53.
[7] *Critical Inquiry*, 8 (1981–2), 265–79.
[8] *ELH* 50 (1983), 261–77.
[9] *SQ* 45 (1994), 297–303.

thy hand": metaphor and mayhem in *Titus Andronicus*[1] is also concerned with mutilation, as is Lynn Enterline in *The Rhetoric of the Body from Ovid To Shakespeare* (2000). The notion of dismemberment forges a link with Robert S. Miola's analysis of the way in which sixteenth-century religious divisions are embedded in the play. In '"An alien people clutching their gods"? Shakespeare's ancient religions'[2] Miola observes that the dismembered body parts in *Titus Andronicus* represent 'a barbarity that is familiar as well as alien. The display of *disjecta membra*, the cut-off tongue, heads and hands evokes the . . . controversy over relics',[3] a doctrinal conflict contributing to the fervid religious intolerance of the period.

Renaissance cultural divisions also inform Heather James's *Shakespeare's Troy: Drama, Politics, and the Translation of Empire* (1997). James explores *Titus Andronicus, Troilus and Cressida, Antony and Cleopatra, Cymbeline* and *The Tempest*, tracing the way in which Shakespeare utilises the Troy legend, and examining the degree to which his work may be aligned with Tudor and Stuart notions of 'empire', particularly during periods of political uncertainty. Ania Loomba provides a useful route into the related critical field of race through a consideration of *Titus Andronicus, Othello, Antony and Cleopatra* and *The Merchant of Venice* in her *Shakespeare, Race and Colonialism* (2002). Loomba argues that to understand the meaning of race in Shakespeare we must also consider gender, religion and culture, a point that also underlies Jeanette S. White's ' "Is black so base a hue?": Shakespeare's Aaron and the politics of race',[4] which suggests that Aaron's actions are driven by his need for empowerment and his desire to challenge the European Renaissance stereotype that determines him evil by his colour. Two further works by Ania Loomba, *Gender, Race, Renaissance Drama* (1989) and '"Delicious traffick": alterity and exchange on early modern stages',[5] also explore the place of blacks and similarly marginalised groups in a white patriarchal society, while Geraldo U. De Sousa in *Shakespeare's Cross-Cultural Encounters* (1999) looks at race and gender in early modern Europe and Shakespeare's exploration of cultural stereotypes. Finally, Pascale Aebischer in *Shakespeare's Violated Bodies: Stage and Screen Performance* (2004) explores how bodies marginalised in the written text due to race, disability or silence can dominate the stage in performance, focusing on post-1980 theatre and film productions of *Titus Andronicus, King Lear, Othello* and *Hamlet*.

---

[1] *SQ* 40 (1989), 299–316.
[2] *S. Sur.* 54 (2001), 31–45.
[3] *Ibid.*, 35.
[4] *CLA Journal* 40 (1997), 336–66.
[5] *S. Sur.* 52 (1999), 201–14.

NOTE ON THE TEXT

Between 1594 and 1623, four editions of *Titus Andronicus* were published. The first was a quarto: these were cheap and often poorly printed editions. Fortunately, the first quarto of *Titus* (Q, 1594) was produced with some care. It was probably printed from a manuscript in Shakespeare's own hand, or a scribal copy: we cannot be sure which.[1] The second quarto (Q2, 1600) was printed from a slightly damaged copy of the first, with many minor corrections and additions. Chief amongst these are the omission of three and a half lines (between 1.1.35 and 36) which Shakespeare seems to have forgotten to cut when he revised Act 1, and an attempt to restore a number of lines in Act 5 that were obliterated in the damaged copy of Q. Q3 (1611) was printed from Q2. It contains nothing new except a compositor's corrections of Q2, and a number of fresh errors. Details of these editions are discussed in the Textual Analysis (pp. 159–66 below).

The First Folio edition of *Titus Andronicus* (F, 1623) was printed with some editorial care, using a copy of Q3 collated with a playhouse text, perhaps a prompt copy belonging to Shakespeare's company, the King's Men. It introduces act divisions and alters many stage directions, no doubt to conform with established stage practice. It is the only source we have for 3.2, which Shakespeare seems to have added sometime after 1594 to exploit a vogue for mad scenes.

The present edition is based upon the premise that Q is our best authority for the words which Shakespeare wanted spoken on the stage, except of course in 3.2, where I have followed F because it seems to be Shakespeare's authentic addition. For the rest of the dialogue, I have followed Q where there is any reasonable chance that it represents the words Shakespeare wrote, rather than a compositor's errors or alterations. Many stage directions in F supplement those in Q, and some are alterations. The Q directions may reflect Shakespeare's thoughts in his study, actual events in an early performance, or a combination of both. But since those in F seem to derive from his company's working prompt copy, I have normally included them, on the assumption that they may represent what was actually done in performance. In the Commentary I have drawn attention to verbal stage directions – dialogue which requires specific actions to take place on-stage: 'Open the gates and let me in' (1.1.62).

I have adopted the First Folio act divisions, and added the scene divisions introduced in Nicholas Rowe's 1709 edition, because these are now traditional.

The early compositors made errors and corrections which must be noted. My text is supported by a collation of these variations, and attempts by subsequent editors to correct ('emend') them. Each note in the collation begins with a lemma – a word or

[1] See discussion of Q in the Textual Analysis, pp. 160–1 below.

phrase from the text followed by a square bracket. This edition collates the three quartos and the First Folio, noting all significant variations. The collation names the editors who first proposed all emendations which I have adopted, together with those who have made emendations which I have considered plausible but have rejected for various reasons. Suggested emendations which I have rejected, but which are of special interest, are shown as conjectures (*conj.*). My new readings are marked *This edn.*

In order to clarify the action for the reader I have sometimes amplified or added stage directions. These additions are printed in square brackets. Speech headings in Q and F are not always consistent. I have silently expanded abbreviations, and regularised variations: for example, Saturninus's speeches are sometimes headed *Emperour* or *King*, Tamora is sometimes *Queene* and Aaron is frequently *Moore*. The name Young Lucius has been silently adopted from the stage direction at the beginning of 4.2 and used for his speech headings, where Q calls him *Puer*. I have silently normalised proper names both in the speech headings and the text.[1] Sometimes the text includes redundant speech headings after a stage direction; I have silently removed the surplus speech headings (e.g. TITUS at 2.2.11). When a speech heading is unclear I have conjectured the name of a probable speaker, and collated the change: thus *Titus sonne speakes* (1.1.360) is omitted in favour of a speech heading which conjectures that the speaker is Martius.[2] A number of speech headings in Acts 1 and 4 are centred in Q. I have silently regularised them. Whenever centred stage directions also serve as speech headings, I have silently inserted a speech heading in the conventional location, for example MARCUS and CAPTAIN at 1.1.18 and 64. However, where the centred stage directions give useful information for performance, I have retained them. For example, the Q stage direction *Enter a CAPTAIN* (1.1.63) doubles as a speech heading, but is retained and F's speech heading (CAPTAIN) is silently inserted.[3]

I have removed the italics in which the quartos and First Folio print proper nouns. Both editions usually italicise speech quoted in dialogue: the letter Saturninus reads at 2.3.268, for example, or *Long live our Emperor Saturnine* at 1.1.233. I have substituted quotation marks in these places, and wherever speech is quoted: "'And shall"! What villain was it spake that word?' (1.1.359). Italics have been retained for words in foreign languages, such as Latin, *Suum cuique* (1.1.280). Wherever necessary I have corrected the Latin, and the spelling of classical names, collating Q and F readings.

I have silently modernised spelling and obsolete variants of words still in use: thus 'stroke' becomes 'struck' and 'race', 'raze' (1.1.364, 451). Punctuation in Q differs significantly from modern practice, and while I have modernised it, I have punctuated as lightly as possible. I have modernised by adding hyphens to compound adjectives like 'high-witted' (4.4.35) or 'first-born' (1.1.5, 120). Wherever the metre of Shakespeare's

---

[1] For example, 'Bascianus' at 1.1.278, 285, 401, 411, and 2.3.55.
[2] The same practice is used at 2.3.268, when Saturninus reads a letter.
[3] See also SDs signifying entrances for Aaron at 2.3.191, and for Marcus at 1.1.17 and 2.4.10, or directing the Andronici to kneel at 1.1.388.

verse requires pronunciation of a syllable which is elided in modern usage, or stresses a syllable which is unstressed in modern English, I have added an accent: rollèd, banishèd, receptàcle.

For a more detailed description of the text as it is found in the quartos and Folio, together with a discussion of their relationship to each other, to Shakespeare's MS. and to the prompt copy, see the Textual Analysis, pp. 159–66 below.

Titus Andronicus

LIST OF CHARACTERS

SATURNINUS, *older son of the late Emperor of Rome*
BASSIANUS, *his brother*
MARCUS ANDRONICUS, *Tribune of the People*
TITUS ANDRONICUS, *General, brother of Marcus*
LUCIUS ⎫
QUINTUS ⎪
MARTIUS ⎬ *Titus's sons*
MUTIUS ⎭
LAVINIA, *Titus's daughter*
TAMORA, *Queen of the Goths*
ALARBUS ⎫
CHIRON ⎬ *Tamora's sons*
DEMETRIUS ⎭
AARON, *a Moor, Tamora's lover*
YOUNG LUCIUS, *Lucius's son*
PUBLIUS, *Marcus's son*
SEMPRONIUS ⎫
CAIUS ⎬ *kinsmen of Titus*
VALENTINE ⎭
AEMILIUS, *a noble Roman*
CAPTAIN, MESSENGER, NURSE, CLOWN, GOTHS,
Senators, Tribunes, followers of Saturninus and Bassianus, Soldiers, Attendants, Romans

Notes

There is no list of characters in the quartos or the Folio. The traditional list is based on Rowe's first *dramatis personae*. I have listed named characters in order of appearance.

Many actors no doubt appeared both as speaking characters and in silent parts, 'as many as can be'. I have proposed one scheme of 'doubling' for a company of fourteen men and boys: see pp. 174–5 below.

SEMPRONIUS appears only in 4.3. In 5.2 his place among Titus's kinsmen is taken by VALENTINE. Titus addresses each by name, but neither speaks. It is possible that Shakespeare forgot the name he had assigned to the character, and gave him a new one in the later scene.

THE LAMENTABLE TRAGEDY
OF TITUS ANDRONICUS

[1.1] *Flourish. Enter the Tribunes and Senators aloft; and then enter*
[below] SATURNINUS *and his followers at one door, and* BASSIANUS
and his followers at the other, with drum and colours

SATURNINUS Noble patricians, patrons of my right,
      Defend the justice of my cause with arms;
      And countrymen, my loving followers,
      Plead my successive title with your swords.
      I am his first-born son that was the last   5
      That wore the imperial diadem of Rome;
      Then let my father's honours live in me,
      Nor wrong mine age with this indignity.
BASSIANUS Romans, friends, followers, favourers of my right,
      If ever Bassianus, Caesar's son,   10
      Were gracious in the eyes of royal Rome,
      Keep then this passage to the Capitol,

Title] F; The most Lamentable Romaine Tragedie of *Titus Andronicus* Q, Q2; The Most Lamentable Tragedie of
Titus Andronicus Q3   Act 1, Scene 1   1.1] *Actus Primus. Scaena Prima.* F; *not in* Qq   0 SD.1 *Flourish.*] F; *not in*
Qq   0 SD.2 *below*] *Capell (subst.)*   0 SD.3 *at the other*] F; *not in* Qq   0 SD.3 *drum and colours*] F; *Drums and*
Trumpets Q   5 am his] Qq; was the F

Act 1, Scene 1

*0 SD The play starts with a bang. Two factions enter through opposite tiring-house doors.
Saturninus and followers try to force their way
back in, through the door held by Bassianus and
party, which is established as the 'passage to the
Capitol' by 12. Conflict is immediate, swords are
out; a scuffle seems imminent. But the pretenders'
rhetoric, the presence of sober tribunes and senators in the gallery over the doors, and the balanced
formality of staging give the events a ceremonial
quality. The tension between savage violence and
formal ceremony is characteristic of the whole of
Act 1.

1–17 Saturninus and Bassianus may address the
audience as well as the dignitaries aloft and their
followers.

1 patricians aristocrats. 'Patrician' derives from
pater (Latin), 'father'. Saturninus appeals to the
senators, members of the Roman ruling (paternal)
class.

1 patrons protectors, defenders. The word
derives from *patronus* (Latin), a rich man or patrician who protected his 'clients' or courtiers in
exchange for their services; see also 65 n. below.

4 successive title title to the succession.

8 age seniority.

8 this indignity i.e. physical exclusion from the
Capitol by Bassianus and his followers; see 12 n.

11 gracious acceptable (as at 429 and 2.1.32);
used elsewhere in its modern sense.

12 Bassianus establishes one door as the entrance
to the Capitol; he and his followers hold it, while
Saturninus tries to enter.

12 Keep Guard.

12 Capitol Supposed seat of Roman government. Elizabethans often confused the Temple of
Jupiter Capitolinus on the Capitoline Hill with the
Senate House (Curia Julia) near the Forum at its
foot; see another example at *JC* 2.4.1 and 11.

And suffer not dishonour to approach
The imperial seat, to virtue consecrate,
To justice, continence and nobility;   15
But let desert in pure election shine,
And Romans, fight for freedom in your choice.

Enter MARCUS ANDRONICUS *aloft with the crown*

MARCUS   Princes that strive by factions and by friends
Ambitiously for rule and empery,
Know that the people of Rome, for whom we stand   20
A special party, have by common voice
In election for the Roman empery
Chosen Andronicus, surnamèd Pius,
For many good and great deserts to Rome.
A nobler man, a braver warrior   25
Lives not this day within the city walls.
He by the Senate is accited home
From weary wars against the barbarous Goths,
That with his sons, a terror to our foes,
Hath yoked a nation strong, trained up in arms.   30
Ten years are spent since first he undertook
This cause of Rome and chastisèd with arms
Our enemies' pride; five times he hath returned
Bleeding to Rome, bearing his valiant sons
In coffins from the field.   35
And now at last, laden with honour's spoils,

---

17 SD] F; *Marcus Andronicus with the Crowne* / centred as SH Qq   23–4 Pius, . . . Rome.] F, Q2–3 *(subst.)*; Pius: . . . Rome, Q   *35–6 field. / And] Q2–3, F *(subst.)*; field, and at this day, / To the Monument of that *Andronicy* / Done sacrifice of expiation / And slaine the Noblest prisoner of the *Gothes*, / And Q

16 pure election free choice (rather than primogeniture, succession by the eldest son).

17 SD From here to 45, Marcus 'aloft' is the focus of the action; thus other actors would have been oriented in a direction we have come to think of as 'upstage'.

17 SD, 18 SH Since all Q speech headings before Bassianus's at 63 are centred, Marcus's long centred heading could be regularised as MARCUS ANDRONICUS [*with the crown*]. However, this edition prefers F's stage direction.

19 empery emperorship, as at 22 and 201; 'empire' is used metaphorically in the same sense at 183.

21 A special party Chosen representatives. Marcus speaks as tribune (see 181), representing the 'plebeians' or common people.

23 Pius Religious, patriotic, just (Latin). Titus's character displays all three meanings of the name.

27 accited summoned.

28 barbarous The metre requires this word to be pronounced as a disyllable, 'barb'rous'.

30 yoked vanquished. It was the Roman custom to make vanquished enemies pass under a yoke; see 69 and 111.

*35–6 Three and a half lines are found only in Q, between 35 and 36. The grammatical relationship of the passage to its context (33–5) is insecure, and it describes as completed a sacrifice which is subsequently dramatised (96–147). This is probably a relic of an earlier draft, accidentally printed in Q but deleted from later texts (see Textual Analysis, p. 160 below).

Returns the good Andronicus to Rome,
Renownèd Titus, flourishing in arms.
Let us entreat, by honour of his name
Whom worthily you would have now succeed,   40
And in the Capitol and Senate's right,
Whom you pretend to honour and adore,
That you withdraw you and abate your strength,
Dismiss your followers, and as suitors should,
Plead your deserts in peace and humbleness.   45
SATURNINUS How fair the tribune speaks to calm my thoughts!
BASSIANUS Marcus Andronicus, so I do affy
In thy uprightness and integrity,
And so I love and honour thee and thine,
Thy noble brother Titus and his sons,   50
And her to whom my thoughts are humbled all,
Gracious Lavinia, Rome's rich ornament,
That I will here dismiss my loving friends,
And to my fortune's and the people's favour
Commit my cause in balance to be weighed.   55
                             Exeunt [followers of Bassianus]
SATURNINUS Friends that have been thus forward in my right,
I thank you all and here dismiss you all,
And to the love and favour of my country
Commit myself, my person, and the cause.
                             [Exeunt followers of Saturninus]
Rome, be as just and gracious unto me   60
As I am confident and kind to thee.
Open the gates and let me in.
BASSIANUS Tribunes, and me, a poor competitor.
                   Flourish. They go up into the Senate-house.
                   [Exeunt aloft Marcus, Tribunes and Senators]

---

54 fortune's] *Delius;* fortunes Qq; Fortunes F   55 SD] *Capell;* Exit Soldiers Qq, F   59 SD] *Capell; not in* Qq, F   63 SD.1
Flourish.] F; *not in* Qq   63 SD.2 *Exeunt . . . Senators] This edn*

39–40 by honour . . . succeed The sense
depends on the interpretation of 'his'; either 'for
the honour of *the dead emperor*' (Capell) or 'for
the sake of *whichever candidate* you favour' (Waith,
subst.).
  41 in the . . . right in the name of the Capitol
and Senate.
  42 pretend claim.
  47 affy put faith in, trust.
  61 confident and kind trusting and trustwor-
thy. In Shakespeare, 'kind' may mean 'natural',
behaving consistently with the obligations of kin-

ship.
  62 Open the gates This verbal SD suggests that
one of the tiring-house doorways may have been
shut. Judging by the de Witt sketch, solid double
doors could have stood very effectively for gates
(see Appendix 1, p. 169 below).
  63 competitor co-petitioner (Wells).
  63 SD Saturninus and Bassianus exit into the
tiring-house. None of the party aloft has anything
to do until Marcus's speech at 169, obviously a re-
entry; all hands will be needed to swell the crowd
for the triumph, which enters at 69.

Enter a CAPTAIN

CAPTAIN Romans, make way. The good Andronicus,
    Patron of virtue, Rome's best champion,   65
    Successful in the battles that he fights,
    With honour and with fortune is returned
    From where he circumscribèd with his sword,
    And brought to yoke, the enemies of Rome.

Sound drums and trumpets, and then enter two of Titus' sons [LUCIUS
and MUTIUS]. *After them, men bearing* [*two*] *coffin*[*s*] *covered with
black; then two other sons* [QUINTUS *and* MARTIUS]. *After them,*
TITUS ANDRONICUS, *and then* TAMORA *the Queen of Goths and
her sons,* [ALARBUS,] CHIRON *and* DEMETRIUS, *with* AARON *the
Moor, and others as many as can be. They set down the coffin*[*s*], *and Titus
speaks*

TITUS Hail, Rome, victorious in thy mourning weeds!   70
    Lo, as the bark that hath discharged his fraught
    Returns with precious lading to the bay
    From whence at first she weighed her anchorage,
    Cometh Andronicus, bound with laurel boughs,
    To re-salute his country with his tears,   75
    Tears of true joy for his return to Rome.
    Thou great defender of this Capitol,
    Stand gracious to the rites that we intend.
    Romans, of five-and-twenty valiant sons,
    Half of the number that King Priam had,   80

64 SH] F; *not in* Qq   69 SD.1–2 LUCIUS *and* MUTIUS] *This edn*   69 SD.2 *After them*] F; *and then* Qq   *69 SD.2 *men* . . .
coffins] *Conj. Wells; two men bearing a coffin* Qq, F   69 SD.3 *then*] Qq; *after them* F   69 SD.3 QUINTUS *and* MARTIUS]
This edn   69 SD.3 *After them*] F; *then* Q   69 SD.5 *sons*] *two sonnes* Qq, F   69 SD.5 ALARBUS] *Rowe; not in* Qq, F   69
SD.6 *They*] F; *then* Q   69 SD.6 *coffins*] *Conj. Wells; coffin* Qq, F

64 **Romans** Unless a few followers of Saturninus and Bassianus remain on the stage, the Captain
must address the audience.

65 **Patron** See 1 n. above. The choice of this
word makes Titus protector of his 'client', Virtue.
Here it may have a secondary sense as an archaic
form of 'pattern', an example of excellence (*OED*
Patron *sb* 1a).

68 **circumscribèd** confined, or restricted (*OED*
Circumscribed *ppl a* 1).

69 **SD** The omission of Alarbus from Q may be
an error derived from revision. He is present by
129; it seems logical that he should enter with his
brothers. The order in which Titus's sons enter
is conjectural: Quintus and Martius are linked by

events, Lucius and Mutius by assonance and their
prominence in Act 1. As the oldest, Lucius should
lead the first pair. There must be two coffins; Titus
buries two sons. The fact that he refers to his chariot (249) need not imply that he brings it on to the
stage (Wells, p. 90).

70 **weeds** garments.

71 **bark** ship.

71 **his fraught** its freight.

73 **anchorage** anchors.

77 **Thou** i.e. Jupiter Capitolinus.

80 **Half . . . had** In Homer, King Priam of Troy
had fifty sons, all but one of whom were killed in
the siege; see 136–8 n. below.

Behold the poor remains alive and dead!
These that survive let Rome reward with love;
These that I bring unto their latest home,
With burial amongst their ancestors.
Here Goths have given me leave to sheathe my sword.   85
Titus, unkind and careless of thine own,
Why suffer'st thou thy sons, unburied yet,
To hover on the dreadful shore of Styx?
Make way to lay them by their brethren.

                    They open the tomb

There greet in silence, as the dead are wont,   90
And sleep in peace, slain in your country's wars.
O sacred receptàcle of my joys,
Sweet cell of virtue and nobility,
How many sons hast thou of mine in store,
That thou wilt never render to me more!   95

LUCIUS Give us the proudest prisoner of the Goths,
That we may hew his limbs, and on a pile
Ad manes fratrum sacrifice his flesh
Before this earthy prison of their bones,
That so the shadows be not unappeased,   100
Nor we disturbed with prodigies on earth.

TITUS I give him you, the noblest that survives,
The eldest son of this distressèd queen.

TAMORA [*Kneels*] Stay, Roman brethren; gracious conqueror,
Victorious Titus, rue the tears I shed,   105
A mother's tears in passion for her son;
And if thy sons were ever dear to thee,
O think my son to be as dear to me.

---

98 *manes*] F3; *manus* Qq, F   104 SD *Kneels*] Wells; *kneeling with her sons* / Waith

---

83 **latest** last.
86 **unkind** unnatural; see 5.3.48: 'What hast thou done, unnatural and unkind?', and compare *Ham.* 1.1.65: 'A little more than kin, and less than kind'.
88 **Styx** River or lake in the Underworld; the souls of the unburied dead were trapped on its banks; burial allowed them to cross the Styx into Hades.
*89 SD *tomb* Either one of the tiring-house entrances or a large trap at centre; the latter is more likely, since it would double as the 'subtle hole' in 2.3.
92 **receptàcle** The metre dictates emphasis on

the third syllable. Olivier stressed it very strongly in Brook's 1955 production, perhaps to reflect Elizabethan pronunciation and to agree with the metre.
98 *Ad manes fratrum* To the spirits of our brothers (Latin).
100 **shadows** *manes*, ghosts.
101 **prodigies** omens.
104 Tamora certainly kneels here; see 454–5, and the Longleat drawing (illustration 2, p. 15 above). There is less evidence that her sons should kneel.
105 **rue** pity.
106 **passion** emotion.

Sufficeth not that we are brought to Rome
To beautify thy triumphs and return   110
Captive to thee and to thy Roman yoke;
But must my sons be slaughtered in the streets
For valiant doings in their country's cause?
O if to fight for king and commonweal
Were piety in thine, it is in these;   115
Andronicus, stain not thy tomb with blood.
Wilt thou draw near the nature of the gods?
Draw near them then in being merciful:
Sweet mercy is nobility's true badge;
Thrice-noble Titus, spare my first-born son.   120

TITUS Patient yourself, madam, and pardon me.
These are their brethren whom your Goths beheld
Alive and dead, and for their brethren slain
Religiously they ask a sacrifice;
To this your son is marked, and die he must,   125
T'appease their groaning shadows that are gone.

LUCIUS Away with him, and make a fire straight,
And with our swords upon a pile of wood
Let's hew his limbs till they be clean consumed.

Exeunt Titus' sons with Alarbus

TAMORA O cruel, irreligious piety!   130
CHIRON Was never Scythia half so barbarous!
DEMETRIUS Oppose not Scythia to ambitious Rome.
Alarbus goes to rest and we survive
To tremble under Titus' threat'ning look.
Then, madam, stand resolved, but hope withal   135
The self-same gods that armed the Queen of Troy
With opportunity of sharp revenge
Upon the Thracian tyrant in his tent

---

122 their] Qq; the F   122 your] you Q2–3, F   129 SD *Exeunt*] *Exit* Qq, F   129 SD *Titus'*] Qq; *not in* F   131 never] Q;
euer Q2–3, F   132 not] Qq; me F   134 look] Qq; lookes F

110 **triumphs** Processions in honour of a victorious general who had defeated foreign enemies
of Rome. Captives and spoils were carried in the
procession and shown to the people.
117–18 **Wilt thou . . . being merciful** Compare
MM 2.2.59–63.
121 **Patient yourself** Be calm. Tamora probably rises here.
122 **your** The Q2 compositor emends to 'you',
which makes sense; but since Q is the authoritative text, and also makes sense, emendation is
unnecessary.

131 **Scythia** Ancient name of southern Ukraine,
between the Carpathians and the Don. The
nomadic Scythians had a reputation for being cruel.
132 **Oppose** Compare.
136–8 Hecabe (in Latin, Hecuba), the captive
Queen of Troy, avenged the murder of her last
son Polydoros by scratching out the eyes of his
murderer, the Thracian king Polymnestor (Ovid,
XIII). In *Hecabe*, Euripides has the queen kill
Polymnestor's two sons. Either version might be
the source, but neither corresponds in all details to
this passage.

    May favour Tamora, the Queen of Goths
    (When Goths were Goths, and Tamora was queen),   140
    To quit the bloody wrongs upon her foes.

        Enter the SONS *of Andronicus again*

LUCIUS See, lord and father, how we have performed
    Our Roman rites: Alarbus' limbs are lopped,
    And entrails feed the sacrificing fire
    Whose smoke like incense doth perfume the sky.   145
    Remaineth nought but to inter our brethren,
    And with loud 'larums welcome them to Rome.
TITUS Let it be so, and let Andronicus
    Make this his latest farewell to their souls.
     Flourish. Then sound trumpets, and lay the coffins in the tomb
    In peace and honour rest you here, my sons,   150
    Rome's readiest champions, repose you here in rest,
    Secure from worldly chances and mishaps.
    Here lurks no treason, here no envy swells,
    Here grow no damnèd drugs, here are no storms,
    No noise, but silence and eternal sleep.   155
    In peace and honour rest you here, my sons.

        Enter LAVINIA

LAVINIA In peace and honour live Lord Titus long;
    My noble lord and father, live in fame.
    Lo, at this tomb my tributary tears
    I render for my brethren's obsequies,   160
    And at thy feet I kneel, with tears of joy
    Shed on this earth for thy return to Rome.
    O bless me here with thy victorious hand,
    Whose fortunes Rome's best citizens applaud.
TITUS Kind Rome, that hast thus lovingly reserved   165
    The cordial of mine age to glad my heart!
    Lavinia, live, outlive thy father's days

---

143 rites] F2; rights Qq; rightes F   149 SD *Flourish. Then*] F; *not in* Qq   149 SD *coffins*] F; *coffin* Qq   154 drugs] drugges
Q, Q2; grudgges Q3; grudges F   157 SH] Q3, F; *not in* Q, Q2   162 this] Q; the Q2–3, F

141 **quit** requite, avenge.
147 **'larums** alarums, calls to arms.
150–6 Verbal repetitions mark this speech as a
formal panegyric or praising of the dead.
153 **envy** malice; see 2.1.4.

154 **drugs** Plants from which poison can be
made.
159 **tributary** paying tribute.
160 **obsequies** funeral ceremonies.
166 **cordial** comfort.

And fame's eternal date, for virtue's praise!

[*Enter Tribunes and* MARCUS, *carrying a white robe*]

MARCUS Long live Lord Titus, my beloved brother,
   Gracious triumpher in the eyes of Rome!   170
TITUS Thanks, gentle tribune, noble brother Marcus.
MARCUS And welcome, nephews, from successful wars,
   You that survive, and you that sleep in fame.
   Fair lords, your fortunes are alike in all,
   That in your country's service drew your swords,   175
   But safer triumph is this funeral pomp,
   That hath aspired to Solon's happiness,
   And triumphs over chance in honour's bed.
   Titus Andronicus, the people of Rome,
   Whose friend in justice thou hast ever been,   180
   Send thee by me, their tribune and their trust,
   This palliament of white and spotless hue
   And name thee in election for the empire
   With these our late-deceasèd emperor's sons.
   Be *candidatus* then, and put it on   185
   And help to set a head on headless Rome.
TITUS A better head her glorious body fits
   Than his that shakes for age and feebleness.
   What should I don this robe and trouble you?
   Be chosen with proclamation today,   190
   Tomorrow yield up rule, resign my life,
   And set abroad new business for you all?

---

168 SD] *Dyce (subst.)*

168 fame's . . . date even longer than fame
lives.
***168 SD** Marcus and the tribunes may enter
'aloft'; see 182 n., 233 SD n.
169 Marcus's first speech since 45, a greeting
and an entrance line. He has the 'palliament' for
Titus with him; see 182.
174 alike in all Titus's dead and living sons are
equally fortunate, but the dead are safer; see 177 n.
177 aspired risen.
177 Solon's happiness Herodotus, *Histories*,
1.32, tells how the Lydian king Croesus asked
Solon, the Athenian statesman of the early fifth
century B.C., to name the happiest of men. Solon
chose an obscure Athenian whose life had been fortunate to the end; 'Call no man happy who is not

dead', he said, meaning that disaster can strike the
living at any moment.
***182 palliament** robe. There is only one other
known occurrence of this invented word. It has
been the subject of much controversy with respect
to Peele's hand in the play; see pp. 5 and 11 above.
Marcus offers Titus the 'palliament'. This would
be awkward if Marcus were 'aloft'; see 168 SD n.,
233 SD n.
183 name . . . empire nominate you (i.e. as a
candidate) for emperor.
185 *candidatus* white-robed (Latin); signifying
that one is standing for office. In *Cor.* 2.3.40 it is
called a 'gown of humility'.
189 What Why.
192 set abroad initiate.

Rome, I have been thy soldier forty years,
And led my country's strength successfully,
And buried one-and-twenty valiant sons,   195
Knighted in field, slain manfully in arms
In right and service of their noble country.
Give me a staff of honour for mine age,
But not a sceptre to control the world;
Upright he held it, lords, that held it last.   200
MARCUS Titus, thou shalt obtain and ask the empery.

                      [*Enter* SATURNINUS *aloft*]

SATURNINUS Proud and ambitious tribune, canst thou tell?
TITUS Patience, Prince Saturninus.
SATURNINUS   Romans, do me right.
        Patricians, draw your swords, and sheathe them not
        Till Saturninus be Rome's emperor.   205
        Andronicus, would thou were shipped to hell,
        Rather than rob me of the people's hearts!
LUCIUS Proud Saturnine, interrupter of the good
        That noble-hearted Titus means to thee!
TITUS Content thee, prince; I will restore to thee   210
        The people's hearts, and wean them from themselves.

                      [*Enter* BASSIANUS *aloft*]

BASSIANUS Andronicus, I do not flatter thee,
        But honour thee, and will do till I die.
        My faction if thou strengthen with thy friends,
        I will most thankful be, and thanks to men   215
        Of noble minds is honourable meed.

---

201 SD] *This edn*   212 SD] *This edn*   214 friends] Q; friend Q2–3, F

196 Knighted in field An anachronism: bat-
tlefield knighthoods were conferred by sovereigns
or commanders in medieval Europe, and in
Shakespeare's own time: the Earl of Essex offended
the queen by creating numerous knights while on
campaign in Ireland in 1599.
201 obtain and ask i.e. you have only to ask
and it shall be yours; the verbal figure, prolepsis,
reverses the customary order (ask, obtain) to stress
the ease and justice of Titus's becoming emperor
(obtain, ask).
*201 SD Saturninus and Bassianus might enter at
168, but that would be less dramatic. They could

enter simultaneously, by different doors, if they
were below; but if they are 'aloft' the rivals cannot enter together. It follows, therefore, that each
should enter just before he speaks; see 233 SD n.
202 Saturninus's first speech since his exit at 63.
He and Bassianus may both enter at 168, but a sudden entry here is more dramatic.
211 SD See 201 SD n.
212 Bassianus speaks for the first time since his
exit at 63: see 201 n. The senators may also enter
with Saturninus at 201 SD.
216 meed reward.

TITUS People of Rome, and people's tribunes here,
        I ask your voices and your suffrages:
        Will ye bestow them friendly on Andronicus?
TRIBUNES To gratify the good Andronicus   220
        And gratulate his safe return to Rome,
        The people will accept whom he admits.
TITUS Tribunes, I thank you, and this suit I make,
        That you create our emperor's eldest son,
        Lord Saturnine, whose virtues will, I hope,   225
        Reflect on Rome as Titan's rays on earth
        And ripen justice in this commonweal;
        Then if you will elect by my advice,
        Crown him and say, 'Long live our emperor!'
MARCUS With voices and applause of every sort,   230
        Patricians and plebeians, we create
        Lord Saturninus Rome's great emperor,
        And say, 'Long live our Emperor Saturnine!'
A long flourish till [Saturninus and Bassianus] come down
SATURNINUS Titus Andronicus, for thy favours done
        To us in our election this day,   235
        I give thee thanks in part of thy deserts
        And will with deeds requite thy gentleness;
        And for an onset, Titus, to advance
        Thy name and honourable family,
        Lavinia will I make my empress,   240

217 people's] Qq; Noble F   223 suit] sute Qq; sure F   226 Titan's] Q2–3, F; Tytus Q   230 sort] Q2–3, F; Q *partially obscured*   231 Patricians] Q2–3, F; Q *damaged*   232 Lord] Q2–3, F; Q *damaged*   233 And] Q2–3, F; Q *damaged*   233 SD] F; *not in* Qq   233 SD *Saturninus and Bassianus] this edn; they* F

218 voices votes. Used in this sense in *Cor.* 2.3.105–37.
221 gratulate express joy at; greet, salute (Onions, Wilson).
224 create elect.
226 Titan Hyperion, a Titan, was father of the sun-god Helios, with whom poets sometimes confounded him.
230 sort social class. The last two letters are illegible in the surviving copy of Q, and 'sort' is written in the margin.
231–3 The bottom corner of page B2 in Q is torn, obliterating part of the first word in each line: [Pat]ricians, [Lor]d, [A]nd.
233 SD *come down* i.e. from aloft, using stairs inside the tiring-house. The Folio SD does not tell us which characters come down here, and there is no earlier SD to show who is 'aloft'. The possible

choices are (1) Marcus and the tribunes (see 168 SD n.); (2) Marcus, the tribunes, Saturninus and Bassianus; (3) Saturninus and Bassianus (see 168 SD n.). Each presents difficulties: (1) and (2) Marcus must hand the 'palliament' to Titus below at 182; (2) Marcus must proclaim Saturninus emperor from above his head, and five actors would look awkward exiting 'aloft' and entering below during a 'flourish'; (2) and (3) fail to mirror the play's opening action. There is also doubt about the movements of the senators. Like a stage director, an editor must make the choice which seems least difficult, but readers should be aware that other choices are valid.

236 in part of as partial reward for.
237 gentleness nobility.
238 onset beginning.

          Rome's royal mistress, mistress of my heart,

          And in the sacred Pantheon her espouse.

          Tell me, Andronicus, doth this motion please thee?

TITUS It doth, my worthy lord, and in this match

          I hold me highly honoured of your grace,   245

          And here in sight of Rome to Saturnine,

          King and commander of our commonweal,

          The wide world's emperor, do I consecrate

          My sword, my chariot, and my prisoners,

          Presents well worthy Rome's imperious lord.   250

          Receive them then, the tribute that I owe,

          Mine honour's ensigns humbled at thy feet.

SATURNINUS Thanks, noble Titus, father of my life.

          How proud I am of thee and of thy gifts

          Rome shall record, and when I do forget   255

          The least of these unspeakable deserts,

          Romans, forget your fealty to me.

TITUS [*To Tamora*] Now, madam, are you prisoner to an emperor,

          To him that for your honour and your state

          Will use you nobly and your followers.   260

SATURNINUS A goodly lady, trust me, of the hue

          That I would choose, were I to choose anew.

          Clear up, fair queen, that cloudy countenance;

          Though chance of war hath wrought this change of cheer,

          Thou com'st not to be made a scorn in Rome.   265

          Princely shall be thy usage every way.

          Rest on my word and let not discontent

          Daunt all your hopes. Madam, he comforts you

          Can make you greater than the Queen of Goths –

          Lavinia, you are not displeased with this?   270

LAVINIA Not I, my lord, sith true nobility

---

242 Pantheon] F2; Pathan Qq, F   250 imperious] Q, Q2; imperiall Q3, F   258 SD] *Johnson; not in* Qq, F   264 chance] Q2–3, F; change Q   269 you] Qq; your F

242 **Pantheon** A temple sacred to all the gods. Shakespeare treats the temple as the equivalent of a Christian church, where this marriage can be solemnised.

  243 **motion** proposal.

  250 **imperious** imperial.

  252 **ensigns** tokens; here Titus seems to refer to the sword, chariot and prisoners mentioned in 249.

  253 **father of my life** A metaphor acknowledging that Titus has crowned him, and agreed to be his father-in-law.

256 **unspeakable** inexpressible.

  257 **fealty** The loyalty a feudal vassal owes his lord.

  261–2 Capell and subsequent editors have marked these lines as an aside. While this is a valid intepretation of the moment, others are possible. The choice is better left open.

  264 **cheer** facial expression.

  268 **he** i.e. he who.

  271 **sith** since.

> Warrants these words in princely courtesy.

SATURNINUS Thanks, sweet Lavinia. Romans, let us go.
> Ransomless here we set our prisoners free.
> Proclaim our honours, lords, with trump and drum.   275

BASSIANUS Lord Titus, by your leave, this maid is mine.

TITUS How, sir! Are you in earnest then, my lord?

BASSIANUS Ay, noble Titus, and resolved withal
> To do myself this reason and this right.

MARCUS *Suum cuique* is our Roman justice;   280
> This prince in justice seizeth but his own.

LUCIUS And that he will and shall, if Lucius live.

TITUS Traitors, avaunt! Where is the emperor's guard?
> Treason, my lord! Lavinia is surprised.

SATURNINUS Surprised! By whom?

BASSIANUS   By him that justly may   285
> Bear his betrothed from all the world away.

>   [*Exit Bassianus with Lavinia*]

MUTIUS Brothers, help to convey her hence away
> And with my sword I'll keep this door safe.

>   [*Exeunt Quintus and Martius*]

TITUS Follow, my lord, and I'll soon bring her back.

MUTIUS My lord, you pass not here.

TITUS   What, villain boy,   290
> Barr'st me my way in Rome?

>   [*Strikes him*]

MUTIUS   Help, Lucius, help!   [*Dies*]
>   [*Exeunt Saturninus, Tamora, Chiron, Demetrius and Aaron*]

LUCIUS My lord, you are unjust and more than so;
> In wrongful quarrel you have slain your son.

TITUS Nor thou, nor he are any sons of mine;

---

280 *cuique*] F2; *cuiqum* Q, Q2; *cuiquam* Q3, F   286 SD] *Rowe; not in* Qq, F   288 SD] *Malone (subst.); not in* Qq, F   290–1
What . . . Rome?] *Divided as Pope; one line* Qq   291 SD.1 *Strikes him*] *This edn; assailing him / Capell*   291 SD.2 *Dies*]
Capell (subst.); He kills him Q3, F; *not in* Q, Q2   291 SD.3 *Exeunt . . . Aaron*] *Cam. (subst.); not in* Qq, F

*275 Trumpets and drums were heard at (and
may have entered with) Titus's Triumph at 69,
and again at 149. The trumpets may have provided the
flourish at 233. Both instruments probably respond
to this verbal SD. If so, Saturninus and his attendants
may exit; see 285 n.

280 *Suum cuique* To each his own (Latin);
proverbial, Tilley M209.

283 avaunt be gone.

285 Here Saturninus may enter again: he is
unaware of what has just occurred on the stage.

Wells suggests that Shakespeare may have meant
him to enter aloft here: thus the SD (*Enter
aloft . . .*) at 298 would be inserted here, and the
one at 291 (*Exeunt Saturninus . . .*) at 275.

288 Marcus may exit, but it is beneath his dignity
and alien to his office to take part in this
scuffle, however much he may sympathise with his
nephews. If Lucius exits with his brothers (288),
his return in response to Mutius's cry (291) must
be ridiculously quick.

My sons would never so dishonour me.   295
Traitor, restore Lavinia to the emperor.
LUCIUS Dead if you will, but not to be his wife
That is another's lawful promised love.   [*Exit*]

Enter aloft the EMPEROR *with* TAMORA *and her two* SONS, *and*
AARON *the Moor*

SATURNINUS No, Titus, no, the emperor needs her not;
Nor her, nor thee, nor any of thy stock.   300
I'll trust by leisure him that mocks me once;
Thee never, nor thy traitorous haughty sons,
Confederates all thus to dishonour me.
Was none in Rome to make a stale
But Saturnine? Full well, Andronicus,   305
Agree these deeds with that proud brag of thine
That saidst, I begged the empire at thy hands.
TITUS O monstrous! What reproachful words are these?
SATURNINUS But go thy ways; go give that changing piece
To him that flourished for her with his sword.   310
A valiant son-in-law thou shalt enjoy:
One fit to bandy with thy lawless sons,
To ruffle in the commonwealth of Rome.
TITUS These words are razors to my wounded heart.
SATURNINUS And therefore, lovely Tamora Queen of Goths,   315
That like the stately Phoebe 'mongst her nymphs
Dost overshine the gallant'st dames of Rome,
If thou be pleased with this my sudden choice,
Behold, I choose thee, Tamora, for my bride
And will create thee Empress of Rome.   320
Speak, Queen of Goths, dost thou applaud my choice?
And here I swear by all the Roman gods,

---

298 SD. *Exit*] Capell; *not in* Qq, F   316 *Phoebe*] F2; *Thebe* Qq, F

301 I'll . . . leisure I'll be slow to trust.

304 stale Meaning uncertain. Possibly a person (sometimes a prostitute) used as a cover for sinister designs (*OED* Stale *sb*³ 5).

306 proud brag Titus has said no such thing.

309 go thy ways Expression of dismissal.

309 changing piece small coin, i.e. 'small change' (Maxwell), punning on (ex)change; or a girl regarded sexually (Partridge), elliptic for 'piece of flesh'. Compare 'Master, I have gone through for this piece you see' (*Per.* 4.2.43–4); and modern vernacular, 'piece of ass'; thus, 'fickle little thing'.

310 flourished . . . sword brandished his sword for her.

312 bandy brawl.

313 ruffle swagger.

316 Phoebe Diana, goddess of the moon. Saturninus means that Tamora's beauty exceeds that of the fairest Roman ladies as much as Diana's surpasses the beauty of her attendant demi-goddesses.

Sith priest and holy water are so near,
And tapers burn so bright, and everything
In readiness for Hymenaeus stand;   325
I will not re-salute the streets of Rome,
Or climb my palace, till from forth this place
I lead espoused my bride along with me.

TAMORA And here in sight of heaven to Rome I swear,
If Saturnine advance the Queen of Goths,   330
She will a handmaid be to his desires,
A loving nurse, a mother to his youth.

SATURNINUS Ascend, fair queen, Pantheon. Lords, accompany
Your noble emperor and his lovely bride,
Sent by the heavens for Prince Saturnine,   335
Whose wisdom hath her fortune conquerèd.
There shall we consummate our spousal rites.

Exeunt [all but Titus]

TITUS I am not bid to wait upon this bride.
Titus, when wert thou wont to walk alone,
Dishonoured thus and challengèd of wrongs?   340

Enter MARCUS, *and Titus' sons* [LUCIUS, QUINTUS *and*
MARTIUS]

MARCUS O Titus, see! O see what thou hast done!
In a bad quarrel slain a virtuous son.

TITUS No, foolish tribune, no; no son of mine,
Nor thou, nor these confederates in the deed
That hath dishonoured all our family: 345

---

333 queen, Pantheon.] *Rowe (subst.)*; Queene: Panthean Qq; Queene, / Pantheon F   337 SD *all but Titus] Manet Titus /*
Hanmer; Omnes Qq, F   340 SD. LUCIUS . . . MARTIUS] *Rowe (subst.); not in* Qq, F   344 these confederates] F *(subst.)*;
these, confederates Q

*323 holy water Another Christian
anachronism; see 242 n. above. In this case
and at 3.1.149, they are Roman Catholic.
  325 Hymenaeus Hymen, god of marriage.
  326 re-salute greet again.
  327 climb enter the Capitol, which was on a
hill; see 12 n. above.
  331 handmaid servant.
  336 Whose wisdom The antecedent is unclear,
but is probably 'bride'; i.e. Tamora has wisely
accepted Saturninus's proposal.
  337 SD Neither Q nor F provides a specific exit
for Marcus. If he has not left the stage at 286,

he may exit here, but not with the wedding party.
Saturninus has established one of the tiring-house
doors as the entrance to the Pantheon. Marcus can
exit through the other door to recall his nephews
at 340.
  339 bid invited.
  339 wont accustomed.
  340 challengèd accused.
  344 these confederates In Q there is a comma
after 'these', which couples Marcus with his
nephews in Titus's accusation; but since he takes no
real part in the scuffle, the charge would be unjustified. I have followed F in omitting the comma.

        Unworthy brother and unworthy sons!
LUCIUS But let us give him burial as becomes,
        Give Mutius burial with our brethren.
TITUS   Traitors, away! He rests not in this tomb.
        This monument five hundred years hath stood,   350
        Which I have sumptuously re-edified.
        Here none but soldiers and Rome's servitors
        Repose in fame; none basely slain in brawls.
        Bury him where you can, he comes not here.
MARCUS My lord, this is impiety in you.   355
        My nephew Mutius' deeds do plead for him,
        He must be buried with his brethren.
QUINTUS *and* MARTIUS And shall, or him we will accompany.
TITUS   'And shall'! What villain was it spake that word?
MARTIUS He that would vouch it in any place but here.   360
TITUS   What, would you bury him in my despite?
MARCUS No, noble Titus, but entreat of thee
        To pardon Mutius and to bury him.
TITUS   Marcus, even thou hast struck upon my crest
        And with these boys mine honour thou hast wounded.   365
        My foes do I repute you every one,
        So trouble me no more, but get you gone.
LUCIUS He is not with himself; let us withdraw.
MARTIUS Not I, till Mutius' bones be burièd.
                The brother and the sons kneel
MARCUS Brother, for in that name doth nature plead –   370
MARTIUS Father, and in that name doth nature speak –
TITUS   Speak thou no more, if all the rest will speed.
MARCUS Renownèd Titus, more than half my soul –

---

348 Mutius] Q3, F; *Mucius* Q, Q2   358 SH QUINTUS *and* MARTIUS] *Capell; Titus two sonnes speakes.* Qq, F *centred*   360
SH MARTIUS] *Capell; Titus sonne speakes.* Qq, F *centred*   368 SH] *Rowe; 3.Sonne* Qq; *1.Sonne* F   368 with] Qq; *not
in* F   369 SH, 371 SH MARTIUS] *Capell; 2.Sonne* Qq, F

347 **becomes** is fitting.
351 **re-edified** rebuilt.
*358–71 Variety of speech ascription amongst
the sons is almost as great as the number of editors who have attempted it. The choices made in
this edition are based on characterisation. Lucius –
1.Sonne (368) – is moderate (see 374); the youngest,
Martius (from Mars, god of war) is belligerent (see
360, and *2.Sonne* at 369 and 371).
358 SH QUINTUS *and* MARTIUS J. S. G. Bolton
suggests ('Two notes on *Titus Andronicus*', *MLN*
45 (1930), 140–1) that the Q SH, *Titus two sonnes
speakes* (centred), may be an error for '*2.Sonne*'.

But the Q SH is quite reasonable, and F does not
alter it. There is no need to emend.
360 **vouch** uphold.
364 **crest** A plume or heraldic symbol sur-
mounting a helmet. A metaphor for his pride or
honour (*OED* Crest *sb*[1] 2, 3).
366 **repute** consider, reckon.
368 **not with** beside.
372 **if . . . speed** Obscure; 'if the rest of you
wish to live' (Wilson) or 'if the others are to succeed', i.e. in this plea (Waith); 'if everything else is
to go well' (Maxwell).

LUCIUS Dear father, soul and substance of us all –

MARCUS Suffer thy brother Marcus to inter   375
　　　　　His noble nephew here in virtue's nest,
　　　　　That died in honour and Lavinia's cause.
　　　　　Thou art a Roman, be not barbarous;
　　　　　The Greeks upon advice did bury Ajax,
　　　　　That slew himself, and wise Laertes' son   380
　　　　　Did graciously plead for his funerals.
　　　　　Let not young Mutius, then, that was thy joy,
　　　　　Be barred his entrance here.

TITUS 　　　　　　　　　　　　　　　　　　Rise, Marcus, rise.
　　　　　　　　　　　　[They rise]
　　　　　The dismall'st day is this that e'er I saw,
　　　　　To be dishonoured by my sons in Rome.   385
　　　　　Well, bury him, and bury me the next.
　　　　　　　　　　They put him in the tomb

LUCIUS There lie thy bones, sweet Mutius, with thy friends,
　　　　　Till we with trophies do adorn thy tomb.
　　　　　　　　　　They all kneel and say:

ALL BUT TITUS No man shed tears for noble Mutius;
　　　　　He lives in fame, that died in virtue's cause.   390
　　　　　　　　　[Exeunt] all but Marcus and Titus

MARCUS My lord, to step out of these dreary dumps,
　　　　　How comes it that the subtle Queen of Goths
　　　　　Is of a sudden thus advanced in Rome?

TITUS I know not, Marcus, but I know it is;
　　　　　Whether by device or no, the heavens can tell.   395
　　　　　Is she not then beholding to the man

---

379 Ajax] F; Ayax Q   380 wise] Qq; *not in* F   383 SD] *Bevington; not in* Qq, F   388 SD] F; *they . . . say*, Q; *all [but Titus] / Waith*   389 SH] *Capell; not in* Qq, F   390 SD *Exeunt*] *This edn; Exit* Qq, F   391 dreary] Qq; *sudden* F

379 **advice** deliberation.

379 **Ajax** Latin name of Aias, a Homeric hero. Losing a dispute with Odysseus (Laertes' son: 380) over the armour of the dead Achilles, he went mad and slew himself. The Greeks debated whether to give him honourable burial. See Ovid, XIII.

388 **trophies** memorials.

388 SD It seems improbable that Titus would kneel here, or join in the eulogy (389–90), but this scene is not notable for probability.

390 Proverbial: Tilley V74.

390 SD This edn follows Qq and F, which call for Titus's sons to leave the stage; but Tamora seems

to address them at 471, and one of them (probably Lucius) speaks at 474. Some editors direct them to stand aside here.

*391 **dumps** melancholy; or a mournful song, referring to the dirge for Mutius (*OED* Dump sb¹ 3). The abrupt non-sequitur here is awkward and supports Wilson's suggestion that 341–90 and Mutius's death are revisions; see Textual Analysis, p. 162 below.

395 **device** stratagem, trickery.

396 **beholding . . . man** indebted to Titus, her captor.

That brought her for this high good turn so far?
Yes, and will nobly him remunerate.

Flourish

| *Enter the* EMPEROR, TAMORA *and her two* SONS, *with the* MOOR *at one door* | *Enter at the other door* BASSIANUS *and* LAVINIA, *with* [*Titus's* SONS] |

SATURNINUS So, Bassianus, you have played your prize.
    God give you joy, sir, of your gallant bride.   400
BASSIANUS And you of yours, my lord. I say no more
    Nor wish no less, and so I take my leave.
SATURNINUS Traitor, if Rome have law or we have power,
    Thou and thy faction shall repent this rape.
BASSIANUS 'Rape' call you it, my lord, to seize my own,   405
    My true betrothèd love and now my wife?
    But let the laws of Rome determine all;
    Meanwhile am I possessed of that is mine.
SATURNINUS 'Tis good, sir; you are very short with us,
    But if we live we'll be as sharp with you.   410
BASSIANUS My lord, what I have done, as best I may,
    Answer I must, and shall do with my life.
    Only thus much I give your grace to know:
    By all the duties that I owe to Rome,
    This noble gentleman, Lord Titus here,   415
    Is in opinion and in honour wronged,
    That in the rescue of Lavinia
    With his own hand did slay his youngest son,
    In zeal to you and highly moved to wrath
    To be controlled in that he frankly gave.   420
    Receive him then to favour, Saturnine,
    That hath expressed himself in all his deeds
    A father and a friend to thee and Rome.
TITUS Prince Bassianus, leave to plead my deeds;

398] F; *not in* Qq; *attributed to Marcus, Dyce (conj. Malone)*   398 SD.1 *Flourish*] F; *not in* Qq   *398 SD.2–4] In two columns* Q   398 SD.4 *Titus'* SONS] *This edn; others.* Qq, F   408 am I] Q, Q2; I am Q3, F

398 SD The symmetrical form of the Q SD, in double columns, may reflect Shakespeare's intended staging, and has therefore been retained.

399 **played your prize** won your bout (a term from fencing).

408 **that** that which; see 420.

416 **opinion** reputation.

420 **controlled** restrained. This sense of the word applies to every use of it in *Titus Andronicus* except 1.1.199, where it has the modern meaning.

420 **frankly** freely.

422 **expressed** manifested, revealed.

424 **leave to plead** cease urging as a plea; i.e. cease treating my deeds as if they extenuated an offence.

'Tis thou, and those, that have dishonoured me.   425
Rome and the righteous heavens be my judge
How I have loved and honoured Saturnine. [*Kneels*]
TAMORA My worthy lord, if ever Tamora
　　　　Were gracious in those princely eyes of thine,
　　　　Then hear me speak indifferently for all;   430
　　　　And at my suit, sweet, pardon what is past.
SATURNINUS What, madam, be dishonoured openly,
　　　　And basely put it up without revenge?
TAMORA Not so, my lord; the gods of Rome forfend
　　　　I should be author to dishonour you.   435
　　　　But on mine honour dare I undertake
　　　　For good Lord Titus' innocence in all,
　　　　Whose fury not dissembled speaks his griefs.
　　　　Then at my suit look graciously on him;
　　　　Lose not so noble a friend on vain suppose,   440
　　　　Nor with sour looks afflict his gentle heart.
　　　　[*Aside to Saturninus*] My lord, be ruled by me, be won at
　　　　　　last.
　　　　Dissemble all your griefs and discontents;
　　　　You are but newly planted in your throne;
　　　　Lest then the people and patricians too,   445
　　　　Upon a just survey take Titus' part
　　　　And so supplant you for ingratitude,
　　　　Which Rome reputes to be a heinous sin,
　　　　Yield at entreats, and then let me alone
　　　　I'll find a day to massacre them all   450
　　　　And raze their faction and their family,
　　　　The cruel father and his traitorous sons,
　　　　To whom I sued for my dear son's life;
　　　　And make them know what 'tis to let a queen
　　　　Kneel in the streets and beg for grace in vain.   455
　　　　Come, come, sweet emperor; come, Andronicus;

---

427 SD] *Bevington; not in* Qq, F　　442 SD] *Rowe; not in* Qq, F　　447 you] Q, Q2; us Q3, F

425 **those** Marcus and his sons.
430 **indifferently** impartially.
433 **put it up** sheathe it, i.e. like a sword; see
2.1.53.
435 **be author . . . you** be the instigator of any
dishonour to you.
436 **undertake** vouch.
438 **Whose fury . . . griefs** i.e. his grief is
plainly real, because he cannot conceal his rage.

440 **suppose** supposition.
442 **be won at last** allow yourself to be persuaded, i.e. won over.
449 **at entreats** to entreaties.
449 **let me alone** leave it to me.
451 **raze** The Q spelling, 'race', 'suggests both
"raze" and the obsolete "arace", to root out'
(Waith).

Take up this good old man, and cheer the heart
That dies in tempest of thy angry frown.
SATURNINUS Rise, Titus, rise; my empress hath prevailed.
TITUS [*Rises*] I thank your majesty and her, my lord.   460
These words, these looks infuse new life in me.
TAMORA Titus, I am incorporate in Rome,
A Roman now adopted happily,
And must advise the emperor for his good.
This day all quarrels die, Andronicus.   465
And let it be mine honour, good my lord,
That I have reconciled your friends and you.
For you, Prince Bassianus, I have passed
My word and promise to the emperor
That you will be more mild and tractable.   470
And fear not, lords and you, Lavinia;
By my advice, all humbled on your knees
You shall ask pardon of his majesty.
    [*Marcus, Lavinia and Titus's sons kneel*]
LUCIUS We do, and vow to heaven and to his highness
That what we did was mildly as we might,   475
Tend'ring our sister's honour and our own.
MARCUS That on mine honour here do I protest.
SATURNINUS Away, and talk not; trouble us no more.
TAMORA Nay, nay, sweet emperor, we must all be friends.
The tribune and his nephews kneel for grace.   480
I will not be denied; sweetheart, look back.
SATURNINUS Marcus, for thy sake, and thy brother's here
And at my lovely Tamora's entreats
I do remit these young men's heinous faults:
Stand up.   485
    [*They rise*]
Lavinia, though you left me like a churl,

---

460 SD] *Bevington; not in* Qq, F   473 SD] *Witherspoon (subst.); not in* Qq, F   474 SH LUCIUS] *Rowe; Tamora continued*
Q; *indented without* SH Q2; *All* Q3; *Son* F   477 do I] Q; *I doe* Q2–3, F   485 Stand up. / Lavinia . . . churl,] *Rowe;*
Stand vp: *Lauinia . . . Churle,* Qq, F   485 SD] *Chambers (subst.); not in* Qq, F

457 **Take . . . man** Raise Titus (from his kneeling position).
462 **incorporate in** bound up in one body with.
See *Cor.* 1.1.130: in a metaphor for the Roman state,
the belly calls the limbs 'my incorporate friends',
meaning that all are parts of an indivisible whole.
*473 Verbal SDs at 472 and 480 show that
Marcus, Titus's sons and perhaps Lavinia kneel.
474 SH Rowe's SH is based on F, 'Son'.
475 **mildly . . . might** done as mildly as

we could, i.e. under the circumstances; see *Cor.*
3.2.139–41, where 'mildly' is used five times in this
sense.
476 **Tend'ring** Having regard for.
485 SD Titus has been kneeling since 427; he
rises with the rest.
486 **churl** peasant, ill-bred person. Since 'churl'
is a male word, he can only mean that Lavinia has
left him as though *he* were a churl.

I found a friend and sure as death I swore
I would not part a bachelor from the priest.
Come, if the emperor's court can feast two brides,
You are my guest, Lavinia, and your friends.   490
This day shall be a love-day, Tamora.

TITUS Tomorrow, and it please your majesty
   To hunt the panther and the hart with me,
   With horn and hound we'll give your grace *bonjour.*

SATURNINUS Be it so, Titus, and gramercy too.   495

Flourish. Exeunt [all but Aaron]

[2.1]

AARON ????Now climbeth Tamora Olympus' top,
   Safe out of Fortune's shot and sits aloft,
   Secure of thunder's crack or lightning flash,
   Advanced above pale envy's threatening reach.
   As when the golden sun salutes the morn   5
   And having gilt the ocean with his beams,
   Gallops the zodiac in his glistering coach,
   And overlooks the highest-peering hills:
   So Tamora.
   Upon her wit doth earthly honour wait,   10
   And virtue stoops and trembles at her frown.
   Then Aaron, arm thy heart and fit thy thoughts
   To mount aloft with thy imperial mistress
   And mount her pitch, whom thou in triumph long
   Hast prisoner held, fettered in amorous chains   15
   And faster bound to Aaron's charming eyes

---

495 SD *Flourish.*] F, *to open Act 2; sound trumpets,* Q   *495 SD *all but Aaron*] *manet* Moore Qq   Act 2, Scene 1   2.1]
Rowe; *Actus Secunda.* F; *not in* Qq; *Flourish. Enter Aaron alone.* F; *not in* Qq   4 above] Qq; *about* F   8 highest-peering]
Theobald; highest piering Qq, F   8 hills:] F; hills. Qq   9 So Tamora.] *Indented* Q

487 **sure as death** Proverbial: Tilley D136.
491 **love-day** A day set aside for settling
disputes; or a day for love-making.
   492 **and** if.
   494 *bonjour* good day (French).
   495 **gramercy** thanks; from *grand merci*
(French); see 4.2.7.
   *495 SD Since Aaron remains on-stage, the
action continues. I have retained the traditional
act division to facilitate study in conjunction with
reference works such as concordances.

Act 2, Scene 1
   1 **Olympus** Mountain home of the gods.
   3 **Secure of** Safe from.
   7 **Gallops** i.e. gallops through.
   8 **overlooks** looks down on.
   14 **mount her pitch** rise to the highest part of
her flight (from falconry).
   16 **charming eyes** eyes that cast a magical
spell.

Than is Prometheus tied to Caucasus.
Away with slavish weeds and servile thoughts!
I will be bright, and shine in pearl and gold
To wait upon this new-made empress.   20
To wait, said I? To wanton with this queen,
This goddess, this Semiramis, this nymph,
This siren that will charm Rome's Saturnine
And see his shipwrack and his commonweal's.
Hollo, what storm is this?   25

    Enter CHIRON *and* DEMETRIUS *braving*

DEMETRIUS Chiron, thy years wants wit, thy wits wants edge
  And manners, to intrude where I am graced,
  And may, for aught thou knowest, affected be.
CHIRON Demetrius, thou dost overween in all,
  And so in this, to bear me down with braves.   30
  'Tis not the difference of a year or two
  Makes me less gracious or thee more fortunate;
  I am as able and as fit as thou
  To serve, and to deserve my mistress' grace,
  And that my sword upon thee shall approve   35
  And plead my passions for Lavinia's love.
AARON Clubs, clubs! These lovers will not keep the peace.
DEMETRIUS Why, boy, although our mother, unadvised,
  Gave you a dancing-rapier by your side,
  Are you so desperate grown to threat your friends?   40
  Go to; have your lath glued within your sheath
  Till you know better how to handle it.
CHIRON Meanwhile, sir, with the little skill I have,
  Full well shalt thou perceive how much I dare.

---

18 servile] Q, Q2; idle Q3, F   22 nymph] Q, Q2; Queene Q3, F   25 Hollo] Qq, F; Holla F2–4; Holloa *Cam.*; Hullo *Alexander*

17 **Prometheus . . . Caucasus** Zeus chained the Titan Prometheus to the Caucasus for stealing fire from heaven for the benefit of mortals.

22 **Semiramis** Assyrian queen, builder of Babylon, and conqueror. Her beauty and lust were as legendary as her power; see 2.3.118.

25 SD *braving* defying (each other); see 30, 2.3.126, 4.2.36, 4.2.137.

27 **graced** favoured.

28 **affected** loved.

29 **overween** arrogantly presume.

35 **approve** prove.

37 **Clubs, clubs!** A brawl! Elizabethan street cry, summoning the Watch to stop a fight – or apprentices to join in one.

38 **unadvised** ill-advisedly.

39 **dancing-rapier** An ornamental light sword.

41 **lath** Wooden stage-sword.

DEMETRIUS Ay, boy, grow ye so brave?
                                They draw
AARON   Why how now, lords?   45
      So near the emperor's palace dare ye draw
      And maintain such a quarrel openly?
      Full well I wot the ground of all this grudge.
      I would not for a million of gold
      The cause were known to them it most concerns,   50
      Nor would your noble mother for much more
      Be so dishonoured in the court of Rome.
      For shame, put up.
DEMETRIUS   Not I, till I have sheathed
      My rapier in his bosom, and withal
      Thrust those reproachful speeches down his throat,   55
      That he hath breathed in my dishonour here.
CHIRON For that I am prepared and full resolved,
      Foul-spoken coward, that thund'rest with thy tongue
      And with thy weapon nothing dar'st perform.
AARON Away, I say!   60
      Now by the gods that warlike Goths adore,
      This petty brabble will undo us all.
      Why, lords, and think you not how dangerous
      It is to jet upon a prince's right?
      What, is Lavinia then become so loose,   65
      Or Bassianus so degenerate,
      That for her love such quarrels may be broached
      Without controlment, justice, or revenge?
      Young lords, beware; and should the empress know
      This discord's ground, the music would not please.   70
CHIRON I care not, I, knew she and all the world;
      I love Lavinia more than all the world.
DEMETRIUS Youngling, learn thou to make some meaner choice;
      Lavinia is thine elder brother's hope.
AARON Why, are ye mad? Or know ye not in Rome   75
      How furious and impatient they be,
      And cannot brook competitors in love?

---

46 ye] Q; you Q2–3, F   55 those] Q, Q2; these Q3, F   62 petty] Qq; pretty F   64 jet] Qq; set F   75 Why,] *Theobald;*
Why Qq, F

---

46 With a gesture, Aaron may establish that the
tiring-house represents the palace.
  48 **wot** know.
  62 **brabble** brawl.

64 **jet** encroach.
  70 **ground** reason; with a musical pun on the
bass over which a descant is 'raised' (Onions).
  71 **knew she** if she knew.

               I tell you, lords, you do but plot your deaths
               By this device.
CHIRON   Aaron, a thousand deaths
               Would I propose, to achieve her whom I love.   80
AARON To achieve her how?
DEMETRIUS   Why makes thou it so strange?
               She is a woman, therefore may be wooed;
               She is a woman, therefore may be won;
               She is Lavinia, therefore must be loved.
               What, man! More water glideth by the mill   85
               Than wots the miller of, and easy it is
               Of a cut loaf to steal a shive, we know:
               Though Bassianus be the emperor's brother,
               Better than he have worn Vulcan's badge.

AARON [*Aside*] Ay, and as good as Saturninus may.   90
DEMETRIUS Then why should he despair that knows to court it
               With words, fair looks and liberality?
               What, hast not thou full often struck a doe
               And borne her cleanly by the keeper's nose?

AARON Why then it seems some certain snatch or so   95
               Would serve your turns.
CHIRON   Ay, so the turn were served.
DEMETRIUS Aaron, thou hast hit it.
AARON   Would you had hit it too!
               Then should not we be tired with this ado.
               Why hark ye, hark ye, and are you such fools
               To square for this? Would it offend you then   100

79–80] *Divided as Hanmer; Aaron . . . propose / To . . . love Qq, F, Waith*   **80** I love] Q, Q2; I do love Q3, F   **81** her
how?] Qq; her, how? F   **81** Why makes] Q; Why, makes Q2–3; Why, mak'st F; Why mak'st *Wilson*   **90** SD] *Theobald;
not in Qq, F*

80 propose be prepared to meet (Onions).
81 Why . . . strange? Why do you seem so
surprised?
*82–3 Proverbial: Tilley w681, *ODEP*, p. 911;
see *1H6* 5.3.78–9: 'She's beautiful; and therefore to
be wooed / She is a woman; therefore to be won.'
See also *R3* 1.2.227–8: 'Was ever woman in this
humour wooed? Was ever woman in this humour
won?' This misogynistic remark begins a string of
proverbs.
85–6 More . . . of Proverbial: Tilley w99,
ODEP, p. 870.
86–7 easy . . . shive Proverbial: Tilley T34.
Demetrius means that since Lavinia is married, and
hence no longer a virgin, Bassianus need be none
the wiser if she takes a lover.

87 shive slice.
89 Vulcan's badge i.e. cuckold's horns; Ovid,
IV, repeats Homer's story of Venus's adultery with
Mars; Vulcan is her husband.
  91 court it play the suitor.
  94 cleanly cleverly, adroitly.
  95 snatch A sudden grab or snap at something;
or, a small amount or portion (*OED* sv *sb* 3a; 7a). In
the latter sense, perhaps figuratively 'a quick one'
(sexually). Slang, 'woman's genitals', is not found
before 1904 (Rubinstein).
  96 serve your turns serve (sexually) your sexual bouts (Rubinstein).
  100 square quarrel.

              That both should speed?

CHIRON Faith, not me.

DEMETRIUS   Nor me, so I were one.

AARON For shame, be friends and join for that you jar.
        'Tis policy and stratagem must do
        That you affect, and so must you resolve   105
        That what you cannot as you would achieve,
        You must perforce accomplish as you may.
        Take this of me: Lucrece was not more chaste
        Than this Lavinia, Bassianus' love.
        A speedier course than ling'ring languishment   110
        Must we pursue, and I have found the path.
        My lords, a solemn hunting is in hand;
        There will the lovely Roman ladies troop.
        The forest walks are wide and spacious
        And many unfrequented plots there are,   115
        Fitted by kind for rape and villainy.
        Single you thither then this dainty doe
        And strike her home by force, if not by words;
        This way, or not at all, stand you in hope.
        Come, come, our empress, with her sacred wit   120
        To villainy and vengeance consecrate,
        Will we acquaint withal what we intend,
        And she shall file our engines with advice
        That will not suffer you to square yourselves,
        But to your wishes' height advance you both.   125
        The emperor's court is like the house of Fame,
        The palace full of tongues, of eyes and ears:
        The woods are ruthless, dreadful, deaf, and dull.

101 That . . . speed] Qq; *not in* F   110 than] *Rowe;* this Qq, F   122 withal what] withall what Q; with all that Q2–3, F; with all what *Alexander*   127 and] Q, Q2; of Q3, F

101 **speed** succeed.

102 **so** so long as; see 5.3.172.

103 **for that . . . jar** to get what you are making discord over.

104 **policy** crafty scheming; see 4.2.149.

105 **affect** aim at.

*108 **Lucrece** Chaste wife raped by Tarquin; she then killed herself. Shakespeare's *Rape of Lucrece* (1593) has important links with *Titus Andronicus*.

112 **solemn** i.e. belonging to a celebration or festivity (Onions).

115 **plots** places; i.e. plots of ground.

116 **kind** nature; see 1.1.61.

121 **consecrate** dedicated.

122 **withal** with. Alexander's emendation alters the meaning to 'with *all that* we intend'.

123 **engines** It is uncertain whether this is meant literally; 'wits' (Maxwell), 'stratagem' (Waith) or as part of a metaphorical phrase with 'file', i.e. 'sharpen our machinery'.

126 **Fame** Rumour. Possibly an allusion to Chaucer's *Hous of Fame*, but more probably to Ovid, XII, or Virgil, IV.

128 **ruthless** pitiless.

There speak and strike, brave boys, and take your turns;
There serve your lust shadowed from heaven's eye,   130
And revel in Lavinia's treasury.
CHIRON Thy counsel, lad, smells of no cowardice.
DEMETRIUS *Sit fas aut nefas,* till I find the stream
    To cool this heat, a charm to clam these fits,
    Per Stygia, per manes vehor.   135

                                         Exeunt

[2.2] *Enter* TITUS ANDRONICUS *and his three sons* [LUCIUS,
QUINTUS *and* MARTIUS], *with hounds and horns, and* MARCUS

TITUS The hunt is up, the morn is bright and grey,
    The fields are fragrant, and the woods are green.
    Uncouple here, and let us make a bay,
    And wake the emperor and his lovely bride,
    And rouse the prince, and ring a hunter's peal   5
    That all the court may echo with the noise.
    Sons, let it be your charge, as it is ours,
    To attend the emperor's person carefully;
    I have been troubled in my sleep this night,
    But dawning day new comfort hath inspired.   10

Here a cry of hounds, and wind horns in a peal; then enter
SATURNINUS, TAMORA, BASSIANUS, LAVINIA, CHIRON,
DEMETRIUS *and their Attendants*

    Many good morrows to your majesty;
    Madam, to you as many and as good.
    I promisèd your grace a hunter's peal.

---

130 lust] Qq; lusts F   133 stream] Qq; streames F   **Act 2, Scene 2**   2.2] *Rowe; not in* Qq, F   0 SD.1–2 LUCIUS . . .
MARTIUS] *Not in* Qq, F   0 SD.2 *and* MARCUS] F; *not in* Qq   1 morn] Q3, F; Moone Q, Q2

133 *Sit . . . nefas* Be it right of wrong (Latin).
135 *Per . . . vehor* I am borne through the Stygian regions, through the shades (Latin). Probably an inaccurate memory of Seneca: *Per Stygia, per amnes igneos amens sequar* (*Phaedra* 1180); see below, 4.3.44.

Act 2, Scene 2
1 **grey** The colour of early morning light was sometimes described as 'grey' without connotations of cloud; see *2H4* 2.3.19, *Rom.* 2.3.1, and Peele, *The Old Wives Tale* 4.11, Malone Society Reprint, 1908. This last may owe something to *Titus*: see notes in

Maxwell and Wilson.
3 **Uncouple** Unleash the hounds.
3 **bay** i.e. baying of hounds.
4–6 If Aaron has not already done so at 2.1.46, Titus establishes that the action takes place before the palace.
10 SD.1 *cry* pack; i.e. a 'cry' of hounds is heard to make a 'bay'. See *Ham.* 3.2.278: 'a cry of players'.
10 SD.1 *hounds* Even if real hounds were used (Waith), it is difficult to imagine how they could have been induced to 'yellow' on cue. A cry of players in the tiring-house, imitating a cry of hounds, is more probable.

SATURNINUS And you have rung it lustily, my lords,
        Somewhat too early for new-married ladies.   15
BASSIANUS Lavinia, how say you?
LAVINIA   I say no;
        I have been broad awake two hours and more.
SATURNINUS Come on then; horse and chariots let us have,
        And to our sport. Madam, now shall ye see
        Our Roman hunting.
MARCUS   I have dogs, my lord,   20
        Will rouse the proudest panther in the chase,
        And climb the highest promontory top.
TITUS And I have horse will follow where the game
        Makes way and runs like swallows o'er the plain.
DEMETRIUS Chiron, we hunt not, we, with horse nor hound,   25
        But hope to pluck a dainty doe to ground.

                                 Exeunt

[2.3] *Enter* AARON *alone* [*with gold*]

AARON He that had wit would think that I had none,
        To bury so much gold under a tree
        And never after to inherit it.
        Let him that thinks of me so abjectly
        Know that this gold must coin a stratagem   5
        Which, cunningly effected, will beget
        A very excellent piece of villainy;
        And so repose, sweet gold, for their unrest
        That have their alms out of the empress' chest.

        Enter TAMORA *alone to the Moor*

TAMORA My lovely Aaron, wherefore look'st thou sad   10
        When everything doth make a gleeful boast?

16–17 I say . . . more] F; *one line in* Qq   17 broad] Qq; *not in* F   24 runs] Qq, F; run F2, *Wilson*   24 like] Qq;
likes F   **Act 2, Scene 3**   2.3] *Capell; not in* Qq, F   0 SD *with gold*] *Capell (subst.); not in* Qq, F   9 SD *alone*] Qq;
not in F

Act 2, Scene 3
  3 **inherit** enjoy possession of.
  4 **thinks . . . abjectly** i.e. thinks me abject, con-
temptible.
  *8 The verbal SD requires Aaron to hide some
gold, perhaps at the foot of a column like those
shown in the de Witt sketch (see illustration 10,

p. 170 below). If a property tree were intended, it
is difficult to see why Tamora must set the scene
verbally (12–16).
  9 **That . . . chest** Who benefit from Tamora's
charity by finding her gold (ironic).
  11 **boast** display.

The birds chant melody on every bush,
The snakes lies rollèd in the cheerful sun,
The green leaves quiver with the cooling wind
And make a chequered shadow on the ground;   15
Under their sweet shade, Aaron, let us sit,
And whilst the babbling echo mocks the hounds,
Replying shrilly to the well-tuned horns,
As if a double hunt were heard at once,
Let us sit down and mark their yellowing noise;   20
And after conflict such as was supposed
The wand'ring prince and Dido once enjoyed
When with a happy storm they were surprised,
And curtained with a counsel-keeping cave,
We may, each wreathèd in the other's arms,   25
Our pastimes done, possess a golden slumber,
Whiles hounds and horns and sweet melodious birds
Be unto us as is a nurse's song
Of lullaby, to bring her babe asleep.
AARON Madam, though Venus govern your desires,   30
Saturn is dominator over mine;
What signifies my deadly-standing eye,
My silence, and my cloudy melancholy,
My fleece of woolly hair that now uncurls
Even as an adder when she doth unroll   35
To do some fatal execution?
No, madam, these are no venereal signs;
Vengeance is in my heart, death in my hand,
Blood and revenge are hammering in my head.
Hark, Tamora, the empress of my soul,   40

---

13 snakes] Q, Q2; snake Q3, F   20 yellowing] Qq; yelping F   32 deadly-standing] *Theobald;* deadlie standing Qq, F

13 snakes lies While this does not agree with modern usage, it resembles the construction at 2.1.26, and derives from Q, the best text.

20 yellowing yelping; apparent extension of 'yell' on the analogy of 'bell' – 'bellow' (*OED* Yellow *v²*).

21–4 And after . . . cave Fleeing the fall of Troy, Aeneas is entertained by Dido, Queen of Carthage. Virgil, IV, tells how they shelter from a storm while hunting; the resulting love-affair almost deflects the hero from his divinely ordained mission to found the Trojan settlement which will become Rome.

31 dominator dominant astrological influence.

Ironically, Aaron is a 'saturnine' man, which means that he is by nature 'sluggish, cold and gloomy in temperament' (*OED* Saturnine *adj* 1a).

32 deadly-standing fixed in a death-dealing stare (Maxwell).

37 venereal of Venus, i.e. love.

38–9 Compare Thomas Lodge, *The Wounds of Civil War*, ed. Joseph W. Houppert, 1969, 3.4.62–3: 'Within my breast, care, danger, sorrow dwells, / Hope and revenge sit hammering in my heart.' There are also similarities between the Lodge speech and 93–8 below.

Which never hopes more heaven than rests in thee,
This is the day of doom for Bassianus;
His Philomel must lose her tongue today,
Thy sons make pillage of her chastity,
And wash their hands in Bassianus' blood.   45
Seest thou this letter? Take it up, I pray thee,
And give the king this fatal-plotted scroll.
Now question me no more; we are espied.
Here comes a parcel of our hopeful booty
Which dreads not yet their lives' destruction.   50

Enter BASSIANUS *and* LAVINIA

TAMORA Ah my sweet Moor, sweeter to me than life!
AARON No more, great empress; Bassianus comes.
    Be cross with him, and I'll go fetch thy sons
    To back thy quarrels, whatsoe'er they be.   [*Exit*]
BASSIANUS Who have we here? Rome's royal empress   55
    Unfurnished of her well-beseeming troop?
    Or is it Dian, habited like her,
    Who hath abandonèd her holy groves
    To see the general hunting in this forest?
TAMORA Saucy controller of my private steps,   60
    Had I the power that some say Dian had,
    Thy temples should be planted presently
    With horns, as was Actaeon's, and the hounds
    Should drive upon thy new-transformèd limbs,
    Unmannerly intruder as thou art!   65
LAVINIA Under your patience, gentle empress,
    'Tis thought you have a goodly gift in horning
    And to be doubted that your Moor and you

47 fatal-plotted] *Theobald;* fatal plotted Qq, F   54 quarrels] Q, Q2; quarrel Q3, F   54 SD] *Rowe; not in* Qq, F   55 Who]
Qq; Whom F   56 her] Q, Q2; our Q3, F   60 my] Q, Q2; our Q3, F   64 thy] Q, Q2; his Q3, F

43 **Philomel** The first of many references to the
story of Philomela's rape by Tereus, a source of the
Lavinia-plot (Ovid, VI); see p. 10 above, and 2.4.26–
7, 38–43; 4.1.47–8; 5.2.194–5.
46 Aaron gives Tamora a letter.
47 **fatal-plotted** devised with deadly purpose.
49 **parcel** part.
49 **hopeful** hoped-for.
53 **cross** quarrelsome.
56 **Unfurnished . . . troop?** Unaccompanied by
her appropriate retinue.
57 **Dian, habited like her** i.e. Diana, goddess

of the hunt, disguised as Tamora.
60 **Saucy controller** Insolent restrainer.
62–4 **Thy temples . . . limbs** Actaeon spied on
Diana bathing. She changed him into a stag, and
he was killed by his own hounds (Ovid, III).
62 **presently** immediately; see 4.4.44, 5.3.58.
63 **Actaeon** The accent is on the second syllable.
66 **Under your patience** By your leave.
67 **horning** cuckolding.
68 **to be doubted** is suspected.

Are singled forth to try thy experiments.
Jove shield your husband from his hounds today!   70
'Tis pity they should take him for a stag.

BASSIANUS Believe me, queen, your swarthy Cimmerian
Doth make your honour of his body's hue,
Spotted, detested, and abominable.
Why are you sequestered from all your train,   75
Dismounted from your snow-white goodly steed
And wandered hither to an òbscure plot,
Accompanied but with a barbarous Moor,
If foul desire had not conducted you?

LAVINIA And being intercepted in your sport,   80
Great reason that my noble lord be rated
For sauciness. I pray you, let us hence,
And let her joy her raven-coloured love;
This valley fits the purpose passing well.

BASSIANUS The king my brother shall have notice of this.   85

LAVINIA Ay, for these slips have made him noted long;
Good king to be so mightily abused.

TAMORA Why, I have patience to endure all this.

Enter CHIRON *and* DEMETRIUS

DEMETRIUS How now, dear sovereign and our gracious mother,
Why doth your highness look so pale and wan?   90

TAMORA Have I not reason, think you, to look pale?
These two have ticed me hither to this place,

---

69 thy] Q; *not in* Q2–3, F   72 swarthy] *Bevington;* swartie Q, Q2; swarty Q3; swarth F; swart *Maxwell*   78 but] Q, Q2; *not in* Q3, F   85 notice] Qq, F; note *Pope, Wilson*   88 Why, I have . . . this] Qq *(subst.);* Why I have . . . this? F; Why have I . . . this? F2, *Wilson*   90 doth] Qq, F; does *Rowe, Waith*

---

69 **singled . . . experiments** alone together to experiment, i.e. at horning.

69 **thy** Between 69 and 95, various editors have attempted emendations with a view to correcting some of the eight lines of eleven syllables. Singly, many of these emendations are plausible, but taken together, they strain credulity. I have thought it safer to trust Q; in a play that is full of irregular verse, it is easier to accept these as authorial than to challenge the copy-text.

72 **swarthy** dark-skinned. F's 'swarth', sometimes emended as 'swart', scans better; but many lines in this play fail to scan, and the Q reading ('swarty') is more likely to be what Shakespeare wrote.

72 **Cimmerian** A people who live in darkness near the realm of the dead (*Odyssey* XI). Cimmerians were proverbially dark-skinned; Tilley C389.1.

74 **Spotted** Stained, polluted; see *Ham.* 3.4.90–1: 'I see such black and grainèd spots / As will not leave their tinct.'

81 **rated** chided, scolded.

83 **joy** enjoy.

86 **noted** notorious.

86 **long** Tamora met and married the emperor on the previous day. This rudimentary instance of the 'double time' that Shakespeare manipulates advantageously in *Othello* probably derives from the chapbook story (Waith).

92 **ticed** enticed.

A barren detested vale you see it is;
The trees, though summer, yet forlorn and lean,
Overcome with moss and baleful mistletoe;   95
Here never shines the sun, here nothing breeds
Unless the nightly owl or fatal raven;
And when they showed me this abhorrèd pit,
They told me, here at dead time of the night
A thousand fiends, a thousand hissing snakes,   100
Ten thousand swelling toads, as many urchins,
Would make such fearful and confusèd cries
As any mortal body hearing it
Should straight fall mad, or else die suddenly.
No sooner had they told this hellish tale   105
But straight they told me they would bind me here
Unto the body of a dismal yew
And leave me to this miserable death.
And then they called me foul adulteress,
Lavicious Goth, and all the bittrest terms   110
That ever ear did hear to such effect.
And had you not by wondrous fortune come,
This vengeance on me had they executed.
Revenge it as you love your mother's life,
Or be ye not henceforth called my children.   115

DEMETRIUS This is a witness that I am thy son.
CHIRON And this for me, struck home to show my strength.

                    [*They*] *stab* [*Bassianus*]

LAVINIA Ay, come, Semiramis, nay, barbarous Tamora,
For no name fits thy nature but thy own.
TAMORA Give me the poniard; you shall know, my boys,   120
Your mother's hand shall right your mother's wrong.

---

95 Overcome] Q; Orecome Q2–3, *Wilson*   *110 Lavicious] Lauicious Q, Q2; Lasciuious Q3, F   117 SD] *Capell (subst.)*;
stab him Qq, F *after 116*   119 Ay, come] *Hanmer*; I come Qq, F; I, come *Theobald*   120 the] Q, Q2; thy Q3, F

93–7 Compare Tamora's description of the same
spot at 12–16.
  95 **Overcome** Overgrown.
  97 **fatal** ominous; see 202.
  *98 **pit** A large trap is now open. In Act 1, it
may have served as the tomb of the Andronici.
  107 **dismal yew** The graveyard tree; see H. T.
Price, 'The yew-tree in *Titus Andronicus*', *N&Q*
208 (1963), 98–9.
  *110 **Lavicious** Editors unanimously emend
here, but there need be no compositor's error. The

Elizabethan ear that was hospitable to words like
'abhominable' could easily accept a coinage like
this, names like Ariachne (*Tro.* 5.2.152) and Abhor-
son (*MM*) or words like 'palliament' (1.1.182),
'yellowing' (2.3.20), 'satisfice' (2.3.180) and 'successantly' (4.4.112).
  110 **Goth** Possibly with a pun on Goth/goat;
goats are proverbially lustful.
  117 SD The verbal SD in 116 shows that both
brothers stab Bassianus.

DEMETRIUS Stay, madam, here is more belongs to her.
　　　　　First thresh the corn, then after burn the straw.
　　　　　This minion stood upon her chastity,
　　　　　Upon her nuptial vow, her loyalty,   125
　　　　　And with that painted hope braves your mightiness;
　　　　　And shall she carry this unto her grave?
CHIRON And if she do I wish I were an eunuch.
　　　　　Drag hence her husband to some secret hole
　　　　　And make his dead trunk pillow to our lust.   130
TAMORA But when ye have the honey ye desire,
　　　　　Let not this wasp outlive, us both to sting.
CHIRON I warrant you, madam, we will make that sure.
　　　　　Come, mistress, now perforce we will enjoy
　　　　　That nice-preservèd honesty of yours.   135
LAVINIA O Tamora, thou bearest a woman's face –
TAMORA I will not hear her speak; away with her.
LAVINIA Sweet lords, entreat her hear me but a word.
DEMETRIUS Listen, fair madam, let it be your glory
　　　　　To see her tears, but be your heart to them   140
　　　　　As unrelenting flint to drops of rain.
LAVINIA When did the tiger's young ones teach the dam?
　　　　　O do not learn her wrath; she taught it thee.
　　　　　The milk thou suck'st from her did turn to marble;
　　　　　Even at thy teat thou hadst thy tyranny.   145
　　　　　Yet every mother breeds not sons alike;
　　　　　[*To Chiron*] Do thou entreat her show a woman's pity.
CHIRON What, wouldst thou have me prove myself a bastard?
LAVINIA 'Tis true, the raven doth not hatch a lark;
　　　　　Yet I have heard – O, could I find it now! –   150

126 braves] Qq, F; she braves F2　　131 ye desire] F2; we desire Qq, F　　132 outlive, us] *Theobald (subst.)*; out liue vs Q; out-liue vs Q2–3, F　　135 nice-preservèd] F; nice preserued Qq　　136 bearest a woman's] Qq, F; bears't a woman F 147 SD] *Dyce; not in* Qq, F　　147 woman's] womans Q; woman Q2–3, F

　　122 belongs to her which she has coming to her, i.e. deserves.
　　124 minion stood upon hussy made much of.
　　126 painted hope braves Attempts to make this line scan have centred on these words. Wilson follows F2, and Maxwell suggests inserting 'and' without doing so himself. Both turn the line into an Alexandrine. Others make it a pentameter by emending 'painted' as 'fals'd' (Robertson), or 'quainte' (Wells).
　　129–30 Drag . . . lust We hear no more of this

atrocity; this may point to a change of plan as a result of revision.
　　135 nice-preservèd honesty fastidiously guarded chastity.
　　143 learn teach.
　　145 From the proverb, 'He sucked evil from the dug' (Dent E198).
　　149 Parallel to the proverbs, 'An eagle does not hatch a dove', and 'An evil bird lays an evil egg' (Tilley E2, B376).

The lion, moved with pity, did endure
To have his princely paws pared all away.
Some say that ravens foster forlorn children
The whilst their own birds famish in their nests.
O be to me, though thy hard heart say no,   155
Nothing so kind, but something pitiful.

TAMORA I know not what it means; away with her.

LAVINIA O let me teach thee for my father's sake,
That gave thee life when well he might have slain thee;
Be not obdùrate, open thy deaf ears.   160

TAMORA Hadst thou in person ne'er offended me,
Even for his sake am I pitiless.
Remember, boys, I poured forth tears in vain
To save your brother from the sacrifice
But fierce Andronicus would not relent.   165
Therefore away with her and use her as you will;
The worse to her, the better loved of me.

LAVINIA O Tamora, be called a gentle queen
And with thine own hands kill me in this place,
For 'tis not life that I have begged so long;   170
Poor I was slain when Bassianus died.

TAMORA What begg'st thou then? Fond woman, let me go.

LAVINIA 'Tis present death I beg, and one thing more
That womanhood denies my tongue to tell.
O keep me from their worse-than-killing lust   175
And tumble me into some loathsome pit
Where never man's eye may behold my body;
Do this, and be a charitable murderer.

TAMORA So should I rob my sweet sons of their fee.
No, let them satisfice their lust on thee.   180

---

160 ears] Q3, F; years Q, Q2   172 then? Fond . . . go.] F3; then fond . . . go? Qq; then? fond . . . go? F, F2; then, fond woman? *Maxwell*   *180 satisfice] Q, *Maxwell*; satisfie Q2–3, F, *Wilson*

151–2 In Aesop's fable 'The Lion in Love', the lion allows his claws to be drawn for love. Since the story was well enough known to be proverbial (Tilley L313, L316), it is probably futile to seek sources for minor details.

154 **birds** young (*OED* Bird 1a).

156 **Nothing . . . pitiful** Not so kind (as the raven) but somewhat pitying.

172 **Fond** Foolish.

172 **let me go** Lavinia may cling to Tamora here.

173 **present** immediate.

174 **denies** forbids.

179 **So** Thus.

179 **fee** reward.

*180 **satisfice** Q is unclear; but even if it should be read as 'satisfiee' this may be a compositor's error for 'satisfice', an authentic sixteenth-century compound from 'satisfy' and 'suffice' (Maxwell).

DEMETRIUS Away! For thou hast stayed us here too long.

LAVINIA No grace, no womanhood? Ah beastly creature,
　　　　The blot and enemy to our general name!
　　　　Confusion fall –

CHIRON Nay then, I'll stop your mouth. Bring thou her husband;　　185
　　　　This is the hole where Aaron bid us hide him.
　　　　　　　　　　　　[*Chiron and Demetrius throw the body
　　　　　　　　　　　of Bassianus in the pit, and exeunt with Lavinia]

TAMORA Farewell, my sons; see that you make her sure.
　　　　Ne'er let my heart know merry cheer indeed
　　　　Till all the Andronici be made away.
　　　　Now will I hence to seek my lovely Moor　　　　　　190
　　　　And let my spleenful sons this trull deflower.　　　　*Exit*

Enter AARON *with two of Titus' sons* [QUINTUS *and* MARTIUS]

AARON Come on, my lords, the better foot before;
　　　　Straight will I bring you to the loathsome pit
　　　　Where I espied the panther fast asleep.

QUINTUS My sight is very dull, whate'er it bodes.　　　　　195

MARTIUS And mine, I promise you. Were it not for shame,
　　　　Well could I leave our sport to sleep awhile.

QUINTUS What, art thou fallen? What subtle hole is this,
　　　　Whose mouth is covered with rude-growing briers
　　　　Upon whose leaves are drops of new-shed blood　　　200
　　　　As fresh as morning dew distilled on flowers?
　　　　A very fatal place it seems to me.
　　　　Speak, brother, hast thou hurt thee with the fall?

MARTIUS O brother, with the dismal'st object hurt
　　　　That ever eye with sight made heart lament.　　　　　205

AARON Now will I fetch the king to find them here,
　　　　That he thereby may have a likely guess

---

186 SD] *Capell (subst.); Exeunt* F2; *not in* Qq, F　　191 SD.1 *Exit*] F; *not in* Qq　　191 SD.2 QUINTUS *and* MARTIUS]
Capell; not in Qq, F　　192 SH AARON] F; *not in* Qq　　199 rude-growing] *Pope;* rude growing Qq, F　　201 morning] Q,
Q2; mornings Q3, F　　203 hurt] Q, Q2; *not in* Q3, F

184 Confusion Destruction; see 5.2.8.

185 I'll . . . mouth He gags her, or covers her mouth with his hand.

185–6 Bring . . . him Chiron and Demetrius probably drop Bassianus down the trap.

187 sure harmless.

189 made away killed; see 208.

191 spleenful lustful.

191 trull whore. The absurdity of 'deflowering' a 'trull' seems to be lost on Tamora.

195 sight . . . dull Perhaps a common belief: 'Men's sences, sudden altering out of reason / Doe bode ill lucke, or doe fore-show some treason' (Thomas Andrewe, *The Unmasking of a Female Machiavel* (1604), sig. E1ᵛ).

198 What, . . . fallen? Martius has fallen down the trap: now Quintus speaks down to him. They must both mime the dimness mentioned at 195–6.

204 object sight; see 3.1.64.

How these were they that made away his brother.   *Exit*

MARTIUS Why dost not comfort me and help me out

From this unhallowed and bloodstainèd hole?   210

QUINTUS I am surprisèd with an uncouth fear;

A chilling sweat o'erruns my trembling joints;

My heart suspects more than mine eye can see.

MARTIUS To prove thou hast a true-divining heart,

Aaron and thou look down into this den   215

And see a fearful sight of blood and death.

QUINTUS Aaron is gone, and my compassionate heart

Will not permit mine eyes once to behold

The thing whereat it trembles by surmise.

O tell me who it is, for ne'er till now   220

Was I a child to fear I know not what.

MARTIUS Lord Bassianus lies berayed in blood

All on a heap, like to a slaughtered lamb

In this detested, dark, blood-drinking pit.

QUINTUS If it be dark, how dost thou know 'tis he?   225

MARTIUS Upon his bloody finger he doth wear

A precious ring that lightens all this hole,

Which, like a taper in some monument,

Doth shine upon the dead man's earthy cheeks

And shows the ragged entrails of this pit;   230

So pale did shine the moon on Pyramus

When he by night lay bathed in maiden blood.

O brother, help me with thy fainting hand –

If fear hath made thee faint as me it hath –

Out of this fell devouring receptàcle,   235

---

208 SD] Q2–3; *after 207*, Q; *Exit Aron* F   210 unhallowed] vnhallow'd F; vnhollow Qq   214 true-divining] *Theobald;* True diuining Qq, F   220 who] Q, Q2; how Q3, F   222 berayed in blood] *Wilson (subst.);* bereaud in blood Q; embrewed heere Q2–3, F   223 to a] Qq; to the F   227 this] Q, Q2; the Q3, F   229 earthy] Q, Q2; earthly Q3, F   230 this] Qq; the F   231 Pyramus] Q2–3, F; Priamus Q

210 **bloodstainèd** That the suffix should be pronounced here and not on 'unhallowed' is suggested by F's elision in the latter.

211 **surprisèd** bewildered.

211 **uncouth** uncanny.

219 **by surmise** even in imagination.

*222 **berayed** fouled, defiled. The Q reading ('bereaud') is conceivably an image. We would say 'bereaved of', however, and the preposition is wrong in Elizabethan usage, too. Both the Q2 compositor and an early owner of Q perceived it as an error.

227 **A precious . . . hole** Carbuncles were thought to generate light.

230 **ragged entrails** rugged interior.

231 **Pyramus** In Ovid, IV, the lovers Pyramus and Thisbe were to meet by night. Frightened by a lion, Thisbe left her cloak for the beast to maul with bloody jaws. Finding it, Pyramus killed himself; see *MND* 3.1.50 ff. The absurd Q error, 'Priamus', is characteristic of that edition; classical allusion was not the compositors' strong point.

As hateful as Cocytus' misty mouth.
QUINTUS Reach me thy hand that I may help thee out,
    Or wanting strength to do thee so much good,
    I may be plucked into the swallowing womb
    Of this deep pit, poor Bassianus' grave.   240
    I have no strength to pluck thee to the brink.
MARTIUS Nor I no strength to climb without thy help.
QUINTUS Thy hand once more; I will not loose again
    Till thou art here aloft or I below.
    Thou canst not come to me; I come to thee.   245
        [He] falls in

Enter the EMPEROR *and* AARON *the Moor [with Attendants]*

SATURNINUS Along with me; I'll see what hole is here
    And what he is that now is leapt into it.
    Say, who art thou that lately didst descend
    Into this gaping hollow of the earth?
MARTIUS The unhappy sons of old Andronicus,   250
    Brought hither in a most unlucky hour
    To find thy brother Bassianus dead.
SATURNINUS My brother dead! I know thou dost but jest;
    He and his lady both are at the lodge
    Upon the north side of this pleasant chase;   255
    'Tis not an hour since I left them there.
MARTIUS We know not where you left them all alive,
    But, out alas! here have we found him dead.

Enter TAMORA, ANDRONICUS *and* LUCIUS

TAMORA Where is my lord the king?
SATURNINUS Here, Tamora, though grieved with killing grief.   260
TAMORA Where is thy brother Bassianus?

---

236 Cocytus'] F2; Ocitus Qq, F   245 SD.1 *He falls in] Pope (subst.); Boths fall in* F; *not in* Qq   245 SD.2 *with Attendants]*
This edn; not in Qq, F   250 sons] Q; sonne Q2–3, F   257 them] Qq; him F   260 grieved] griude Q; greeu'd Q2–3;
grieu'd F; grip'd *conj. Maxwell*

236 Cocytus' misty mouth Hell's gate. Cocytus is a river in Epiros, thought in antiquity to be an entrance to the Underworld.

*237–45 This business is potentially ludicrous, like Gloucester's leap from a non-existent cliff (*Lear* 4.6.40 ff.).

245 SD.2 *Attendants* These will be needed at 283; Alexander and Waith follow Capell in bringing them on with Tamora at 258, but they are more likely to be members of the emperor's retinue.

260 grieved Maxwell's conjecture returns to eighteenth-century methods, in which editorial taste is preferred to the authority of Qq and F; there is too much inept and careless writing in *Titus Andronicus* to justify us in blaming the compositor for this clumsy wording.

SATURNINUS Now to the bottom dost thou search my wound.
        Poor Bassianus here lies murderèd.
TAMORA Then all too late I bring this fatal writ,
        The complot of this timeless tragedy,   265
        And wonder greatly that man's face can fold
        In pleasing smiles such murderous tyranny.
                    She giveth Saturnine a letter
SATURNINUS *Reads the letter*
        'And if we miss to meet him handsomely,
        Sweet huntsman – Bassianus 'tis we mean –
        Do thou so much as dig the grave for him;   270
        Thou know'st our meaning. Look for thy reward
        Among the nettles at the elder tree
        Which overshades the mouth of that same pit
        Where we decreed to bury Bassianus.
        Do this and purchase us thy lasting friends.'   275
        O Tamora, was ever heard the like?
        This is the pit, and this the elder tree.
        Look, sirs, if you can find the huntsman out
        That should have murdered Bassianus here.
AARON My gracious lord, here is the bag of gold.   280
SATURNINUS [*To Titus*] Two of thy whelps, fell curs of bloody kind,
        Have here bereft my brother of his life.
        Sirs, drag them from the pit unto the prison;
        There let them bide until we have devised
        Some never-heard-of torturing pain for them.   285
TAMORA What, are they in this pit? O wondrous thing!
        How easily murder is discoverèd.
TITUS [*Kneels*] High emperor, upon my feeble knee
        I beg this boon with tears not lightly shed,
        That this fell fault of my accursèd sons –   290
        Accursèd if the faults be proved in them –

---

268 SD] *Saturninus reads the letter* Qq, F *centred*   281 SD] *Capell; not in* Qq, F   288 SD] *Bevington; not in* Qq, F   291
faults] Qq, F; fault *Theobald, Waith*

262 **search** probe.
265 **complot** plot; see 5.1.65; 5.2.147.
265 **timeless** not subject to the passage of time (*OED* Timeless *a* 2).
266 **fold** conceal. More common is 'unfold', display, disclose, reveal, bring to light, *Ham.* 1.1.2: 'Stand and unfold yourself.'
268 **handsomely** conveniently.
279 **should** was to.
*283 **drag . . . prison** The verbal SD calls upon

someone to bring the brothers up through the trap; 300 seems to indicate that the corpse is raised as well; see 245 n. above.

291 **faults** It is clear that Elizabethans did not share our view of grammatical agreement, or even Theobald's; see 2.1.26. Emendation of the authoritative text on no better grounds than to confer agreement is rash. In 291 Shakespeare may have felt the need to agree with 'them' rather than with 'fault' in 290.

SATURNINUS If it be proved! You see it is apparent.
     Who found this letter? Tamora, was it you?
TAMORA Andronicus himself did take it up.
TITUS I did, my lord, yet let me be their bail;   295
     For by my fathers' reverent tomb I vow
     They shall be ready at your highness' will
     To answer their suspicion with their lives.
SATURNINUS Thou shalt not bail them; see thou follow me.
     Some bring the murdered body, some the murderers.   300
     Let them not speak a word; the guilt is plain,
     For by my soul, were there worse end than death,
     That end upon them should be executed.
TAMORA Andronicus, I will entreat the king.
     Fear not thy sons; they shall do well enough.   305
TITUS [*Rising*] Come, Lucius, come; stay not to talk with them.

                                                Exeunt

[2.4] *Enter the Empress' sons* [CHIRON *and* DEMETRIUS] *with*
LAVINIA, *her hands cut off, and her tongue cut out, and ravished*

DEMETRIUS So now go tell, and if thy tongue can speak,
     Who 'twas that cut thy tongue and ravished thee.
CHIRON Write down thy mind, bewray thy meaning so,
     And if thy stumps will let thee play the scribe.
DEMETRIUS See how with signs and tokens she can scrowl.   5
CHIRON Go home, call for sweet water, wash thy hands.
DEMETRIUS She hath no tongue to call, nor hands to wash,
     And so let's leave her to her silent walks.

---

296 reverent] Qq, F; reverend F4, *Wilson and most editors; see 3.1.23, 5.3.136*   306 SD.1 Rising] *Bevington; not in*
Qq, F   306 SD.2 Exeunt] F; *not in* Qq   **Act 2, Scene 4**   2.4] *Dyce (subst.); not in* Qq, F   0 SD CHIRON *and*
DEMETRIUS] *Capell; not in* Qq, F   5 scrowl] Qq; scrowle F; scrawl *Steevens, Waith*

292 **apparent** obvious.

294 Compare 46–7: the change of plan is less likely to be Tamora's than Shakespeare's.

296 Since, as Maxwell says, 'reverent' and 'reverend' were used practically interchangeably, there is no real reason to emend here.

298 **their suspicion** suspicion of them.

299 **bail them** release them, by being their security; see 295.

305 **Fear not** Fear not for.

Act 2, Scene 4

0 SD No doubt Elizabethan players used blood and false stumps to make this entrance horrible, but Peter Brook and Brian Bedford both made it shocking with neither; see pp. 43–4 above.

3 **bewray** reveal; see 5.1.28.

5 **scrowl** A variant of 'scrawl', with play on 'scroll'; 'write' (Onions).

6 **sweet** perfumed (see *Rom.* 5.3.13); fresh (*OED* sv *a* 3b), current in this sense since A.D. 1000 (Onions).

CHIRON And 'twere my cause I should go hang myself.

DEMETRIUS If thou hadst hands to help thee knit the cord.   10

Exeunt [Chiron and Demetrius]

Wind horns. Enter MARCUS *from hunting*

MARCUS Who is this? My niece, that flies away so fast?
Cousin, a word; where is your husband?
If I do dream, would all my wealth would wake me;
If I do wake, some planet strike me down
That I may slumber an eternal sleep!   15
Speak, gentle niece, what stern ungentle hands
Hath lopped and hewed and made thy body bare
Of her two branches, those sweet ornaments
Whose circling shadows kings have sought to sleep in,
And might not gain so great a happiness   20
As half thy love? Why dost not speak to me?
Alas, a crimson river of warm blood,
Like to a bubbling fountain stirred with wind,
Doth rise and fall between thy rosèd lips,
Coming and going with thy honey breath.   25
But sure some Tereus hath deflowered thee,
And, lest thou shouldst detect him, cut thy tongue.
Ah, now thou turn'st away thy face for shame,
And notwithstanding all this loss of blood,
As from a conduit with three issuing spouts,   30
Yet do thy cheeks look red as Titan's face,
Blushing to be encountered with a cloud.
Shall I speak for thee? Shall I say 'tis so?
O that I knew thy heart, and knew the beast,
That I might rail at him to ease my mind.   35
Sorrow concealèd, like an oven stopped,

10 SD.1 *Exeunt*] F; *not in* Qq   10 SD.1 *Chiron and Demetrius*] Theobald; *not in* Qq, F   10 SD.2 *Wind horns*] F; *not in* Qq   15 an] Q; *in* Q2–3, F   27 him] *Rowe;* them Qq, F   30 three] *Hanmer;* their Qq, F

9 cause case, condition.

*11–57 The spirit of this speech is poetic rather than dramatic as we understand drama today. It anticipates the baroque *tirade*, in which the depth of the speaker's passion is to be measured by the length of his speech and the complexity of its figures. Lavinia must do nothing to distance herself, e.g. by breaking convention to remind an audience that in the real world she would be bleeding to death as Marcus spoke. Bradbrook and Waith show that Shakespeare is indebted to Ovid here; see Bradbrook, *Shakespeare and Elizabethan Poetry*,

1951, pp. 60–6, and Waith, 'The metamorphosis of violence in *Titus Andronicus*', *S.Sur.* 10 (1957), 39–49.

12 Cousin Niece. Used to denote almost any relative.

27 detect expose. In Ovid's story, Tereus cut out Philomela's tongue.

31 Titan The sun.

36 stopped shut. It is proverbial that 'an oven dammed up bakes soonest' (Dent 089.1).

36–7 Sorrow . . . it is Baldwin (II, 435–6) finds a parallel in *Venus and Adonis*, while Maxwell cites

Doth burn the heart to cinders where it is.
Fair Philomela, why she but lost her tongue
And in a tedious sampler sewed her mind:
But lovely niece, that mean is cut from thee;   40
A craftier Tereus, cousin, hast thou met,
And he hath cut those pretty fingers off
That could have better sewed than Philomel.
O had the monster seen those lily hands
Tremble like aspen leaves upon a lute,   45
And make the silken strings delight to kiss them,
He would not then have touched them for his life.
Or had he heard the heavenly harmony
Which that sweet tongue hath made,
He would have dropped his knife and fell asleep,   50
As Cerberus at the Thracian poet's feet.
Come, let us go and make thy father blind,
For such a sight will blind a father's eye.
One hour's storm will drown the fragrant meads;
What will whole months of tears thy father's eyes?   55
Do not draw back, for we will mourn with thee;
O could our mourning ease thy misery!

                                                            Exeunt

[3.1] *Enter the Judges and Senators with Titus' two sons* [QUINTUS
and MARTIUS] *bound, passing on the stage to the place of execution, and*
TITUS *going before, pleading*

TITUS Hear me, grave fathers; noble tribunes, stay.
       For pity of mine age, whose youth was spent

---

38 Philomela] Qq, F; Philomel *Cam.*   38 why] Q, Q2; *not in* Q3, F   41 cousin] Q, Q2; *not in* Q3, F   41 met] Qq; met
withall F   55 What will] Qq; What, will F   **Act 3, Scene 1   3.1**] *Rowe; Actus Tertius* F; *not in* Qq   0 SD.1–2 QUINTUS
and MARTIUS] *Not in* Qq, F

Gorboduc 3.1.101–2. All may derive from the same
proverb, Tilley F266.
  39 tedious sampler laboriously sewn embroi-
dery. Philomela told Procne, her sister and Tereus's
wife, the identity of her ravisher by embroidering
her story in a tapestry.
  51 Cerberus . . . feet When Orpheus descended
to recover Eurydice from the Underworld, his
music charmed the three-headed dog that kept the
gate.

Act 3, Scene 1
  1–22 There is plenty of time for a slow procession to pass from one tiring-house door to the
other. In Brian Bedford's production at Stratford,
Ontario (1978 and 1980), the silent figures emerged
from a cold light and crossed to the other vomitorium (see p. 45 above). It was very effective.
  1 tribunes Referred to as 'Judges' in SDs.

In dangerous wars whilst you securely slept;
For all my blood in Rome's great quarrel shed,
For all the frosty nights that I have watched, 5
And for these bitter tears which now you see,
Filling the agèd wrinkles in my cheeks,
Be pitiful to my condemnèd sons
Whose souls is not corrupted as 'tis thought.
For two-and-twenty sons I never wept 10
Because they died in honour's lofty bed.
Andronicus lieth down, and the Judges pass by him
For these, tribunes, in the dust I write
My heart's deep languor and my soul's sad tears.
Let my tears stanch the earth's dry appetite;
My sons' sweet blood will make it shame and blush. 15
O earth, I will befriend thee more with rain

Exeunt [Judges]

That shall distil from these two ancient ruins,
Than youthful April shall with all his showers.
In summer's drought I'll drop upon thee still;
In winter with warm tears I'll melt the snow 20
And keep eternal springtime on thy face,
So thou refuse to drink my dear sons' blood.

Enter LUCIUS *with his weapon drawn*

O reverent tribunes; O gentle agèd men!
Unbind my sons, reverse the doom of death
And let me say, that never wept before, 25
My tears are now prevailing orators.
LUCIUS O noble father, you lament in vain;
The tribunes hear you not, no man is by,
And you recount your sorrows to a stone.

---

9 is] Qq, F; are F2, *Wilson* 16 SD *Exeunt*] F; *not in* Qq 16 SD *Judges*] *This edn; not in* Qq, F 17 ruins] Qq, F; urns *Hanmer, Wilson* 23 reverent] Qq, F, *Maxwell*; reverend F3, *Wilson and most editors; see* 2.3.296, 5.3.136 28 you] Qq, F2–4; *not in* F

*10 **two-and-twenty** Compare 1.1.195, where Titus refers to 'one-and-twenty sons' slain in battle. Either he has added Mutius to the roll of those who have 'died in honour's lofty bed' or someone has lost count. Waith sees this as evidence of revision, but it could as easily be taken as evidence of insufficient revision.
13 **languor** mourning.
14 **stanch** satisfy.
15 **shame** be ashamed.

16 The SD in F suggests that the last Judge should exit at about this point; Titus may not notice. He can rise anywhere before 48.
17 **ruins** Modern editors except Barnet adopt Hanmer's tempting emendation; but since the Q reading makes sense, if not great poetry, it is retained here.
19 **still** continuously; see 3.2.30, 45; 4.1.98; 5.3.41.
22 **So** Provided that.

TITUS Ah Lucius, for thy brothers let me plead: 30
      Grave tribunes, once more I entreat of you.
LUCIUS My gracious lord, no tribune hears you speak.
TITUS Why 'tis no matter, man; if they did hear
      They would not mark me; if they did mark
      They would not pity me, yet plead I must   35
      And bootless unto them.
      Therefore I tell my sorrows to the stones,
      Who, though they cannot answer my distress,
      Yet in some sort they are better than the tribunes
      For that they will not intercept my tale;   40
      When I do weep, they humbly at my feet
      Receive my tears and seem to weep with me,
      And were they but attirèd in grave weeds
      Rome could afford no tribunes like to these.
      A stone is soft as wax, tribunes more hard than stones;   45
      A stone is silent and offendeth not
      And tribunes with their tongues doom men to death.
      But wherefore stand'st thou with thy weapon drawn?
LUCIUS To rescue my two brothers from their death,
      For which attempt the judges have pronounced   50
      My everlasting doom of banishment.
TITUS O happy man! They have befriended thee.
      Why, foolish Lucius, dost thou not perceive
      That Rome is but a wilderness of tigers?
      Tigers must prey, and Rome affords no prey   55
      But me and mine; how happy art thou then
      From these devourers to be banishèd!
      But who comes with our brother Marcus here?

              Enter MARCUS *with* LAVINIA

MARCUS Titus, prepare thy agèd eyes to weep,
      Or if not so, thy noble heart to break.   60
      I bring consuming sorrow to thine age.
TITUS Will it consume me? Let me see it then.

---

34 if . . . mark] Q; or if . . . mark Q2–3; oh, if . . . heare F   35 Q, Q2; *not in* F   36 And] Q, Q2; All Q3   37 to] Q,
Q2; bootles to Q3, F   44 tribunes] Q; Tribune Q2–3, F   45 A stone . . . stones] Qq; *two lines in* F   45 soft as] Qq; as
soft F   56 and] Qq; and and F   59 agèd] Q, Q2; noble Q3, F

36 **bootless** in vain; see 75, 5.3.18. Maxwell sug-   itor may have returned to the prompt copy, but
gests that 36 was a 'false start', cut by Shakespeare   omitted 'yet plead . . . them' because it was cut
but accidentally printed in both Q and F. This   there.
is possible; finding Q3 meaningless, the compos-   40 **intercept** interrupt.

MARCUS This was thy daughter.
TITUS   Why, Marcus, so she is.
LUCIUS Ay me! This object kills me.
TITUS Faint-hearted boy, arise and look upon her.   65
    Speak, Lavinia, what accursèd hand
    Hath made thee handless in thy father's sight?
    What fool hath added water to the sea
    Or brought a faggot to bright-burning Troy?
    My grief was at the height before thou cam'st   70
    And now like Nilus it disdaineth bounds.
    Give me a sword, I'll chop off my hands too,
    For they have fought for Rome and all in vain;
    And they have nursed this woe in feeding life;
    In bootless prayer have they been held up   75
    And they have served me to effectless use.
    Now all the service I require of them
    Is that the one will help to cut the other.
    'Tis well, Lavinia, that thou hast no hands;
    For hands to do Rome service is but vain.   80
LUCIUS Speak, gentle sister, who hath martyred thee?
MARCUS O that delightful engine of her thoughts
    That blabbed them with such pleasing eloquence
    Is torn from forth that pretty hollow cage
    Where like a sweet melodious bird it sung   85
    Sweet varied notes, enchanting every ear.
LUCIUS O say thou for her, who hath done this deed?
MARCUS O thus I found her straying in the park,
    Seeking to hide herself, as doth the deer
    That hath received some unrecuring wound.   90
TITUS It was my dear, and he that wounded her
    Hath hurt me more than had he killed me dead;
    For now I stand as one upon a rock,

69 bright-burning] F3; bright burning Qq, F, F2

64 **Ay me** Alas.
65 The verbal SD shows that Lucius has fallen or knelt, but it is too imprecise to allow an editor to specify which: the choice is the actor's.
69 **faggot** A bundle of sticks bound together as fuel.
71 **Nilus . . . bounds** i.e. like the river Nile, which floods annually.
76 **effectless** fruitless.
81 **martyred** mutilated; see 3.2.36, 5.2.180.

82 **engine** instrument; see 5.3.85, and *Venus and Adonis* 367: 'once more the engine of her thoughts began'.
83 **blabbed** freely spoke. Here the word is free of the implication that she spoke too much, or inappropriately.
90 **unrecuring** incurable.
91 **dear** A pun on Marcus's proverb, 'As the stricken deer withdraws himself to die' (Tilley D189, *ODEP*, p. 780).

Environed with a wilderness of sea,
Who marks the waxing tide grow wave by wave,   95
Expecting ever when some envious surge
Will in his brinish bowels swallow him.
This way to death my wretched sons are gone;
Here stands my other son, a banished man,
And here my brother, weeping at my woes;   100
But that which gives my soul the greatest spurn
Is dear Lavinia, dearer than my soul.
Had I but seen thy picture in this plight
It would have madded me; what shall I do
Now I behold thy lively body so?   105
Thou hast no hands to wipe away thy tears
Nor tongue to tell me who hath martyred thee.
Thy husband he is dead, and for his death
Thy brothers are condemned, and dead by this.
Look, Marcus; ah, son Lucius, look on her!   110
When I did name her brothers, then fresh tears
Stood on her cheeks as doth the honey-dew
Upon a gathered lily almost withered.
MARCUS Perchance she weeps because they killed her husband,
Perchance because she knows them innocent.   115
TITUS If they did kill thy husband, then be joyful
Because the law hath ta'en revenge on them.
No no, they would not do so foul a deed;
Witness the sorrow that their sister makes.
Gentle Lavinia, let me kiss thy lips   120
Or make some sign how I may do thee ease.
Shall thy good uncle, and thy brother Lucius,
And thou and I sit round about some fountain,
Looking all downwards to behold our cheeks,
How they are stained, like meadows yet not dry   125
With miry slime left on them by a flood?
And in the fountain shall we gaze so long
Till the fresh taste be taken from that clearness,

---

115 them] Q, Q2; him Q3, F   121 sign] Qq; signes F   125 like] Q; in Q2–3, F

96 **Expecting ever** Always waiting.
96 **envious** malicious. 'Envy' is used as a noun
in this sense at 1.1.153 and 2.1.4.
  97 **his** its.
  101 **spurn** humiliating blow; literally, a kick.

105 **lively** living.
109 **by this** i.e. by this time; see 4.3.67.
  119 **sorrow** lamentation, mourning (*OED* sv
4a).
  121 **do thee ease** relieve thee.

And made a brine-pit with our bitter tears?
Or shall we cut away our hands like thine?   130
Or shall we bite our tongues and in dumb shows
Pass the remainder of our hateful days?
What shall we do? Let us that have our tongues
Plot some device of further misery
To make us wondered at in time to come.   135

LUCIUS Sweet father, cease your tears, for at your grief
See how my wretched sister sobs and weeps.

MARCUS Patience, dear niece. Good Titus, dry thine eyes.

TITUS Ah Marcus, Marcus! Brother, well I wot
Thy napkin cannot drink a tear of mine,   140
For thou, poor man, hast drowned it with thine own.

LUCIUS Ah my Lavinia, I will wipe thy cheeks.

TITUS Mark, Marcus, mark. I understand her signs;
Had she a tongue to speak, now would she say
That to her brother which I said to thee.   145
His napkin, with his true tears all bewet,
Can do no service on her sorrowful cheeks.
O what a sympathy of woe is this,
As far from help as limbo is from bliss!

Enter AARON *the Moor alone*

AARON Titus Andronicus, my lord the emperor   150
Sends thee this word, that if thou love thy sons,
Let Marcus, Lucius or thyself, old Titus,
Or any one of you, chop off your hand
And send it to the king; he for the same
Will send thee hither both thy sons alive   155
And that shall be the ransom for their fault.

TITUS O gracious emperor! O gentle Aaron!
Did ever raven sing so like a lark
That gives sweet tidings to the sun's uprise?

134 misery] Qq; miseries F   146 with his] F4; with her Qq, F, F2–3

129 **And made** And the fountain turned into.
131 **bite our tongues** i.e. bite them out, to be
tongueless like Lavinia. The idea of biting rather
than cutting may come from Kyd, 4.4.194.
131 **dumb shows** mimes; frequently a part of
Elizabethan theatrical performances.
139 **wot** know.
140 **napkin** handkerchief; Marcus may offer his
to Titus.

148 **sympathy of woe** likeness in suffering
(Onions).
149 **limbo** Region near hell, where the souls
of the unbaptised await the Second Coming. In a
Roman play, this is a Christian (Roman Catholic)
anachronism: see 1.1.323 n.
149 **bliss** heaven.
149 SD *alone* i.e. without attendants.

With all my heart I'll send the emperor my hand.   160
Good Aaron, wilt thou help to chop it off?
LUCIUS Stay father, for that noble hand of thine
That hath thrown down so many enemies
Shall not be sent; my hand will serve the turn,
My youth can better spare my blood than you,   165
And therefore mine shall save my brothers' lives.
MARCUS Which of your hands hath not defended Rome
And reared aloft the bloody battle-axe,
Writing destruction on the enemy's castle?
O none of both but are of high desert.   170
My hand hath been but idle; let it serve
To ransom my two nephews from their death;
Then have I kept it to a worthy end.
AARON Nay, come, agree whose hand shall go along,
For fear they die before their pardon come.   175
MARCUS My hand shall go.
LUCIUS   By heaven, it shall not go!
TITUS Sirs, strive no more; such withered herbs as these
Are meet for plucking up, and therefore mine.
LUCIUS Sweet father, if I shall be thought thy son
Let me redeem my brothers both from death.   180
MARCUS And for our father's sake, and mother's care,
Now let me show a brother's love to thee.
TITUS Agree between you; I will spare my hand.
LUCIUS Then I'll go fetch an axe.
MARCUS   But I will use the axe.
                    Exeunt [Lucius and Marcus]
TITUS Come hither, Aaron. I'll deceive them both;   185
Lend me thy hand, and I will give thee mine.
AARON [*Aside*] If that be called deceit, I will be honest,
And never whilst I live deceive men so;
But I'll deceive you in another sort,
And that you'll say ere half an hour pass.   190
                    He cuts off Titus' hand

                Enter LUCIUS *and* MARCUS *again*

---

184 But . . . axe] *Malone, Waith; as separate line* Qq, F, *Wilson and most editors*   187 SD] *Rowe; not in* Qq, F

169 **castle** A medieval anachronism.   probably Titus wore a false hand. Note that while
179 **shall** am to.   Marcus and Lucius must go for an axe, Aaron can
*190 SD.1 A trick must have been used here: act without one: he wears his scimitar.

TITUS Now stay your strife; what shall be is dispatched.
　　　Good Aaron, give his majesty my hand;
　　　Tell him it was a hand that warded him
　　　From thousand dangers; bid him bury it.
　　　More hath it merited; that let it have.   195
　　　As for my sons, say I account of them
　　　As jewels purchased at an easy price,
　　　And yet dear too, because I bought mine own.
AARON I go, Andronicus; and for thy hand
　　　Look by and by to have thy sons with thee.   200
　　　[*Aside*] Their heads, I mean. O how this villainy
　　　Doth fat me with the very thoughts of it!
　　　Let fools do good, and fair men call for grace;
　　　Aaron will have his soul black like his face.   *Exit*
TITUS [*Kneels*] O here I lift this one hand up to heaven   205
　　　And bow this feeble ruin to the earth;
　　　If any power pities wretched tears,
　　　To that I call. What, wouldst thou kneel with me?
　　　Do then, dear heart, for heaven shall hear our prayers,
　　　Or with our sighs we'll breathe the welkin dim   210
　　　And stain the sun with fog, as sometime clouds
　　　When they do hug him in their melting bosoms.
MARCUS O brother, speak with possibility
　　　And do not break into these deep extremes.
TITUS Is not my sorrow deep, having no bottom?   215
　　　Then be my passions bottomless with them.
MARCUS But yet let reason govern thy lament.
TITUS If there were reason for these miseries,
　　　Then into limits could I bind my woes;

201 SD] *Rowe; not in* Qq, F   205 SD] *Waith; not in* Qq, F   208 wouldst] Q; would Q2–3; wilt F   213 possibility]
Q, Q2; possibilities Q3, F   215 Is . . . sorrow] Qq, F; Is . . . sorrows *Maxwell (conj. Dyce²)*

193 **warded** guarded.
200 **Look** Expect.
202 **fat** fatten; an image of feeding to delightful repletion; see *Tro.* 2.2.48–9: 'would they but fat
their thoughts / With this cramm'd reason'.
206 **ruin** The image denotes his body here; compare 3.1.17.
206–8 **bow . . . with me** The verbal SDs require
Titus and Lavinia to kneel. They may not rise until
the messenger enters at 232.
210 **breathe . . . dim** cloud the sky with our
breath.
213 **speak with possibility** speak of doing

things which may happen or exist (*OED* Possibility
2).
215–16 **Is not . . . them** There can be no grammatical agreement here. Maxwell refers to 2.1.26
to show that Elizabethans tolerated disagreement;
see also 2.2.23–4, 2.3.13 and 3.1.224. Since it cannot even satisfy an anachronistic sense of grammar,
emendation is unjustified.
216 **passions** The passions or 'perturbations
of the mind' express themselves spontaneously in
physical symptoms which Marcus urges Titus to
control.

When heaven doth weep, doth not the earth o'erflow?   220
If the winds rage, doth not the sea wax mad,
Threat'ning the welkin with his big-swoll'n face?
And wilt thou have a reason for this coil?
I am the sea. Hark how her sighs doth flow!
She is the weeping welkin, I the earth;   225
Then must my sea be movèd with her sighs;
Then must my earth with her continual tears
Become a deluge, overflowed and drowned;
For why my bowels cannot hide her woes
But like a drunkard must I vomit them.   230
Then give me leave, for losers will have leave
To ease their stomachs with their bitter tongues.

Enter a MESSENGER *with two heads and a hand*

MESSENGER Worthy Andronicus, ill art thou repaid
For that good hand thou sent'st the emperor.
Here are the heads of thy two noble sons   235
And here's thy hand in scorn to thee sent back:
Thy grief their sports, thy resolution mocked,
That woe is me to think upon thy woes,
More than remembrance of my father's death.   *Exit*
MARCUS Now let hot Etna cool in Sicily   240
And be my heart an ever-burning hell!
These miseries are more than may be borne.
To weep with them that weep doth ease some deal
But sorrow flouted at is double death.

---

224 doth] Q; doe Q2–3, F   **224** flow] Qq, F; blow F2, *Rowe, Wilson and most editors*   **237** grief] Q, Q2; griefes Q3, F
239 SD] Q3, F; *not in* Q, Q2

223 coil turmoil.
224 flow It is unclear why many editors have emended the authoritative text here; the image is unconventional, but far from meaningless.
229–32 For why . . . tongues This image stresses the physiological nature of the passions and their affections. Titus says that since his woes are undesired they have no rational course, and are therefore not subject to rational control in the Stoic manner; rather, they are like elemental forces, subject to strict laws of cause and effect. Thus a passion (grief) is inevitably accompanied by its appropriate affect (tears, hyperbole).
231–2 Then give . . . tongues Proverbial: 'Give losers leave to speak' (Tilley L458, *ODEP*, p. 485).

*232 SD This Messenger has character: he is sympathetic to Titus. The part may be assigned to Aemilius; see 4.4.59, 5.3.136. The heads were probably recognisable; compare *Mac.* 5.9.19. Modern directors mostly prefer to confine them to a sack. At 5.1.114–17 Aaron claims to have observed this scene 'through the crevice of a wall'; he may be visible to the audience.
237 their sports i.e. entertainment for the emperor and his circle.
238 That So that.
240 Etna Sicilian volcano.
243 some deal somewhat.
244 flouted at mocked.

LUCIUS Ah, that this sight should make so deep a wound,   245
    And yet detested life not shrink thereat!
    That ever death should let life bear his name,
    Where life hath no more interest but to breathe!
    [Lavinia kisses Titus]
MARCUS Alas poor heart, that kiss is comfortless
    As frozen water to a starvèd snake.   250
TITUS When will this fearful slumber have an end?
MARCUS Now farewell flatt'ry; die Andronicus,
    Thou dost not slumber: see thy two sons' heads,
    Thy warlike hand, thy mangled daughter here,
    Thy other banished son with this dear sight   255
    Struck pale and bloodless, and thy brother, I,
    Even like a stony image, cold and numb.
    Ah, now no more will I control thy griefs;
    Rent off thy silver hair, thy other hand
    Gnawing with thy teeth, and be this dismal sight   260
    The closing up of our most wretched eyes.
    Now is a time to storm; why art thou still?
TITUS Ha ha ha!
MARCUS Why dost thou laugh? It fits not with this hour.
TITUS Why, I have not another tear to shed;   265
    Besides, this sorrow is an enemy,
    And would usurp upon my wat'ry eyes
    And make them blind with tributary tears.
    Then which way shall I find Revenge's cave?
    For these two heads do seem to speak to me   270
    And threat me I shall never come to bliss
    Till all these mischiefs be returned again,
    Even in their throats that hath committed them.
    Come, let me see what task I have to do;
    You heavy people, circle me about   275
    That I may turn me to each one of you
    And swear upon my soul to right your wrongs.

---

248 SD] *Johnson (subst.); not in* Qq, F   258 thy] Q; my Q2–3, F   259 Rent] Qq, F; Rend *Rowe*², *Wilson*   273 hath] Q;
haue Q2–3, F

246 **shrink** withdraw; i.e. it is surprising that he
and Titus have not died of the wound.
  247 **bear his name** i.e. be called 'life'.
  250 **starvèd** numb with cold.
  255 **dear** dire; with a pun on 'dear' = 'costly'.

268 **tributary tears** tears paid in tribute, i.e. to
sorrow.
  271 **threat** threaten.
  275 **heavy** sorrowful.
  275 **circle me about** Probable verbal SD.

The vow is made. Come, brother, take a head,
And in this hand the other will I bear;
And Lavinia, thou shalt be employed in these arms;   280
Bear thou my hand, sweet wench, between thy teeth.
As for thee, boy, go get thee from my sight;
Thou art an exile, and thou must not stay;
Hie to the Goths and raise an army there;
And if ye love me, as I think you do,   285
Let's kiss and part, for we have much to do.
                                    Exeunt [all but Lucius]
LUCIUS Farewell, Andronicus, my noble father,
The woefullest man that ever lived in Rome!
Farewell proud Rome till Lucius come again;
He loves his pledges dearer than his life.   290
Farewell Lavinia my noble sister,
O would thou wert as thou tofore hast been;
But now nor Lucius nor Lavinia lives
But in oblivion and hateful griefs.
If Lucius live he will requite your wrongs   295
And make proud Saturnine and his empress
Beg at the gates like Tarquin and his queen.
Now will I to the Goths and raise a power
To be revenged on Rome and Saturnine.   *Exit Lucius*

[3.2] *A banquet. Enter* ANDRONICUS, MARCUS, LAVINIA, *and the boy*
[YOUNG LUCIUS, *with Servants*]

TITUS So so, now sit, and look you eat no more
        Than will preserve just so much strength in us

---

*280 in these arms] Qq; in these things F; in this *Hudson (conj. Lettson); omitted, Riverside (conj. Cam.)*   285 ye] Q;
you Q2–3, F   286 SD *all but Lucius] Manet Lucius* F; *not in* Qq   290 loves] Qq, F; leaves *Rowe, Wilson*   Act 3, Scene 2
3.2] *Capell (subst.); not in* F, *where the scene is first found*   0 SD.1 *banquet] F2–4; Bnaket* F   0 SD.2 YOUNG LUCIUS]
Theobald; the Boy F   0 SD.2 *with Servants] This edn*

278–81 Modern audiences laugh at this sort of
grand guignol: Peter Brook cut the verbal SD. Perhaps it was too much, even for Elizabethans; W. A.
Wright (Cam.) saw the textual difficulties as a confusion arising from an early attempt to substitute
'arms' for 'teeth'.
  *280 And . . . arms Maxwell finds this line
'hopelessly corrupt', and it must be admitted that
the image is weak. Nevertheless, it is an image;
Lavinia is 'taking arms' in a war of revenge. Compare *R2* 2.3.152: 'I see the issue of these arms'; and
2H4 4.2.118: 'Most shallowly did you these arms
commence.'

292 tofore heretofore.
  297 Beg . . . queen Tarquinius Superbus, last
king of Rome, expelled after his son Sextus raped
Lucrece; see *The Rape of Lucrece*. This episode is
neither in *Lucrece* nor in any of its major sources,
except for hints in Livy, *Historia* 1.60, and William
Painter, *The Palace of Pleasure* (1566).

Act 3, Scene 2
  0 SD.1 *banquet* Riverside and others emend F as
'banket' and gloss as a 'light repast'; but the same
word in Act 5 (5.2.76, 193, 202) obviously means
'banquet' in the modern sense.

As will revenge these bitter woes of ours.
Marcus, unknit that sorrow-wreathen knot;
Thy niece and I, poor creatures, want our hands   5
And cannot passionate our tenfold grief
With folded arms. This poor right hand of mine
Is left to tyrannise upon my breast,
Who, when my heart, all mad with misery,
Beats in this hollow prison of my flesh,   10
Then thus I thump it down.
[*To Lavinia*] Thou map of woe, that thus dost talk in signs,
When thy poor heart beats with outrageous beating
Thou canst not strike it thus to make it still.
Wound it with sighing, girl, kill it with groans;   15
Or get some little knife between thy teeth,
And just against thy heart make thou a hole
That all the tears that thy poor eyes let fall
May run into that sink, and soaking in,
Drown the lamenting fool in sea-salt tears.   20

MARCUS   Fie, brother, fie! Teach her not thus to lay
Such violent hands upon her tender life.

TITUS   How now! Has sorrow made thee dote already?
Why, Marcus, no man should be mad but I.
What violent hands can she lay on her life?   25
Ah wherefore dost thou urge the name of hands,
To bid Aeneas tell the tale twice o'er,
How Troy was burnt and he made miserable?
O handle not the theme, to talk of hands,
Lest we remember still that we have none.   30

---

9 Who] F; And *Rowe*   12 SD] *Johnson; not in* F

4–7 Marcus . . . folded arms Marcus's attitude denotes melancholy; 'Deep in a dump Jack Ford was got / With folded arms and melancholy hat' (*Elegy on Randolph's Finger* (1630–2)). Compare *TGV* 2.1.19, *LLL* 3.1.181.

6 passionate express; i.e. manifest the symptoms or 'affects' of the passions.

7–11 This poor . . . down Titus feels the rising vapours that Lear calls 'the mother' or 'hysterica passio', mounting from abdomen to throat, where they would choke him if he did not thump his chest to drive them down (*Lear* 2.4.57: 'down, thou climbing sorrow'; and 2.4.121: 'O me, my heart! my rising heart! But down!').

12 map image, picture.

15 Wound . . . sighing It was believed that sighs drew blood from the heart.

19 sink A pool or pit formed in the ground for the receipt of water, sewage, etc. (*OED* Sink *sb*[1] 1a); or a conduit for the same purpose, i.e. a sewer (*OED* sv 1b). The image seems inappropriate.

20 fool An affectionate term.

27–8 To bid . . . miserable Probably a memory of Virgil, 11.3: Dido asks Aeneas to tell his story again, from the beginning. He replies, *Infandum, regina, iubes renovare dolorem . . .* (Unspeakable, queen, is the grief you bid me revive . . .).

*29 handle Titus is punning grotesquely on 'hands'.

Fie, fie, how franticly I square my talk,
As if we should forget we had no hands
If Marcus did not name the word of hands!
Come, let's fall to; and gentle girl, eat this.
Here is no drink! Hark, Marcus, what she says;   35
I can interpret all her martyred signs;
She says she drinks no other drink but tears,
Brewed with her sorrow, mashed upon her cheeks.
Speechless complainer, I will learn thy thought;
In thy dumb action will I be as perfect   40
As begging hermits in their holy prayers.
Thou shalt not sigh, nor hold thy stumps to heaven,
Nor wink, nor nod, nor kneel, nor make a sign,
But I of these will wrest an alphabet
And by still practice learn to know thy meaning.   45
YOUNG LUCIUS Good grandsire, leave these bitter deep laments;
                 Make my aunt merry with some pleasing tale.
MARCUS Alas, the tender boy, in passion moved,
            Doth weep to see his grandsire's heaviness.
TITUS Peace, tender sapling; thou art made of tears,   50
          And tears will quickly melt thy life away.
                    Marcus strikes the dish with a knife
          What dost thou strike at, Marcus, with thy knife?
MARCUS At that that I have killed, my lord, a fly.
TITUS Out on thee, murderer! Thou kill'st my heart.
          Mine eyes are cloyed with view of tyranny;   55
          A deed of death done on the innocent
          Becomes not Titus' brother. Get thee gone;
          I see thou art not for my company.
MARCUS Alas, my lord, I have but killed a fly.
TITUS 'But'? How if that fly had a father and mother?   60
          How would he hang his slender gilded wings
          And buzz lamenting doings in the air!
          Poor harmless fly,

---

38 mashed] *Dyce²*, *Waith;* meshed F   39 complainer, I] *Capell;* complayne, I F *(uncorr.);* complaynet, I F *(miscorr.);*
complaint O I F2–4; *see Hinman, I, 289–90*   52 thy] F2–4; *not in* F   53 fly] F2–4; Flys F   55 are] F2–4; *not in* F   60
father and mother] F; father, brother? *Hudson (conj. Ritson)*

31 **square** shape; see *OED* Square *v* 4a: regulate
according to some principle – in this case, a frantic
principle.
36 **I can . . . sings** I can (learn to) interpret
all of her gestures and expressions, despite her
mutilation.
40 **dumb action** pantomime.

40 **perfect** i.e. 'word' perfect.
45 **still** increasing, more and more.
49 **heaviness** dejection, grief.
61 **gilded wings** Compare *Lear* 4.6.114: 'the
small gilded fly', and 5.3.13: 'gilded butterflies'.
62 **lamenting doings** The exact meaning is
unclear; perhaps 'sad stories'.

That with his pretty buzzing melody
Came here to make us merry, and thou hast killed him.   65
MARCUS Pardon me, sir; it was a black ill-favoured fly
Like to the empress' Moor; therefore I killed him.
TITUS: O O O!
Then pardon me for reprehending thee
For thou hast done a charitable deed.   70
Give me thy knife; I will insult on him,
Flattering myself as if it were the Moor
Come hither purposely to poison me.
There's for thyself, and that's for Tamora.
Ah, sirrah!   75
Yet I think we are not brought so low
But that between us we can kill a fly
That comes in likeness of a coal-black Moor.
MARCUS Alas, poor man, grief has so wrought on him
He takes false shadows for true substances.   80
TITUS Come, take away. Lavinia, go with me;
I'll to thy closet, and go read with thee
Sad stories chancèd in the times of old.
Come, boy, and go with me; thy sight is young,
And thou shalt read when mine begin to dazzle.   85

Exeunt

[4.1] *Enter* YOUNG LUCIUS *and* LAVINIA *running after him and the
boy flies from her with his books under his arm. Enter* TITUS *and*
MARCUS

YOUNG LUCIUS Help, grandsire, help! My aunt Lavinia
Follows me everywhere, I know not why.

65 Came . . . him] Capell; *two lines, divided* merry, / And F   72 myself] F2–4; *my selfes* F   75 Ah, sirrah!] *As one line,
Capell; as part of 74* F   **Act 4, Scene 1**   4.1] *Rowe; Actus Quartus.* F; *not in* Qq   0 SD.1 YOUNG LUCIUS] F; *Lucius
sonne* Qq

66 **ill-favoured** ugly.
71 **insult on** triumph over.
72 **as if** with the pretence that.
74–5 **There's . . . sirrah!** Titus takes the knife
(71) and strikes the fly several more times.
81 **Come, take away** Remove the table. At the
start of the scene, servants must have brought on a
table set for a 'banket'; now they remove it. Their
number, and whether they stay to serve the meal,
would help establish the degree of formality of the
occasion.
82 **closet** private room.

85 **mine** i.e. my eyes.
85 **dazzle** blur with tears; see *LLL* 1.1.180–4;
and *Duchess of Malfi* 4.2.264: 'mine eyes dazzle'.

Act 4, Scene 1

*0 SD It would be awkward to play this entrance
immediately after 3.2, because the same four actors
have just made their exit. This suggests that by the
time Shakespeare added 3.2, an interval between
acts had become customary.
1–4 Young Lucius drops his books here; see the
verbal SD at 25.

Good uncle Marcus, see how swift she comes.
Alas, sweet aunt, I know not what you mean.
MARCUS Stand by me, Lucius; do not fear thine aunt.   5
TITUS She loves thee, boy, too well to do thee harm.
YOUNG LUCIUS Ay, when my father was in Rome she did.
MARCUS What means my niece Lavinia by these signs?
TITUS Fear her not, Lucius; somewhat doth she mean;
        See, Lucius, see how much she makes of thee;   10
        Somewhither would she have thee go with her.
        Ah, boy, Cornelia never with more care
        Read to her sons than she hath read to thee
        Sweet poetry and Tully's *Orator*.
        Canst thou not guess wherefore she plies thee thus?   15
YOUNG LUCIUS My lord, I know not, I, nor can I guess,
        Unless some fit or frenzy do possess her;
        For I have heard my grandsire say full oft,
        Extremity of griefs would make men mad.
        And I have read that Hecuba of Troy   20
        Ran mad for sorrow; that made me to fear,
        Although, my lord, I know my noble aunt
        Loves me as dear as e'er my mother did,
        And would not but in fury fright my youth,
        Which made me down to throw my books and fly,   25
        Causeless perhaps. But pardon me, sweet aunt
        And madam, if my uncle Marcus go,
        I will most willingly attend your ladyship.
MARCUS Lucius, I will.
TITUS How now, Lavinia? Marcus, what means this?   30
        Some book there is that she desires to see.
        Which is it, girl, of these? Open them, boy.
        [*To Lavinia*] But thou art deeper read and better skilled;

---

5 thine] Qq; *thy* F   9 her] Qq; *not in* F   10–15] *Attributed to Titus* Qq, F; *attributed to Marcus, Maxwell (after W. S. Walker)*   12 Ah] F; A Q   15] *Attributed to Titus* Qq, F; *attributed to Marcus, Capell, Waith*   21 for] Q, Q2; *through* Q3, F   33 SD] *This edn; not in* Qq, F

9 **somewhat** something.

12 **Cornelia** Daughter of Scipio Africanus and mother of the Gracchi, reforming tribunes whose education Plutarch attributes to her.

14 **Tully's *Orator*** Cicero's *Ad M. Brutum Orator* (46 B.C.; Baldwin, II, 63–4).

20 **Hecuba of Troy** After taking her revenge, Hecuba went mad; see 1.1.136.

24 **but in fury** except in madness.

30 Capell adds a SD, *seeing her turn over the Books Lucius has let fall*, which in substance has acquired the weight of tradition. Other business might be devised, however, without contradicting 26, 30 and 31.

33 **deeper read** i.e. than Young Lucius. The fact that Titus is addressing Lavinia again is not immediately clear from the dialogue, but tradition offers no SD.

Come and take choice of all my library
And so beguile thy sorrow, till the heavens   35
Reveal the damned contriver of this deed.
Why lifts she up her arms in sequence thus?

MARCUS I think she means that there were more than one
Confederate in the fact; ay, more there was;
Or else to heaven she heaves them for revenge.   40

TITUS Lucius, what book is that she tosseth so?

YOUNG LUCIUS Grandsire, 'tis Ovid's *Metamorphosis*;
My mother gave it me.

MARCUS   For love of her that's gone,
Perhaps she culled it from the rest.

TITUS Soft, so busily she turns the leaves!   45
Help her; what would she find? Lavinia, shall I read?
This is the tragic tale of Philomel
And treats of Tereus' treason and his rape;
And rape, I fear, was root of thy annoy.

MARCUS See, brother, see; note how she quotes the leaves.   50

TITUS Lavinia, wert thou thus surprised, sweet girl?
Ravished and wronged as Philomela was,
Forced in the ruthless, vast, and gloomy woods?
See, see!
Ay, such a place there is where we did hunt –   55
O had we never, never hunted there! –
Patterned by that the poet here describes,
By nature made for murders and for rapes.

MARCUS O why should nature build so foul a den
Unless the gods delight in tragedies?   60

TITUS Give signs, sweet girl, for here are none but friends,
What Roman lord it was durst do the deed?
Or slunk not Saturnine, as Tarquin erst,
That left the camp to sin in Lucrece's bed?

36–7 deed. / Why] Qq; deed. / What booke? / Why F   38 were] Q, Q2; was Q3, F   40 for] Qq; to F   49 thy] Q;
thine Q2–3, F   50 quotes] Q2–3, F; cotes Q   54 See, see! / Ay,] *As Pope;* See, see, I Qq, F

37 **in sequence** one after the other.
39 **fact** crime.
41 **tosseth** i.e. she is trying to turn the pages.
42 *Metamorphosis* The spelling used by Qq, F
and Golding.
46 **what . . . find?** Titus's failure to understand
Lavinia without Ovid's aid contradicts his claim at
3.2.36, 'I can interpret all her martyred signs.'
47 **Philomel** See 2.3.43 n.
49 **annoy** injury.
50 **quotes** scans.

53 **vast** waste, desolate.
57 **Patterned by** On the pattern of.
57 **poet here describes** Neither Ovid, VI.520–1,
nor Golding offers much description. In the latter,
the scene of the crime is 'a pelting graunge that
peakishly did stand / In woods forgrowen' (76ʳ–ᵛ).
63–4 **slunk not . . . Lucrece's bed** did Saturninus go in a sneaking or slinking manner as Tarquin sneaked to the bed of Lucrece, to rape her;
see 2.1.108 n. and 3.1.297 n.

MARCUS Sit down, sweet niece; brother, sit down by me.   65
        Apollo, Pallas, Jove, or Mercury
        Inspire me, that I may this treason find.
        My lord, look here; look here, Lavinia.
        He writes his name with his staff, and guides it with feet and mouth
        This sandy plot is plain; guide, if thou canst,
        This after me. I have writ my name   70
        Without the help of any hand at all.
        Cursed be that heart that forced us to this shift!
        Write thou, good niece, and here display at last
        What God will have discovered for revenge.
        Heaven guide thy pen to print thy sorrows plain   75
        That we may know the traitors and the truth.
        She takes the staff in her mouth, and guides it with her stumps, and writes
        O do you read, my lord, what she hath writ?
TITUS '*Stuprum* – Chiron – Demetrius.'
MARCUS What, what! The lustful sons of Tamora
        Performers of this heinous, bloody deed?   80
TITUS *Magni dominator poli,*
        Tam lentus audis scelera, tam lentus vides?
MARCUS O calm thee, gentle lord, although I know
        There is enough written upon this earth
        To stir a mutiny in the mildest thoughts   85
        And arm the minds of infants to exclaims.
        My lord, kneel down with me; Lavinia, kneel;
        And kneel, sweet boy, the Roman Hector's hope;
        And swear with me, as with the woeful fere

72 this] Qq; that F   77–8] *Maxwell; attributed to Marcus Q, Q2; attributed to Titus Q3, F*

66 Apollo The god of prophecy.
66 Pallas Athene (in Latin, Minerva), goddess of wisdom.
66 Jove Jupiter, father of the gods.
66 Mercury The messenger-god.
69 plain flat.
70 after me as I do.
72 shift expedient; here, like 'makeshift'; see 4.2.177.
74 will . . . revenge wishes to have revealed in order that it may be avenged.
*77–9 If Q2 is correct in attributing 77–8 to Marcus, the SH at 79 is redundant; Q3 and F attempt to solve this problem by assigning 77–8 to Titus; Maxwell and Waith both note that Titus nowhere addresses Marcus as 'lord', and propose that 78 be

assigned to Titus.
78 *Stuprum* Rape (Latin).
81–2 *Magni . . . vides?* 'Ruler of great heaven, are you so slow to hear and see crimes?' (Latin). See Seneca's *Phaedra* 671–2: *Magne regnator deum, tam lentus audis scelera? tam lentus vides?*
86 exclaims outcries.
87 kneel Verbal SD. Marcus and Young Lucius must kneel and stand up again, but exactly when, and whether the others join them, is undetermined.
88 Roman Hector's hope i.e. Lucius is the hope of Titus, here seen as the Roman equivalent of the greatest Trojan hero. In Q 'hope' resembles 'hop', with the *h* and *o* apparently damaged, and printed in a different fount in the margin.
89 fere spouse.

And father of that chaste dishonoured dame,   90
Lord Junius Brutus swore for Lucrece's rape,
That we will prosecute by good advice
Mortal revenge against these traitorous Goths,
And see their blood or die with this reproach.

TITUS 'Tis sure enough, and you knew how;   95
But if you hunt these bear-whelps, then beware;
The dam will wake and if she wind ye once.
She's with the lion deeply still in league
And lulls him whilst she playeth on her back,
And when he sleeps will she do what she list.   100
You are a young huntsman, Marcus, let alone;
And come, I will go get a leaf of brass
And with a gad of steel will write these words,
And lay it by. The angry northern wind
Will blow these sands like Sibyl's leaves abroad,   105
And where's our lesson then? Boy, what say you?

YOUNG LUCIUS I say, my lord, that if I were a man
Their mother's bed-chamber should not be safe
For these base bondmen to the yoke of Rome.

MARCUS Ay, that's my boy! Thy father hath full oft   110
For his ungrateful country done the like.

YOUNG LUCIUS And uncle, so will I and if I live.

TITUS Come, go with me into mine armoury.
Lucius, I'll fit thee, and withal my boy
Shall carry from me to the empress' sons   115
Presents that I intend to send them both.
Come, come; thou'lt do my message, wilt thou not?

YOUNG LUCIUS Ay, with my dagger in their bosoms, grandsire.

TITUS No, boy, not so; I'll teach thee another course.
Lavinia, come; Marcus, look to my house;   120
Lucius and I'll go brave it at the court;
Ay marry, will we, sir, and we'll be waited on.

Exeunt [all but Marcus]

97 wake . . . once.] wake . . . once, Q; wake, . . . once, Q2–3, F; wake; . . . once, *Theobald*   97 ye] Q; you Q2–3, F   101
let] Q, Q2; let it Q3, F   106 our] Q; you Q2; your Q3, F   109 base] Q; bad Q2–3, F   117 my] Q; thy Q2–3, F   122 SD
all but Marcus] *Capell (subst.);* not in Qq, F

97 **wind** scent.
100 **list** wishes.
101 **let alone** let it alone.
103 **gad** sharp spike, i.e. a stylus.
105 **Sibyl's leaves** According to Virgil, VI. 74–5, the Sibyl sometimes wrote her prophecies on leaves, which might blow away.
108–9 **Their . . . Rome** Not even their mother's bedroom could keep those low slaves (captives) safe from me.
114 **fit thee** fit thee out, i.e. outfit or furnish you with all you need.
121 **brave it** defiantly show ourselves. Compare 'court it', 2.1.91.
122 **marry** indeed; originally an oath on the Virgin Mary.

MARCUS O heavens, can you hear a good man groan
            And not relent, or not compassion him?
            Marcus, attend him in his ecstasy,   125
            That hath more scars of sorrow in his heart
            Than foemen's marks upon his battered shield,
            But yet so just that he will not revenge.
            Revenge the heavens for old Andronicus!   *Exit*

[4.2]   *Enter* AARON, CHIRON *and* DEMETRIUS *at one door; and at
the other door* YOUNG LUCIUS *and another with a bundle of weapons,
and verses writ upon them*

CHIRON Demetrius, here's the son of Lucius;
            He hath some message to deliver us.
AARON Ay, some mad message from his mad grandfather.
YOUNG LUCIUS My lords, with all the humbleness I may,
            I greet your honours from Andronicus;   5
            [*Aside*] And pray the Roman gods confound you both.
DEMETRIUS Gramercy, lovely Lucius. What's the news?
YOUNG LUCIUS [*Aside*] That you are both deciphered, that's the
                  news,
            For villains marked with rape. – May it please you,
            My grandsire, well-advised, hath sent by me   10
            The goodliest weapons of his armoury
            To gratify your honourable youth,
            The hope of Rome, for so he bid me say;
            And so I do, and with his gifts present
            Your lordships, that whenever you have need   15
            You may be armèd and appointed well;
            And so I leave you both [*Aside*] like bloody villains.   *Exit*
DEMETRIUS What's here? A scroll, and written round about;

Act 4, Scene 2   4.2] *Pope; not in* Qq, F   0 SD.1–2 *at the other*] Q; *at another* Q2–3, F   6 SD] *Capell; not in* Qq, F; *also
8 SD, 17 SD   8 SH YOUNG LUCIUS . . . news*] Qq; *not in* F   13 bid] Q, Q2; *bad* Q3, F   15 that] *Pope; not in* Qq, F

124 **compassion** have compassion for.
125 **ecstasy** fit of madness; see 4.4.21.
129 **Revenge the heavens** May the heavens take
revenge.

Act 4, Scene 2
0 SD.2 *and another* Since Young Lucius is the
spokesman, this 'other' is likely to be a servant

rather than one of Titus's kinsmen from 4.3.
   8 **deciphered** detected.
   10 **well-advised** in his right mind; contradicting Aaron's 'mad grandfather' (3).
   12 **gratify** oblige, show gratitude to.
   16 **appointed** equipped.
   18 **round about** The scroll is wound around the
weapons; see 27.

Let's see:
    Integer vitae, scelerisque purus,   20
    Non eget Mauri iaculis, nec arcu.
CHIRON O, 'tis a verse in Horace; I know it well,
    I read it in the grammar long ago.
AARON Ay just, a verse in Horace; right, you have it.
    [*Aside*] Now what a thing it is to be an ass!   25
    Here's no sound jest! The old man hath found their guilt
    And sends them weapons wrapped about with lines
    That wound, beyond their feeling, to the quick.
    But were our witty empress well afoot
    She would applaud Andronicus' conceit;   30
    But let her rest in her unrest awhile. –
    And now, young lords, was't not a happy star
    Led us to Rome, strangers and more than so,
    Captives, to be advancèd to this height?
    It did me good before the palace gate   35
    To brave the tribune in his brother's hearing.
DEMETRIUS But me more good to see so great a lord
    Basely insinuate and send us gifts.
AARON Had he not reason, Lord Demetrius?
    Did you not use his daughter very friendly?   40
DEMETRIUS I would we had a thousand Roman dames
    At such a bay, by turn to serve our lust.
CHIRON A charitable wish and full of love!
AARON Here lacks but your mother for to say amen.
CHIRON And that would she for twenty thousand more.   45
DEMETRIUS Come, let us go and pray to all the gods
    For our belovèd mother in her pains.

20–1 *Integer . . . arcu*] As Theobald; *one line* Qq, F   **21** *eget*] Qq; *egit* F   **21** *Mauri*] Q, Q2; *Maury* Q3, F   **21** *arcu*] Q; *arcus* Q2–3, F   **25** SD] *Johnson; not in* Qq, F   **27** them] Q, Q2; the Q3, F   **44** your] Qq; you F

20–1 *Integer . . . arcu* 'The man of upright life, and free from crime, has no need of the Moor's javelins or arrows' (Latin); it is Horace, *Odes* 1.22.1–2, quoted twice in William Lily's school grammar, *Brevissima Institutio* (1570); see Baldwin, I, 579.

24 just exactly.

26 no sound jest no laughing matter; perhaps ironical (Maxwell).

28 beyond their feeling i.e. they are too insensitive to feel the wound.

29 witty quick-witted.

29 afoot on her feet; Tamora is pregnant.

30 conceit idea, device.

31 rest . . . unrest Compare Kyd, 3.8.29: 'Thus therefore will I rest me in unrest.'

38 insinuate ingratiate himself.

42 At . . . bay Thus brought to bay. The phrase recalls the hunting metaphors at 2.1.93–4 and 117–18.

43 A . . . love This may refer to a dispute between Puritans and advocates of the Bishops' Bible over the translation of *agape* (Greek) as either 'charity' or 'love' (Baldwin, II, 644).

45 more i.e. more Roman dames.

47 pains labour.

AARON Pray to the devils; the gods have given us over.

Trumpets sound

DEMETRIUS Why do the emperor's trumpets flourish thus?

CHIRON Belike for joy the emperor hath a son.   50

DEMETRIUS Soft, who comes here?

Enter NURSE *with a blackamoor child*

NURSE   God morrow, lords.
　　　O tell me, did you see Aaron the Moor?

AARON Well, more or less, or ne'er whit at all,
　　　Here Aaron is, and what with Aaron now?

NURSE O gentle Aaron, we are all undone!   55
　　　Now help, or woe betide thee evermore!

AARON Why, what a caterwauling dost thou keep!
　　　What dost thou wrap and fumble in thy arms?

NURSE O that which I would hide from heaven's eye,
　　　Our empress' shame and stately Rome's disgrace,   60
　　　She is delivered, lords, she is delivered.

AARON To whom?

NURSE   I mean she is brought abed.

AARON Well, God give her good rest! What hath he sent her?

NURSE A devil.

AARON Why, then she is the devil's dam; a joyful issue.   65

NURSE A joyless, dismal, black, and sorrowful issue.
　　　Here is the babe as loathsome as a toad
　　　Amongst the fair-faced breeders of our clime;
　　　The empress sends it thee, thy stamp, thy seal,
　　　And bids thee christen it with thy dagger's point.   70

AARON Zounds, ye whore! Is black so base a hue?
　　　Sweet blowse, you are a beauteous blossom, sure.

---

48 SD] Qq; *Flourish.* F   51–2 God . . . Moor?] F; *one line* Qq   51 God] Q, Q2; Good Q3, F   58 thy] Q; thine
Q2–3, F   64–5] Qq, F; A devil . . . dam. / A joyful issue. *Hanmer*   68 fair-faced] *Wilson;* fairefast Q, Q2; fairest Q3, F
71 Zounds, ye] Qq *(subst.);* Out, you F

48 While Aaron may speak this line aside, he may with equal validity speak it openly.

50 Belike Probably.

51 God morrow God give you good morning; a contraction.

53 more A pun on 'Moor'; 'whit' is probably a pun on 'white' as well.

***62–5** The verse here, if it is verse at all, is so irregular that no editor has succeeded in rearranging it to scan. Any decision affects the interpretation of an important moment. Hanmer's arrangement dictates a pause after 'issue' (65); this edn,

following Q, prefers a pause after 'devil' (64); but readers and actors should feel free to experiment.

65 issue outcome.

66 issue offspring; with a play on the different sense in 65.

71 Zounds By God's wounds; a contraction of a blasphemy and the only oath in the play to be purged in F.

72 blowse beggar wench; or fat, red-faced wench (*OED* Blowze 1 and 2). Since the current meaning was both derogatory and female, Aaron's meaning must be ironic.

DEMETRIUS Villain, what hast thou done?
AARON That which thou canst not undo.
CHIRON Thou hast undone our mother!   75
AARON Villain, I have done thy mother.
DEMETRIUS And therein, hellish dog, thou hast undone her.
       Woe to her chance and damned her loathèd choice;
       Accursed the offspring of so foul a fiend.
CHIRON It shall not live.   80
AARON It shall not die.
NURSE Aaron, it must; the mother wills it so.
AARON What, must it, nurse? Then let no man but I
       Do execution on my flesh and blood.
DEMETRIUS I'll broach the tadpole on my rapier's point.   85
       Nurse, give it me; my sword shall soon dispatch it.
AARON Sooner this sword shall plough thy bowels up.
       Stay, murderous villains; will you kill your brother?
       Now by the burning tapers of the sky
       That shone so brightly when this boy was got,   90
       He dies upon my scimitar's sharp point
       That touches this, my first-born son and heir.
       I tell you, younglings, not Enceladus
       With all his threat'ning band of Typhon's brood,
       Nor great Alcides, nor the god of war   95
       Shall seize this prey out of his father's hands.
       What, what, ye sanguine shallow-hearted boys,
       Ye white-limed walls, ye alehouse painted signs!
       Coal-black is better than another hue
       In that it scorns to bear another hue,   100
       For all the water in the ocean
       Can never turn the swan's black legs to white
       Although she lave them hourly in the flood.

76] Qq; *not in* F   77 her] Q, Q2; *not in* Q3, F   95 Alcides] Q2–3, F; Alciades Q

76 done had sexual intercourse with; coarse play on 'undone' (75).

78 chance luck.

84–6 Somewhere here Aaron probably takes the child from the Nurse.

85 broach spit, impale.

87 this sword Aaron usually draws a scimitar (see 91), but it could be effective if he cowed the Goths without having to draw.

89 tapers . . . sky Compare *Mac.* 2.1.4–5: 'There's husbandry in heaven; / Their candles are all out.'

90 got begotten.

91 scimitar The reference to this exotic weapon

suggests that Aaron (and perhaps Othello) might have worn equally exotic costume.

93–5 Enceladus . . . Alcides Hundred-headed Typhon led Enceladus and the other Giants in an assault on the gods, who were only able to win with the aid of Heracles (Alcides, i.e. grandson of Alcaeus).

97 sanguine red-faced.

98 white-limed whitewashed; may echo Matt. 23.27, 'whited sepulchres', i.e. hypocrites.

101–3 all . . . flood Proverbial: Tilley B436, *ODEP*, p. 65.

103 lave wash.

Tell the empress from me I am of age
To keep mine own, excuse it how she can.   105
DEMETRIUS Wilt thou betray thy noble mistress thus?
AARON My mistress is my mistress, this myself,
The vigour and the picture of my youth;
This before all the world do I prefer,
This maugre all the world will I keep safe   110
Or some of you shall smoke for it in Rome.
DEMETRIUS By this our mother is forever shamed.
CHIRON Rome will despise her for this foul escape.
NURSE The emperor in his rage will doom her death.
CHIRON I blush to think upon this ignomy.   115
AARON Why there's the privilege your beauty bears.
Fie, treacherous hue that will betray with blushing
The close enacts and counsels of thy heart!
Here's a young lad framed of another leer;
Look how the black slave smiles upon the father,   120
As who should say, 'Old lad, I am thine own.'
He is your brother, lords, sensibly fed
Of that self blood that first gave life to you,
And from your womb where you imprisoned were
He is enfranchisèd and come to light.   125
Nay, he is your brother by the surer side
Although my seal be stampèd in his face.
NURSE Aaron, what shall I say unto the empress?
DEMETRIUS Advise thee, Aaron, what is to be done
And we will all subscribe to thy advice.   130
Save thou the child, so we may all be safe.
AARON Then sit we down and let us all consult.

---

115 ignomy] Qq; ignominie F   118 thy] Q, Q2; the Q3, F   124 your] Q, Q2; that Q3, F, *Wilson*

108 vigour Wells makes a good case for reading 'figure', arguing that 'vigour' here is an obsolete dialect variant which is misleading. Waith agrees without emending. If they are right, this is a tautology (vigour = picture).

110 maugre in spite of.

111 smoke suffer; i.e. have a hot time of it (Onions).

113 escape escapade.

*****115 ignomy** ignominy; an established spelling in the sixteenth century (*OED*).

116 privilege . . . bears i.e. blushing is the privilege of people of your colour (ironic).

118 close enacts secret purposes.

119 leer complexion.

122–3 sensibly fed / Of visibly bred from.

124 your womb i.e. the womb that bred Chiron and Demetrius; Q3 emends unnecessarily.

126 he is . . . side you can be certain that he is your brother, because you can be sure who is your mother (but not your father).

127 my . . . face the fact that I am his father is proved by the colour of his face; with play on 'seal' and 'stampèd', as if the child's face bore a wax seal, stamped with Aaron's signet.

130 subscribe assent.

My son and I will have the wind of you;
Keep there.

[They sit]

Now, talk at pleasure of your safety.

DEMETRIUS *[To Nurse]* How many women saw this child of his?   135

AARON Why so, brave lords, when we join in league
    I am a lamb, but if you brave the Moor
    The chafèd boar, the mountain lioness,
    The ocean swells not so as Aaron storms.
    But say again, how many saw the child?   140

NURSE Cornelia the midwife, and myself,
    And no one else but the delivered empress.

AARON The empress, the midwife, and yourself;
    Two may keep counsel when the third's away.
    Go to the empress, tell her this I said.   145

He kills her

    Weeke weeke!
    So cries a pig preparèd to the spit.

DEMETRIUS What mean'st thou, Aaron? Wherefore didst thou
    this?

AARON O Lord, sir, 'tis a deed of policy.
    Shall she live to betray this guilt of ours,   150
    A long-tongued babbling gossip? No, lords, no.
    And now be it known to you my full intent.
    Not far, one Muliteus, my countryman,
    His wife but yesternight was brought to bed;
    His child is like her, fair as you are.   155
    Go pack with him, and give the mother gold,
    And tell them both the circumstance of all,
    And how by this their child shall be advanced,

---

134 SD] *Rowe (subst.); not in* Qq, F   135 SD] *Waith; not in* Qq, F   139 as] Qq; at F   141 Cornelia the] Qq; Cornelia, the F   142 no one] Qq; none F   146–7 Weeke . . . spit.] *Cam.; one line* Qq, F   153 Muliteus, my] Qq, F; Muly lives, my *conj.* Steevens

133 **have . . . you** sit downwind of you, to watch you without being detected; a hunting and stalking image.

134 SD Most editors place the direction after this line. Aaron need not sit: he must be standing to kill the Nurse, and that will bring Demetrius and Chiron to their feet again.

138 **chafèd** enraged.

141 By following the punctuation in F, Waith implies that Cornelia and the midwife are two separate people; but at 167–9 Aaron is sure that only one more murder will ensure secrecy.

144 **Two . . . away** Proverbial: Tilley T642.1.

146 **Weeke** Aaron mocks the Nurse's dying cries.

153 **Muliteus** Steevens conjectured that this is an error for 'Muly', a common Moorish name in Elizabethan literature, but Maxwell admits that a classicised version might have recommended itself to Shakespeare in this context.

155 Ironically, the child of these inter-racial parents takes the colour of the mother; see 5.1.28–30.

156 **pack** conspire.

And be receivèd for the emperor's heir,
And substituted in the place of mine   160
To calm this tempest whirling in the court,
And let the emperor dandle him for his own.
Hark ye, lords, you see I have given her physic,
And you must needs bestow her funeral;
The fields are near and you are gallant grooms.   165
This done, see that you take no longer days,
But send the midwife presently to me.
The midwife and the nurse well made away,
Then let the ladies tattle what they please.
CHIRON Aaron, I see thou wilt not trust the air   170
    With secrets.
DEMETRIUS   For this care of Tamora,
    Herself and hers are highly bound to thee.
                    Exeunt [Chiron and Demetrius with the dead Nurse]
AARON Now to the Goths as swift as swallow flies,
    There to dispose this treasure in mine arms   175
    And secretly to greet the empress' friends.
    Come on, you thick-lipped slave, I'll bear you hence,
    For it is you that puts us to our shifts.
    I'll make you feed on berries and on roots,
    And feed on curds and whey, and suck the goat,   180
    And cabin in a cave, and bring you up
    To be a warrior and command a camp.   *Exit*

[4.3] *Enter* TITUS, *old* MARCUS, YOUNG LUCIUS, *and other*
gentlemen [PUBLIUS, SEMPRONIUS *and* CAIUS] *with bows, and*
Titus bears the arrows with letters on the ends of them

TITUS Come, Marcus, come; kinsmen, this is the way.
    Sir boy, let me see your archery;
    Look ye draw home enough, and 'tis there straight.

163 you] Q, Q2; ye Q3, F   170–1 Aaron . . . secrets] *As Theobald; one line* Qq, F   172 SD *Chiron . . . Nurse*] Capell; *not in* Qq, F   **Act 4, Scene 3   4.3**] *Capell (subst.); not in* Qq, F   0 SD.2 PUBLIUS . . . CAIUS] *Cam.; not in* Qq, F   0 SD.3 *ends*] Qq; *end* F

163 physic medicine; he refers to the dead Nurse.

165 gallant grooms strong fellows.
167 presently immediately.

181 cabin lodge.

Act 4, Scene 3
    3 draw home i.e. draw your arrow to the head, for maximum force.

Terras Astraea reliquit;
Be you remembered, Marcus, she's gone, she's fled.   5
Sirs, take you to your tools. You, cousins,
Shall go sound the ocean and cast your nets;
Happily you may catch her in the sea,
Yet there's as little justice as at land.
No! Publius and Sempronius, you must do it;   10
'Tis you must dig with mattock and with spade
And pierce the inmost centre of the earth.
Then when you come to Pluto's region,
I pray you deliver him this petition;
Tell him it is for justice and for aid,   15
And that it comes from old Andronicus,
Shaken with sorrows in ungrateful Rome.
Ah Rome! Well, well, I made thee miserable
What time I threw the people's suffrages
On him that thus doth tyrannise o'er me.   20
Go, get you gone, and pray be careful all
And leave you not a man-of-war unsearched;
This wicked emperor may have shipped her hence,
And kinsmen, then we may go pipe for justice.

MARCUS O Publius, is not this a heavy case,   25
To see thy noble uncle thus distract?

PUBLIUS Therefore, my lords, it highly us concerns
By day and night t'attend him carefully,
And feed his humour kindly as we may
Till time beget some careful remedy.   30

MARCUS Kinsmen, his sorrows are past remedy,
But [   ]
Join with the Goths and with revengeful war

4–5 *Terras . . . Marcus] Capell; one line* Qq, F   6–7] *This edn; divided . . . tooles. / You . . . Ocean / And . . . nets* Qq, F; *divided . . . shall / Go . . . nets Capell*   8 catch] Q, Q2; find Q3, F   *32 But] Q *catchword; not in* Q2–3, F

4 *Terras . . . reliquit* Astraea (goddess of Justice) has left the earth (Latin); Ovid, 1.150.
5 **Be you remembered** Remember.
7–11 The actors may carry the tools Titus names; compare Kyd, 12.71–5, 13.108–10.
8 **Happily** Perhaps.
9 **there's** there is; i.e. in the sea.
13 **Pluto** The god of the Underworld.
19 **What time** When.
24 **pipe** whistle.
26 **uncle** Publius is apparently Marcus's son.
26 **distract** distraught, mad.
29 **feed his humour** humour him.

30 **careful** costing trouble, laborious (Wilson, Riverside) or showing care, concern (Witherspoon, Waith).
*32 **But** A catchword at the foot of a printed page was normally the first word on the next page – a device that was used to help the printer ensure that the pages ended up in their proper sequence. The fact that 'But' is printed where the catchword would be, but is *not* found at the top of the next page in Q, suggests that one or more lines were omitted in printing; this is supported by the absence of punctuation at the end of 31 in Q.

  Take wreak on Rome for this ingratitude,

  And vengeance on the traitor Saturnine.   35

TITUS Publius, how now? How now, my masters?

  What, have you met with her?

PUBLIUS No, my good lord, but Pluto sends you word

  If you will have Revenge from hell, you shall;

  Marry, for Justice, she is so employed,   40

  He thinks, with Jove in heaven or somewhere else,

  So that perforce you must needs stay a time.

TITUS He doth me wrong to feed me with delays.

  I'll dive into the burning lake below

  And pull her out of Acheron by the heels.   45

  Marcus, we are but shrubs, no cedars we,

  No big-boned men framed of the Cyclops' size,

  But metal, Marcus, steel to the very back,

  Yet wrung with wrongs more than our backs can bear;

  And sith there's no justice in earth nor hell   50

  We will solicit heaven and move the gods

  To send down justice for to wreak our wrongs.

  Come, to this gear. You are a good archer, Marcus.

      He gives them the arrows

  '*Ad Jovem*', that's for you; here, '*Ad Apollinem*';

  '*Ad Martem*', that's for myself;   55

  Here, boy, 'To Pallas'; here, 'To Mercury';

  'To Saturn', Caius, not to Saturnine;

  You were as good to shoot against the wind.

  To it, boy! Marcus, loose when I bid.

---

54 *Apollinem*] *Rowe*²; *Apollonem* Qq, F 57 Saturn', Caius] *Capell*; Saturnine, to Caius Qq, F

34 wreak vengeance; see 52, 4.4.11, 5.2.32.

36–7 Titus seems to think that his search parties have been away and returned.

37 her i.e. Astraea.

44–5 burning lake . . . Acheron Phlegethon and Pyriphlegethon are fiery rivers in the Underworld; Seneca refers to them (*amnes igneos*) in the passage quoted at 2.1.135. A line earlier, Phaedra speaks of *Tartareus lacus* (the Tartarean lake); Virgil, VI.134 and VIII.296, calls the Styx *lacus*. Acheron is a river in the Underworld, for the whole of which it stands here and in the incantation of Marlowe's Faustus: '*Sint mihi dei Acherontis propitii*' (*Dr Faustus* 3.16). It is not surprising, therefore, that Shakespeare muddled his infernal geography; so did Milton; his Satan is 'chained on the burning

lake' of Hell (*Paradise Lost* I, 210).

46 shrubs . . . we In a proverb, 'High cedars fall when low shrubs remain' (Dent C208, *ODEP*, p. 112).

47 Cyclops A mythical race of giants; see Homer, *Odyssey* IX.

50 sith since.

53 gear business.

54 *Ad Jovem* To Jove (Latin). The other arrows are addressed to Apollo (54) and Mars (55); see 4.1.66 nn.

56 Pallas Athene (Minerva).

58 were as good to might as well (i.e. you might as well shoot straight into the wind as appeal to Saturninus).

59 loose shoot.

Of my word, I have written to effect;   60
There's not a god left unsolicited.
MARCUS Kinsmen, shoot all your shafts into the court;
We will afflict the emperor in his pride.
TITUS Now, masters, draw. O well said, Lucius!
Good boy, in Virgo's lap; give it Pallas.   65
MARCUS My lord, I aim a mile beyond the moon;
Your letter is with Jupiter by this.
TITUS Ha ha! Publius, Publius, what hast thou done?
See, see, thou hast shot off one of Taurus' horns.
MARCUS This was the sport, my lord; when Publius shot,   70
The Bull, being galled, gave Aries such a knock
That down fell both the Ram's horns in the court,
And who should find them but the empress' villain?
She laughed, and told the Moor he should not choose
But give them to his master for a present.   75
TITUS Why there it goes; God give his lordship joy!

Enter the CLOWN *with a basket and two pigeons in it*

News, news from heaven! Marcus, the post is come.
Sirrah, what tidings? Have you any letters?
Shall I have justice? What says Jupiter?
CLOWN Ho, the gibbet-maker? He says that he hath taken them   80
down again, for the man must not be hanged till the next week.
TITUS But what says Jupiter, I ask thee?
CLOWN Alas, sir, I know not Jubiter; I never drank with him in all
my life.

---

66 aim] Qq, F; aim'd *Hudson*   67 Jupiter] Iupiter Q2–3, F; Iubiter Q; *also at 79, 82*   75 his] Q, Q2; your Q3, F   77
News . . . come] *One line, attributed to Titus, Rowe²; two lines, divided . . . heaven! / Marcus / attributed to Clowne* Q; *two
lines, divided . . . heaven! / Marcus / attributed to Titus* Q2–3, F   83–4] *As prose, Hanmer; as verse, divided after* Jubiter
Qq, F   83 Jubiter] Iubiter Q; Iupiter Q2–3, F

60 Of On.
62–5 They shoot their arrows. In a modern theatre, a feeble volley is aimed backstage. Elizabethan
actors probably shot right out of the yard, to the
peril of passersby.
64 said done.
65 Virgo The sixth sign of the Zodiac, known
also as *dikē* (Greek), i.e. Astraea, standing for
Justice.
69 Taurus The Bull, second sign of the Zodiac.
71 Aries The Ram, first sign of the Zodiac.
73 villain servant; with play on the modern
meaning.

75 give . . . master Another joke on cuckoldry;
see 2.3.66–7.
76 there it goes Possibly a hunter's cry of
encouragement (Wilson); but more probably 'that's
right' or 'that's it'; see *Ham*. Q (the 'bad' quarto):
'To die, to sleep, is that all? Ay, all: / No, to sleep,
to dream; Ay marry, there it goes.'
76 SD CLOWN A stock character of pseudo-rustic
type, 'clown' was a recognised 'line of business' for
an actor who might also be known as 'the clown'.
80 gibbet-maker The Clown hears 'Jupiter' as
'Gibbeter'.
80 them the gallows.

TITUS Why, villain, art not thou the carrier?   85

CLOWN Ay, of my pigeons, sir; nothing else.

TITUS Why, didst thou not come from heaven?

CLOWN From heaven? Alas, sir, I never came there. God forbid
I should be so bold to press to heaven in my young days. Why,
I am going with my pigeons to the tribunal plebs, to take up a   90
matter of brawl betwixt my uncle and one of the emperal's
men.

MARCUS Why, sir, that is as fit as can be to serve for your oration;
and let him deliver the pigeons to the emperor from you.

TITUS Tell me, can you deliver an oration to the emperor with a   95
grace?

CLOWN Nay truly, sir, I could never say grace in all my life.

TITUS Sirrah, come hither; make no more ado
But give your pigeons to the emperor;
By me thou shalt have justice at his hands.   100
Hold, hold; meanwhile here's money for thy charges.
Give me pen and ink. Sirrah, can you with a grace deliver
up a supplication?

CLOWN Ay, sir.

TITUS Then here is a supplication for you. And when you come to   105
him, at the first approach you must kneel; then kiss his foot;
then deliver up your pigeons; and then look for your reward.
I'll be at hand, sir; see you do it bravely.

CLOWN I warrant you, sir; let me alone.

TITUS Sirrah, hast thou a knife? Come, let me see it.   110
Here, Marcus, fold it in the oration,
For thou hast made it like an humble suppliant.
And when thou hast given it to the emperor,

---

88 From . . . there.] *As prose, Pope; as verse, divided after* there, Qq, F   88–92 God . . . men.] *As prose* Q2–3, F; *as
verse, divided after* daies: Q *(continuing thereafter as prose)*   91 emperal's] Q; Emperiall's Q2–3, F   102–3 Give . . .
supplication] *As prose, Hanmer; as verse, divided* . . . ink. / Sirrah Qq, F   102–9 Sirrah . . . alone] Qq, F; *omitted, Waith*
113 to] Q, Q2; *not in* Q3, F

---

85 **carrier** messenger who carries the mail, postman.

90 tribunal plebs *tribuni plebis*, protectors of the plebeian order of citizens; the Clown's Malapropian version. The pigeons are a bribe.

91 emperal emperor, the Clown's version.

93 oration petition.

*93–112 The Q text shows signs of incomplete revision; 102–3 repeat 95–6, for example. Wilson believes that 98–103 were meant to replace 93–7; Maxwell finds 95–8 redundant, and Waith omits

102b–9. The whole Q text is given here; perhaps Titus's mind is wandering.

112 **For thou . . . suppliant** The meaning is obscure; since Titus elsewhere addresses Marcus as 'you', 'thou' probably refers to the Clown. 'For' may mean 'because', which suggests that a line may be missing and the overall meaning something like, 'Because you have made the petition look like that of a humble suppliant, the emperor will receive and open it without suspicion.'

> Knock at my door and tell me what he says.
CLOWN God be with you, sir, I will.   *Exit* 115
TITUS Come, Marcus, let us go. Publius, follow me.

                                                                    Exeunt

[4.4] *Enter* EMPEROR *and* EMPRESS *and her two sons* [CHIRON
and DEMETRIUS, *and Attendants*]; *the emperor brings the arrows in his
hand that Titus shot at him*

SATURNINUS Why, lords, what wrongs are these! Was ever seen
        An emperor in Rome thus overborne,
        Troubled, confronted thus, and for the extent
        Of egall justice, used in such contempt?
        My lords, you know, as know the mightful gods,   5
        However these disturbers of our peace
        Buzz in the people's ears, there nought hath passed
        But even with law against the wilful sons
        Of old Andronicus. And what and if
        His sorrows have so overwhelmed his wits?   10
        Shall we be thus afflicted in his wreaks,
        His fits, his frenzy, and his bitterness?
        And now he writes to heaven for his redress;
        See, here's to Jove, and this to Mercury,
        This to Apollo, this to the god of war!   15
        Sweet scrolls to fly about the streets of Rome!
        What's this but libelling against the Senate
        And blazoning our unjustice everywhere?
        A goodly humour, is it not, my lords?
        As who would say, in Rome no justice were.   20
        But if I live, his feignèd ecstasies
        Shall be no shelter to these outrages,
        But he and his shall know that justice lives

Act 4, Scene 4 4.4] *Capell; not in* Qq, F   0 SD.1–2 CHIRON *and* DEMETRIUS, *and Attendants*] *Waith; not in* Qq, F
*5 as know] *Cam.; not in* Qq, F   18 unjustice] Qq; Iniustice F; injustice *Maxwell (in error?)*

Act 4, Scene 4
3–4 the extent . . . justice exercising justice
impartially.
    4 egall equal; the archaic form is too character-
istic to be modernised without loss.
    *5 as know Something is missing here, in both
Q and F, and while 'as know' seems the best of many

guesses, the reader and actor should be aware that
it is only a guess.
    8 even in accord.
    18 Maxwell's commentary gives 'unjustice' in
the lemma, but the text follows F.
    19 humour whim.

In Saturninus' health whom, if he sleep,
He'll so awake as he in fury shall   25
Cut off the proud'st conspirator that lives.
TAMORA My gracious lord, my lovely Saturnine,
Lord of my life, commander of my thoughts,
Calm thee and bear the faults of Titus' age,
Th'effects of sorrow for his valiant sons   30
Whose loss hath pierced him deep and scarred his heart;
And rather comfort his distressèd plight
Than prosecute the meanest or the best
For these contempts. [*Aside*] Why thus it shall become
High-witted Tamora to gloze with all.   35
But Titus, I have touched thee to the quick;
Thy life-blood out, if Aaron now be wise
Then all is safe, the anchor in the port.

Enter CLOWN

How now, good fellow, wouldst thou speak with us?
CLOWN Yea, forsooth, an your mistress-ship be emperial.   40
TAMORA Empress I am, but yonder sits the emperor.
CLOWN 'Tis he. God and Saint Stephen give you godden. I have
  brought you a letter and a couple of pigeons here.
[*Saturninus*] *reads the letter*
SATURNINUS Go, take him away and hang him presently.
CLOWN How much money must I have?   45
TAMORA Come, sirrah, you must be hanged.
CLOWN Hanged, by'Lady! Then have I brought up a
  neck to a fair end.
                                                      Exit [*with Attendants*]
SATURNINUS Despiteful and intolerable wrongs!
Shall I endure this monstrous villainy?   50

24–5 if he . . . as he] Qq, F; if she . . . as she *Rowe, Maxwell*   34 SD] F, *after 35; not in* Qq   38 anchor] Q, Q2; anchor's
Q3, F   42 godden] Q, Q2; good den Q3, F   43 SD *Saturninus*] *He* Qq, F   47 by'] *Maxwell;* be Qq; ber F; bir F2–3; by'r
F4   48 SD *with Attendants*] *Capell (subst.)*

24–5 whom . . . as he Unclear; the possibility that 'he' refers to 'justice' has led some editors
to emend to 'she'. Masculine personification is not
impossible, but unlikely in view of earlier references
to Astraea. The sense might be, 'if Saturninus (the
custodian of justice) should sleep, Titus's outrages
will wake him, so that he will punish the offender'.
  33 meanest or the best the lowest of the
Andronici (or the people who heed them (7)) or
Titus himself. But Saturninus will soon punish one
of the 'meanest', the Clown (44).

35 gloze use fair words.
37 Thy . . . out Once your blood flows.
40–8 It is difficult to tell from the layout of
the lines on the pages whether the compositors of
either Q or F thought this was verse or prose.
  40 emperial imperial, i.e. the empress; see
4.3.91 above and *TGV* 2.3.5, where the word is
a noun. Here it appears to be an adjective.
  42 godden good evening.
  47 by'Lady by Our Lady.

I know from whence this same device proceeds.
May this be borne as if his traitorous sons,
That died by law for murder of our brother,
Have by my means been butchered wrongfully?
Go, drag the villain hither by the hair;   55
Nor age nor honour shall shape privilege.
For this proud mock I'll be thy slaughterman,
Sly frantic wretch, that holpst to make me great
In hope thyself should govern Rome and me.

Enter Nuntius, AEMILIUS

SATURNINUS What news with thee, Aemilius?   60
AEMILIUS Arm, my lords! Rome never had more cause.
The Goths have gathered head and with a power
Of high-resolvèd men, bent to the spoil,
They hither march amain under condùct
Of Lucius, son to old Andronicus,   65
Who threats, in course of this revenge, to do
As much as ever Coriolanus did.
SATURNINUS Is warlike Lucius general of the Goths?
These tidings nip me, and I hang the head
As flowers with frost, or grass beat down with storms.   70
Ay, now begins our sorrows to approach.
'Tis he the common people love so much;
Myself hath often heard them say,
When I have walkèd like a private man,
That Lucius' banishment was wrongfully,   75
And they have wished that Lucius were their emperor.
TAMORA Why should you fear? Is not your city strong?
SATURNINUS Ay, but the citizens favour Lucius
And will revolt from me to succour him.
TAMORA King, be thy thoughts imperious like thy name.   80

59 SD *Nuntius*, AEMILIUS] Q2–3, F; *Nutius Emillius* Q   66 this] Qq, F; *his Rowe*   77 your] Qq; our F

56 **shape privilege** provide exemption.
58 **holpst** helped.
59 SD *Nuntius* Messenger (Latin).
62 **gathered head** raised an army.
62 **power** force.
63 **to the** upon.
64 **condùct** leadership.
67 **Coriolanus** Caius Marcius, hero of *Coriolanus* (1607–8); banished from Rome, he leads the enemy Volscians against his own city.

75 **wrongfully** (1) unjustly, unfairly (*OED* sv *adv* 1a); (2) illegally (*OED adv* 1b). Shakespeare seems to use the adverbial form as an adjective, modifying 'banishment'. It is clearer if we understand it to mean 'Lucius was banished wrongfully.'
80 **imperious** As emperor he is imperial, and ought to think like one, imperiously; see the Clown's unconscious play on empress/imperial (40).

Is the sun dimmed, that gnats do fly in it?
The eagle suffers little birds to sing
And is not careful what they mean thereby,
Knowing that with the shadow of his wings
He can at pleasure stint their melody;   85
Even so mayst thou the giddy men of Rome.
Then cheer thy spirit; for know thou, emperor,
I will enchant the old Andronicus
With words more sweet and yet more dangerous
Than baits to fish, or honey-stalks to sheep,   90
When as the one is wounded with the bait,
The other rotted with delicious feed.

SATURNINUS But he will not entreat his son for us.

TAMORA If Tamora entreat him, then he will;
For I can smooth and fill his agèd ears   95
With golden promises, that were his heart
Almost impregnable, his old ears deaf,
Yet should both ear and heart obey my tongue.
[*To Aemilius*] Go thou before to be our ambassador;
Say that the emperor requests a parley   100
Of warlike Lucius, and appoint the meeting
Even at his father's house, the old Andronicus.

SATURNINUS Aemilius, do this message honourably
And if he stand in hostage for his safety,
Bid him demand what pledge will please him best.   105

AEMILIUS Your bidding shall I do effectually.   *Exit*

TAMORA Now will I to that old Andronicus,
And temper him with all the art I have
To pluck proud Lucius from the warlike Goths.
And now, sweet emperor, be blithe again   110
And bury all thy fear in my devices.

SATURNINUS Then go successantly and plead to him.

Exeunt

---

87 know thou,] *Kittredge;* know thou Qq, F; know, thou F4   92 feed] Q3; seede Q, Q2; foode F   95 ears] Q; eare Q2–3,
F   97 ears] F; yeares Qq   99 SD] *Rowe; not in* Qq, F   99 to be our] Qq; to our F; be our *Capell*   102 Even . . .
Andronicus] Q, Q2; *omitted* Q3, F   112 successantly] Q *(subst.)*, Q2–3, F; incessantly *Capell*   112 to] Qq; for F

83 **is not careful** does not care.
85 **stint** stop.
86 **giddy** foolish.
90 **honey-stalks** stalks of clover flowers; *OED*
notes that Shakespeare is the only writer to use the
term.
92 **rotted** 'Rot' is a liver disease of sheep.

95 **smooth** flatter; see 5.2.140.
99 The verbal SD (103) is unambiguous, but late.
104 **stand in** insist on.
108 **temper** work on, coax.
112 **successantly** in succession (Wilson), with
possible play on 'incessantly', immediately.

[5.1] *Flourish. Enter* LUCIUS *with an army of* GOTHS, *with drum and soldiers*

LUCIUS Approvèd warriors and my faithful friends,
        I have receivèd letters from great Rome
        Which signifies what hate they bear their emperor
        And how desirous of our sight they are.
        Therefore, great lords, be as your titles witness,   5
        Imperious, and impatient of your wrongs;
        And wherein Rome hath done you any scath,
        Let him make treble satisfaction.
GOTH Brave slip, sprung from the great Andronicus,
        Whose name was once our terror, now our comfort,   10
        Whose high exploits and honourable deeds
        Ingrateful Rome requites with foul contempt,
        Be bold in us; we'll follow where thou lead'st,
        Like stinging bees in hottest summer's day
        Led by their master to the flowered fields,   15
        And be avenged on cursèd Tamora.
ALL OTHER GOTHS And as he saith, so say we all with him.
LUCIUS I humbly thank him, and I thank you all.
        But who comes here, led by a lusty Goth?

Enter a GOTH, *leading of* AARON *with his child in his arms*

SECOND GOTH Renownèd Lucius, from our troops I strayed   20
        To gaze upon a ruinous monastery,
        And as I earnestly did fix mine eye
        Upon the wasted building, suddenly
        I heard a child cry underneath a wall.
        I made unto the noise, when soon I heard   25
        The crying babe controlled with this discourse:

Act 5, Scene 1   **5.1**] *Rowe (subst.); Actus Quintus.* F; *not in* Qq   **0 SD.1** *Flourish.*] F; *not in* Qq   **0 SD.1** *drum*] Q3, F; *drums* Q, Q2   **9** SH GOTH] Qq, F; *1 Goth/Capell; also at 121, 162*   **13** Be bold] Qq; Behold F   **16** avenged] Q3, F; advenged Q, Q2   **17** SH] F2 *(Omn.); not in* Qq, F   **20** SH SECOND GOTH] *Capell; Goth* Qq, F

Act 5, Scene 1
1–16 The reasons Lucius offers the Goths for taking his side, their spokesman's response and their apparent motives, defy logic.
1 Approvèd Proven.
9 SH GOTH At least two different Goths speak, here and at 20; but neither Q nor F attributes their speeches, which thus remain matter for speculation or theatrical convenience.
13 bold confident.

15 master It was thought that bees were ruled by a king-bee.
16 cursèd Tamora Convenient as it is for the plot, it is not at all clear what grudges her own people have against Tamora.
19 lusty vigorous, joyful.
21 ruinous monastery This Gothic tourist has been gazing upon an anachronism.
23 wasted ruined.

'Peace, tawny slave, half me and half thy dam,
Did not thy hue bewray whose brat thou art,
Had nature lent thee but thy mother's look,
Villain, thou mightst have been an emperor.   30
But where the bull and cow are both milk-white
They never do beget a coal-black calf.
Peace, villain, peace' – even thus he rates the babe –
'For I must bear thee to a trusty Goth
Who, when he knows thou art the empress' babe,   35
Will hold thee dearly for thy mother's sake.'
With this, my weapon drawn, I rushed upon him,
Surprised him suddenly, and brought him hither
To use as you think needful of the man.

LUCIUS O worthy Goth, this is the incarnate devil   40
That robbed Andronicus of his good hand;
This is the pearl that pleased your empress' eye
And here's the base fruit of her burning lust.
Say, wall-eyed slave, whither wouldst thou convey
This growing image of thy fiendlike face?   45
Why dost not speak? What, deaf? Not a word?
A halter, soldiers, hang him on this tree
And by his side his fruit of bastardy.

AARON Touch not the boy, he is of royal blood.

LUCIUS Too like the sire for ever being good.   50
First hang the child, that he may see it sprawl,
A sight to vex the father's soul withal.
Get me a ladder.

[*Goths bring a ladder and force Aaron to climb it*]

27 dam] Q2–3, F; dame Q   37 this, my] F; this my Qq   43 her] Q, Q2; his Q3, F   *53 Get . . . ladder.] *Attributed to Lucius, Theobald; attributed to Aaron* Qq, F *(reading* Get . . . ladder, *Lucius)*   53 SD] *Capell (subst.); not in* Qq, F

27 **tawny slave** The playful terms of abuse Aaron uses to address the child are not to be taken literally; see 4.2.72.

27 **dam** mother; usually said of animals; not a compliment when applied to human beings.

33 **rates** See 2.3.81 n.

39 **use . . . man** deal with as you think he deserves.

44 **wall-eyed** The most probable of several meanings is 'having a divergent squint, which exposes an excessive proportion of the white of the eye'. The term was commonly used of horses. 'The horse that is whale-eyed, or white eyed, is for the most part shrewd, craftie, full of toyes, and dim sighted' (Gervase Markham, *Cavelarice, or the English Horseman* (1607); *OED* Wall-eyed *a* 1a, 1b).

*47 **this tree** Probably no property tree is needed. One of the fixed columns on the stage of the playhouse would serve. At 53, Aaron would climb the ladder, which could be kicked away to hang him.

51 **sprawl** contort in death agony.

*53 **Get . . . ladder** Most editors have emended, assigning this to Lucius rather than Aaron. It seems improbable that Aaron should call for a ladder for his own hanging, but the possibility remains that Qq and F are right, and this gesture is intended as another instance of his villainous bravado.

53 **SD** There is nothing in the text to show exactly when the ladder should be brought, or when Aaron mounts it.

AARON   Lucius, save the child
          And bear it from me to the empress.
          If thou do this I'll show thee wondrous things   55
          That highly may advantage thee to hear.
          If thou wilt not, befall what may befall,
          I'll speak no more but 'Vengeance rot you all!'
LUCIUS Say on, and if it please me which thou speak'st
          Thy child shall live, and I will see it nourished.   60
AARON And if it please thee? Why assure thee, Lucius,
          'Twill vex thy soul to hear what I shall speak,
          For I must talk of murders, rapes, and massacres,
          Acts of black night, abominable deeds,
          Complots of mischief, treason, villainies   65
          Ruthful to hear yet piteously performed;
          And this shall all be buried in my death
          Unless thou swear to me my child shall live.
LUCIUS Tell on thy mind; I say thy child shall live.
AARON Swear that he shall, and then I will begin.   70
LUCIUS Who should I swear by? Thou believest no god;
          That granted, how canst thou believe an oath?
AARON What if I do not? As indeed I do not;
          Yet, for I know thou art religious,
          And hast a thing within thee callèd conscience,   75
          With twenty popish tricks and ceremonies
          Which I have seen thee careful to observe,
          Therefore I urge thy oath; for that I know
          An idiot holds his bauble for a god
          And keeps the oath which by that god he swears,   80
          To that I'll urge him; therefore thou shalt vow
          By that same god, what god soe'er it be,
          That thou adorest and hast in reverence,
          To save my boy, to nourish and bring him up,
          Or else I will discover nought to thee.   85
LUCIUS Even by my god I swear to thee I will.
AARON First know thou, I begot him on the empress.
LUCIUS O most insatiate and luxurious woman!

67 in] Q, Q2; by Q3, F   88 and] Q, Q2; *not in* Q3, F

66 **Ruthful** Lamentable.   79 **bauble** Court-fool's mock-sceptre.
66 **piteously** pitiably.   88 **insatiate and luxurious** insatiable and lech-
69 **Tell on** Speak, tell your story.   erous.
76 **popish** Another anachronism.

AARON Tut, Lucius, this was but a deed of charity
                To that which thou shalt hear of me anon.   90
                'Twas her two sons that murdered Bassianus;
                They cut thy sister's tongue and ravished her,
                And cut her hands and trimmed her as thou sawest.
LUCIUS O detestable villain! Call'st thou that trimming?
AARON Why, she was washed and cut and trimmed,   95
                And 'twas trim sport for them which had the doing of it.
LUCIUS O barbarous, beastly villains like thyself!
AARON Indeed, I was their tutor to instruct them.
                That codding spirit had they from their mother,
                As sure a card as ever won the set;   100
                That bloody mind I think they learned of me,
                As true a dog as ever fought at head.
                Well, let my deeds be witness of my worth.
                I trained thy brethren to that guileful hole
                Where the dead corpse of Bassianus lay;   105
                I wrote the letter that thy father found
                And hid the gold within that letter mentioned,
                Confederate with the queen and her two sons;
                And what not done, that thou hast cause to rue,
                Wherein I had no stroke of mischief in it?   110
                I played the cheater for thy father's hand
                And when I had it, drew myself apart
                And almost broke my heart with extreme laughter.
                I pried me through the crevice of a wall
                When, for his hand, he had his two sons' heads;   115
                Beheld his tears and laughed so heartily
                That both mine eyes were rainy like to his;
                And when I told the empress of this sport

---

93 hands and] Qq; hands off and, F   95–6] Qq, F; *divided . . . 'twas / Trim Capell, and all modern editors except Waith*   97 barbarous] F; barberous Qq   107 that] Q; the Q2–3, F

90 To Compared with.

97 **barbarous** It is conceivable that Q 'barberous' was intended as a ghastly pun; undeniable puns that are only slightly less atrocious are found at 2.3.110, 3.1.91, 3.2.29. But an actor could not well distinguish between the vowels in 'barbarous' and 'barberous' without making the moment ludicrous; thus, the pun is probably a compositor's error.

99 **codding** Probably from 'cod' = 'testicle' (slang), with an apparent play on the verb mean-

ing 'to hoax', first recorded in 1873 (*OED* Cod *v*³).

100 **set** game of cards (*OED* Set *sb*¹ 25a).

102 **fought at head** i.e. attacked the head of the bull, like a good bulldog.

104 **trained** lured.

111 **cheater** Possibly an officer responsible for escheats, i.e. land forfeit to the crown (Kittredge); more probably Aaron uses the word in its modern sense.

113 **broke my heart** died, bust a gut.

She sounded almost at my pleasing tale,
And for my tidings gave me twenty kisses.   120
A GOTH What, canst thou say all this and never blush?
AARON Ay, like a black dog, as the saying is.
LUCIUS Art thou not sorry for these heinous deeds?
AARON Ay, that I had not done a thousand more.
Even now I curse the day – and yet I think   125
Few come within the compass of my curse –
Wherein I did not some notorious ill;
As kill a man or else devise his death,
Ravish a maid or plot the way to do it,
Accuse some innocent and forswear myself,   130
Set deadly enmity between two friends,
Make poor men's cattle break their necks,
Set fire on barns and haystacks in the night
And bid the owners quench them with their tears.
Oft have I digged up dead men from their graves   135
And set them upright at their dear friends' door,
Even when their sorrows almost was forgot,
And on their skins, as on the bark of trees,
Have with my knife carvèd in Roman letters,
'Let not your sorrow die, though I am dead.'   140
Tut, I have done a thousand dreadful things
As willingly as one would kill a fly,
And nothing grieves me heartily indeed
But that I cannot do ten thousand more.
LUCIUS Bring down the devil, for he must not die   145
So sweet a death as hanging presently.
        [Aaron is brought down from the ladder]
AARON If there be devils would I were a devil,
To live and burn in everlasting fire,
So I might have your company in hell

---

133 haystacks] Q2–3, F; haystalks Q   134 their] Qq; the F   141 Tut] Q2–3, F; But Q   146 SD] *Cross; not in* Qq, F

119 sounded swooned. The archaic word is retained here in order to preserve the metre.
121–2 blush . . . saying is 'To blush like a black dog' is proverbial: Tilley D507, *ODEP*, p. 71.
125–40 Compare Marlowe, *The Jew of Malta* 2.3.176–202.
133 haystacks While 'haystalks' may be legitimate dialect, as Maxwell argues, it conveys the wrong idea to the modern reader or hearer, who thinks of 'stalks' rather than the harvested 'stacks'.

141 Tut Preferred to Q's colourless 'But' because 'Tut' is more consistent with other speeches in this act; see 89, 150.
*145–51 The verbal SD shows that Aaron is brought down from the ladder and gagged at 151. Between the command (145) and its execution, he may rail (147–50) while Goths or other followers of Lucius fetch him down. The placing of these SDs should not be taken as prescriptive; alternative stagings are possible.

But to torment you with my bitter tongue.   150
LUCIUS Sirs, stop his mouth, and let him speak no more.
                    [*Aaron is gagged*]

                    Enter AEMILIUS

A GOTH My lord, there is a messenger from Rome
          Desires to be admitted to your presence.
LUCIUS Let him come near.
          Welcome, Aemilius; what's the news from Rome?   155
AEMILIUS Lord Lucius, and you princes of the Goths,
          The Roman emperor greets you all by me,
          And, for he understands you are in arms,
          He craves a parley at your father's house,
          Willing you to demand your hostages,   160
          And they shall be immediately delivered.
A GOTH What says our general?
LUCIUS Aemilius, let the emperor give his pledges
          Unto my father and my uncle Marcus
          And we will come. March away.   165
                    Flourish
                                        Exeunt

[**5.2**] *Enter* TAMORA *and her two sons* [CHIRON *and* DEMETRIUS],
disguised

TAMORA Thus, in this strange and sad habiliment,
          I will encounter with Andronicus
          And say I am Revenge, sent from below
          To join with him and right his heinous wrongs.
          Knock at his study, where they say he keeps   5
          To ruminate strange plots of dire revenge;
          Tell him Revenge is come to join with him
          And work confusion on his enemies.
                    They knock, and TITUS *opens his study door*
TITUS Who doth molest my contemplation?

151 SD.1] *Wilson (subst.); not in* Qq, F   165 SD.1 *Flourish*] F; *not in* Qq   165 SD.2 *Exeunt*] Q3, F; *not in* Q, Q2   Act 5,
Scene 2 5.2] *Rome; not in* Qq, F

159 parley discussion of disputed terms.

Act 5, Scene 2
1 sad habiliment sober or drab costume; see
82 n. below.
  5 keeps stays.

*8 SD *knock* Tamora has established at 5 that
the point in the playhouse where Titus enters in
answer to her knock is to be taken as the door
to his 'study'. If any part of the stage had been
conventionally identified as a study, as J. Q. Adams
argues (*The Globe Playhouse*, 1942, pp. 167–228),

Is it your trick to make me ope the door   10
That so my sad decrees may fly away
And all my study be to no effect?
You are deceived, for what I mean to do
See here in bloody lines I have set down,
And what is written shall be executed.   15

TAMORA Titus, I am come to talk to thee.

TITUS No, not a word; how can I grace my talk,
Wanting a hand to give it action?
Thou hast the odds of me; therefore no more.

TAMORA If thou didst know me, thou wouldst talk with me.   20

TITUS I am not mad; I know thee well enough.
Witness this wretched stump, witness these crimson lines,
Witness these trenches made by grief and care,
Witness the tiring day and heavy night,
Witness all sorrow that I know thee well   25
For our proud empress, mighty Tamora.
Is not thy coming for my other hand?

TAMORA Know thou sad man, I am not Tamora;
She is thine enemy, and I thy friend.
I am Revenge, sent from th'infernal kingdom   30
To ease the gnawing vulture of thy mind
By working wreakful vengeance on thy foes.
Come down and welcome me to this world's light,
Confer with me of murder and of death.
There's not a hollow cave or lurking place,   35

18 give it action] F; giue that accord Qq; give it that accord *Pope;* give't that accord *Riverside*   28 Know thou sad] Qq, F; Know, thou sad *Capell;* Know thou, sad F4, *Wilson*   31 thy] Qq; the F   32 thy] Qq; my F

this would be unnecessary. In this scene the study was surely 'aloft'; at 33 and 43 Tamora asks Titus to 'come down' and at 70–80 he cannot hear her remarks to her sons because he is descending the stairs inside the tiring-house. How the study door was achieved, and how they reached it to knock, is matter for speculation.

11 sad grave.

14 bloody lines letter written in Titus's own blood. In Kyd, Bel-Imperia calls for revenge in 'bloody writ' (3.2.26).

18 action delivery; a technical term in rhetoric, referring to the expressive gestures that accompany human speech (Waith). The loss of his hand prevents Titus from gesturing expressively. I have accepted the F reading because it makes excellent sense in a play which returns several times to the theme of mutilation as inhibiting the expression of the passions; see 3.2.31–45.

19 odds of advantage over; i.e. she has two hands with which to express herself.

22 crimson lines See 14.

23 trenches furrows or deep wrinkles (*OED* Trench *sb* 4). See *Sonnets* 2.1–2: 'When forty winters shall besiege thy brow, / And dig deep trenches in thy beauty's field . . .'

28 Know . . . man Some editors have taken upon themselves the actor's job of choosing between interpretations of these words by punctuating them. Since Q and F are unpunctuated they offer no guidance; thus, interpretation is subjective.

31 gnawing vulture An allusion to Prometheus; see 2.1.17.

No vast obscurity or misty vale,
Where bloody murder or detested rape
Can couch for fear, but I will find them out
And in their ears tell them my dreadful name,
Revenge, which makes the foul offender quake. 40
TITUS Art thou Revenge? And art thou sent to me
To be a torment to mine enemies?
TAMORA I am; therefore come down and welcome me.
TITUS Do me some service ere I come to thee.
Lo, by thy side where Rape and Murder stands, 45
Now give some surance that thou art Revenge;
Stab them or tear them on thy chariot wheels,
And then I'll come and be thy wagoner,
And whirl along with thee about the globes,
Provide thee two proper palfreys, black as jet, 50
To hale thy vengeful wagon swift away
And find out murderers in their guilty caves;
And when thy car is laden with their heads
I will dismount, and by thy wagon wheel
Trot like a servile footman all day long, 55
Even from Hyperion's rising in the east
Until his very downfall in the sea;
And day by day I'll do this heavy task,
So thou destroy Rapine and Murder there.
TAMORA These are my ministers, and come with me. 60
TITUS Are they thy ministers? What are they called?
TAMORA Rape and Murder, therefore callèd so
'Cause they take vengeance of such kind of men.
TITUS Good lord, how like the empress' sons they are,
And you the empress! But we worldly men 65
Have miserable, mad, mistaking eyes.
O sweet Revenge, now do I come to thee,

---

40 offender] Q, Q2; offenders Q3, F   49 globes] Qq, F; globe *conj. Capell*   50 thee two] Qq, F; two *Rowe*   50 black] Q, Q2; as blacke Q3, F   52 murderers] *Capell*; murder Qq, F   54 thy] Q; the Q2–3, F   56 Hyperion's] F2 *(subst.)*; Epeons Qq; Eptons F   61 Are they] F2; Are them Qq, F; Are these *Dyce*   62 Rape] Qq, F; Rapine F2, *Cam.*

38 couch lie hidden.
46 surance assurance.
48 wagoner charioteer.
49 globes The rest of the speech refers only to this world, but Q makes sense, and need not be emended.
50 proper palfreys fine horses.
50 jet black stone.
53 car carriage, chariot.

56 Hyperion Father of the sun-god. See 1.1.226 n.
59 Rapine Rape.
63 take vengeance of exact retribution from.
64 Good . . . are The obvious irony shows the audience that the convention of impenetrable disguise is not in use here. Titus is not fooled for a moment.
65 worldly mortal; i.e. of this world.

And if one arm's embracement will content thee,
I will embrace thee in it by and by.   *[Exit]*
TAMORA This closing with him fits his lunacy.   70
Whate'er I forge to feed his brain-sick humours,
Do you uphold and maintain in your speeches,
For now he firmly takes me for Revenge,
And, being credulous in this mad thought,
I'll make him send for Lucius his son,   75
And whilst I at a banquet hold him sure,
I'll find some cunning practice out of hand
To scatter and disperse the giddy Goths,
Or at the least make them his enemies.
See, here he comes, and I must ply my theme.   80

[Enter TITUS*]*

TITUS Long have I been forlorn and all for thee.
Welcome, dread Fury, to my woeful house;
Rapine and Murder, you are welcome too.
How like the empress and her sons you are!
Well are you fitted, had you but a Moor;   85
Could not all hell afford you such a devil?
For well I wot the empress never wags
But in her company there is a Moor;
And, would you represent our queen aright,
It were convenient you had such a devil.   90
But welcome as you are, what shall we do?
TAMORA What wouldst thou have us do, Andronicus?
DEMETRIUS Show me a murderer, I'll deal with him.
CHIRON Show me a villain that hath done a rape,
And I am sent to be revenged on him.   95

69 SD] *Exit Titus from above / Rowe; not in* Qq, F   70 fits] Q; humours Q2–3, F   80 ply] Qq; play F   80 SD] *Rowe;
not in* Qq, F

*69 SD Tamora's speech, 70–80, assumes that
Titus is out of earshot; this is confirmed by 80,
'here he comes'. The only reason Titus could have
for an exit would be to descend from his 'study'
aloft.
    70 closing agreeing.
    71 forge invent.
    76 banquet While there may be doubt about
the character of the meal in 3.2, this obviously is a
'banquet' in the modern sense. Accordingly, there
is no particular reason to retain Q's archaic spelling.
    77 practice stratagem.

    77 out of hand on the spur of the moment.
    82 Fury In Greek mythology, the Furies (in
Greek, *Erinyes*) were serpent-haired goddesses who
punished criminals, particularly those who were
guilty of shedding the blood of their kin. Perhaps Titus recognises that the function of Revenge
resembles theirs, rather than believing that she
is actually one of them. This may suggest what
Tamora's 'strange and sad habiliments' looked like.
    87 wags moves about.
    90 convenient fitting.

TAMORA Show me a thousand that hath done thee wrong,
       And I will be revengèd on them all.
TITUS Look round about the wicked streets of Rome
       And when thou findest a man that's like thyself,
       Good Murder, stab him; he's a murderer.   100
       Go thou with him, and when it is thy hap
       To find another that is like to thee,
       Good Rapine, stab him; he is a ravisher.
       Go thou with them, and in the emperor's court
       There is a queen attended by a Moor;   105
       Well shalt thou know her by thine own proportion,
       For up and down she doth resemble thee;
       I pray thee, do on them some violent death;
       They have been violent to me and mine.
TAMORA Well hast thou lessoned us; this shall we do.   110
       But would it please thee, good Andronicus,
       To send for Lucius, thy thrice-valiant son,
       Who leads towards Rome a band of warlike Goths,
       And bid him come and banquet at thy house?
       When he is here, even at thy solemn feast,   115
       I will bring in the empress and her sons,
       The emperor himself and all thy foes,
       And at thy mercy shall they stoop and kneel,
       And on them shalt thou ease thy angry heart.
       What says Andronicus to this device?   120

                    Enter MARCUS

TITUS Marcus, my brother, 'tis sad Titus calls.
       Go, gentle Marcus, to thy nephew Lucius;
       Thou shalt inquire him out among the Goths.
       Bid him repair to me and bring with him
       Some of the chiefest princes of the Goths.   125
       Bid him encamp his soldiers where they are.
       Tell him the emperor and the empress too
       Feast at my house, and he shall feast with them.

96 hath] Q; have Q2–3, F   97 I will] Qq; Ile F   106 shalt] Q; maist Q2–3, F   106 thine] Q, Q2; thy Q3, F   120 SD]
Qq, F; *at 121, Theobald*   128 Feast] Qq; Feasts F

98–109 Attention to the verbal SDs clearly
shows that Titus addresses in turn Demetrius (98),
Chiron (101) and Tamora (104). Editorial SDs
would be gratuitous.
  101 **hap** fortune, luck.
  107 **up and down** all over, head to toe.

120 SD Marcus's entry in Q and F anticipates
Titus's call; but there is no basis for emendation
except a feeling that this should not be so. In performance, however, several plausible justifications
could be found.
  124 **repair** come; see 5.3.2.

This do thou for my love, and so let him,
As he regards his agèd father's life.   130
MARCUS   This will I do, and soon return again.   [*Exit*]
TAMORA   Now will I hence about thy business,
And take my ministers along with me.
TITUS   Nay, nay, let Rape and Murder stay with me,
Or else I'll call my brother back again   135
And cleave to no revenge but Lucius.
TAMORA   [*Aside*] What say you, boys? Will you abide with him
Whiles I go tell my lord the emperor
How I have governed our determined jest?
Yield to his humour, smooth and speak him fair,   140
And tarry with him till I turn again.
TITUS   [*Aside*] I knew them all, though they supposed me mad,
And will o'erreach them in their own devices,
A pair of cursèd hell-hounds and their dam.
DEMETRIUS   Madam, depart at pleasure; leave us here.   145
TAMORA   Farewell, Andronicus; Revenge now goes
To lay a complot to betray thy foes.
TITUS   I know thou dost; and sweet Revenge, farewell.
                                                        [*Exit Tamora*]
CHIRON   Tell us, old man, how shall we be employed?
TITUS   Tut, I have work enough for you to do.   150
Publius, come hither; Caius and Valentine.

[*Enter Titus's kinsmen*, PUBLIUS, VALENTINE *and* CAIUS]

PUBLIUS   What is your will?
TITUS   Know you these two?
PUBLIUS   The empress' sons, I take them, Chiron, Demetrius.
TITUS   Fie, Publius, fie! Thou art too much deceived;   155
The one is Murder, and Rape is the other's name;
And therefore bind them, gentle Publius;
Caius and Valentine, lay hands on them.

131 SD] *Rowe; not in* Qq, F   137 SD] *Hanmer; not in* Qq, F   137 abide] Q; bide Q2–3, F   142 SD] *Rowe; not in* Qq, F   142 knew] Q; know Q2–3, F   142 supposed] Q; suppose Q2–3, F   144 dam] Q3, F; dame Q, Q2   148 SD] *Capell; not in* Qq, F; *after 147, Rowe*   150 Tut] Q, Q2, F; But Q3   151 SD] *This edn; not in* Qq, F   154 Chiron, Demetrius] Qq, F; Chiron, and Demetrius *Theobald*   156 and] Q; *not in* Q2–3, F

136 cleave . . . Lucius trust only to Lucius (not to you) for my revenge.

139 governed . . . jest managed the prank we have planned.

140 speak him fair humour him, 'butter him up'.

141 turn return.

*151 SD kinsmen Titus calls Publius, Sempronius and Caius 'kinsmen' at 4.3.1, and 'cousins' at 6. Valentine is new. Since only Publius speaks in either scene, it is likely enough that the dramatist forgot the name he had given a mute figure in the earlier scene: Sempronius and Valentine would thus be the same person.

> Oft have you heard me wish for such an hour,
> And now I find it; therefore bind them sure   160
> And stop their mouths if they begin to cry.   [*Exit*]

CHIRON Villains, forbear; we are the empress' sons.

PUBLIUS And therefore do we what we are commanded.
> Stop close their mouths; let them not speak a word.
> Is he sure bound? Look that you bind them fast.   165

> > > > > *Exeunt*

Enter TITUS ANDRONICUS *with a knife, and* LAVINIA *with a basin*

TITUS Come, come, Lavinia; look, thy foes are bound.
> Sirs, stop their mouths; let them not speak to me,
> But let them hear what fearful words I utter.
> O villains, Chiron and Demetrius,
> Here stands the spring whom you have stained with mud,   170
> This goodly summer with your winter mixed;
> You killed her husband, and for that vile fault
> Two of her brothers were condemned to death,
> My hand cut off and made a merry jest;
> Both her sweet hands, her tongue, and that more dear   175
> Than hands or tongue, her spotless chastity,
> Inhuman traitors, you constrained and forced.
> What would you say if I should let you speak?
> Villains, for shame you could not beg for grace.
> Hark, wretches, how I mean to martyr you;   180
> This one hand yet is left to cut your throats
> Whiles that Lavinia 'tween her stumps doth hold
> The basin that receives your guilty blood.
> You know your mother means to feast with me,
> And calls herself Revenge and thinks me mad.   185
> Hark, villains, I will grind your bones to dust,
> And with your blood and it I'll make a paste,
> And of the paste a coffin I will rear,
> And make two pasties of your shameful heads,
> And bid that strumpet, your unhallowed dam,   190
> Like to the earth swallow her own increase.
> This is the feast that I have bid her to,

---

161 And . . . cry.] Qq; *not in* F   161 SD] *Rowe; not in* Qq, F   165 SD.1 *Exeunt*] F; *not in* Qq   182 Whiles] Q; Whilst
Q2–3, F   191 own] Qq; *not in* F

163 therefore that is why.	**188 coffin** pie-crust.
168 fearful terrible, causing fear.	**191 Like . . . increase** See *Rom.* 2.3.9–10: 'The
177 constrained took by force, violated (*OED*	earth that's nature's mother is her tomb; / What
Constrain *v* 5b).	is her burying grave, that is her womb.'

And this the banquet she shall surfeit on,
For worse than Philomel you used my daughter
And worse than Procne I will be revenged.   195
And now prepare your throats; Lavinia, come,
Receive the blood, and when that they are dead
Let me go grind their bones to powder small,
And with this hateful liquor temper it,
And in that paste let their vile heads be baked.   200
Come, come, be every one officious
To make this banquet, which I wish may prove
More stern and bloody than the Centaurs' feast.
                    He cuts their throats
So now bring them in, for I'll play the cook
And see them ready against their mother comes.   205

                                                              Exeunt

[5.3] *Enter* LUCIUS, MARCUS, *and the* GOTHS [*with* AARON
prisoner]

LUCIUS Uncle Marcus, since 'tis my father's mind
          That I repair to Rome, I am content.
A GOTH And ours with thine, befall what fortune will.
LUCIUS Good uncle, take you in this barbarous Moor,
          This ravenous tiger, this accursèd devil;   5
          Let him receive no sust'nance, fetter him
          Till he be brought unto the empress' face
          For testimony of her foul proceedings.
          And see the ambush of our friends be strong;
          I fear the emperor means no good to us.   10
AARON Some devil whisper curses in my ear,
          And prompt me that my tongue may utter forth
          The venomous malice of my swelling heart.

---

195 Procne] *Theobald;* Progne Qq, F   202 may] Qq; might F   205 against] Qq; gainst F   **Act 5, Scene 3**   5.3] *Capell*
(subst.); not in Qq, F   0 SD *with* AARON *prisoner*] *Rowe; not in* Qq, F   7 empress'] Q, Q2; Eperours Q3; Emperous F 11
my] Q, F; mine Q2–3

193 banquet See note on 76.
195 Procne Wife of Tereus, who raped her sister Philomel; see 2.3.43 n.
199 with . . . it mix it with the blood.
201 officious busy.
203 Centaurs' feast The wedding of Pirithous
the Lapith, which ended in a battle between human
and Centaur guests. The latter are half man, half
horse; see Ovid, XII.
205 against by the time.

Act 5, Scene 3
3 ours i.e. our minds, presumably; the syntax
does not match that of the previous speech.

LUCIUS Away, inhuman dog, unhallowed slave!
    Sirs, help our uncle to convey him in.   15

                     [Exit Aaron, guarded by Goths]
                     Flourish
    The trumpets show the emperor is at hand.

Sound trumpets. Enter EMPEROR *and* EMPRESS *with* [AEMILIUS,]
               Tribunes and others

SATURNINUS What, hath the firmament more suns than one?
LUCIUS What boots it thee to call thyself a sun?
MARCUS Rome's emperor and nephew, break the parle;
    These quarrels must be quietly debated.   20
    The feast is ready which the carefull Titus
    Hath ordained to an honourable end,
    For peace, for love, for league, and good to Rome.
    Please you, therefore, draw nigh and take your places.
SATURNINUS Marcus, we will.   25

Hoboyes. A table brought in. Trumpets sounding, enter TITUS *like a cook,*
   placing the dishes, and LAVINIA *with a veil over her face*[, YOUNG
              LUCIUS, *and others*]

TITUS Welcome, my lord; welcome, dread queen;
    Welcome, ye warlike Goths; welcome, Lucius;
    And welcome all. Although the cheer be poor,
    'Twill fill your stomachs; please you eat of it.
SATURNINUS Why art thou thus attired, Andronicus?   30
TITUS Because I would be sure to have all well
    To entertain your highness and your empress.
TAMORA We are beholding to you, good Andronicus.

15 SD.1] *This edn; not in* Qq, F   15 SD.2 *Flourish*] F; *not in* Qq   16 SD.1 AEMILIUS] *Dyce; not in* Qq, F   21 carefull]
Qq, F; *care-full Waith*   25 SD.1 *Hoboyes.*] F *(after 25); not in* Qq   25 SD.1 *A . . . in*] F *centred; not in* Qq   25 SD.1
Trumpets sounding, enter] Q; *Sound trumpets, enter* Q2–3; *Enter* F   26 SD.2 *dishes*] Q; *meat on the table* Q2–3, F   26
SD.2–3 YOUNG . . . *others*] *Malone; not in* Qq, F   26 SD.2 *dishes*] Q; *meat on the table* Q2–3, F   26 SD.2–3 YOUNG . . .
others] *Malone; not in* Qq, F   26 lord] Q; *gracious Lord* Q2–3, F

15 SD.1 Capell directs Lucius's command to the
Goths, who take Aaron away, but other escorts
could be used; see 141–2 and 174 nn. below.
Marcus stays behind.

16 SD.2 *others* Shakespeare might well have
added 'as many as can be', as at 1.1.69. This scene
would have taxed the company's manpower to provide enough Goths, tribunes and 'others' to give
both Lucius and Saturninus impressive retinues.

18 What . . . thee What profit is it to thee;
Lucius uses the familiar 'thee' rather than the
respectful 'you'.

19 break the parle begin discussing terms,
under a truce (*OED* Break *v* 24).

21 carefull sorrowful. Waith hyphenates. The
alert reader will distinguish this from the modern
'careful', but spoken in a theatre, the words sound
identical.

23 league alliance.

25 SD.1 *table* Since F probably reflects playhouse
practice, this may record authentic early staging.

25 SD.3 *others* These should probably include
Publius, Caius and Sempronius/Valentine.

TITUS And if your highness knew my heart, you were.
       My lord the emperor, resolve me this: 35
       Was it well done of rash Virginius
       To slay his daughter with his own right hand
       Because she was enforced, stained, and deflowered?
SATURNINUS It was, Andronicus.
TITUS   Your reason, mighty lord?
SATURNINUS Because the girl should not survive her shame,   40
       And by her presence still renew his sorrows.
TITUS A reason mighty, strong, and effectual;
       A pattern, precedent, and lively warrant
       For me, most wretched, to perform the like.
       Die, die, Lavinia, and thy shame with thee,   45
       And with thy shame thy father's sorrow die.
               [He kills her]
SATURNINUS What hast thou done, unnatural and unkind?
TITUS Killed her for whom my tears have made me blind.
       I am as woeful as Virginius was,
       And have a thousand times more cause than he   50
       To do this outrage; and it now is done.
SATURNINUS What, was she ravished? Tell who did the deed.
TITUS Will't please you eat? Will't please your highness feed?
TAMORA Why hast thou slain thine only daughter thus?
TITUS Not I, 'twas Chiron and Demetrius;   55
       They ravished her and cut away her tongue,
       And they, 'twas they that did her all this wrong.
SATURNINUS Go fetch them hither to us presently.
TITUS Why there they are, both bakèd in this pie,
       Whereof their mother daintily hath fed,   60
       Eating the flesh that she herself hath bred.
       'Tis true, 'tis true, witness my knife's sharp point.
            He stabs the empress
SATURNINUS Die, frantic wretch, for this accursèd deed.
              [He kills Titus]
LUCIUS Can the son's eye behold his father bleed?
       There's meed for meed, death for a deadly deed.   65

---

46 SD] Q3, F; *not in* Q, Q2 47 thou] Qq; *not in* F 51] Qq; *not in* F 51 now is] Q, Q2; is now Q3 54 thus] Q, Q2; *not in* Q3, F 59 this] Q; that Q2–3, F 63 SD] *Rowe (subst.); not in* Qq, F

36 Virginius Heroic centurion, who publicly stabbed his daughter. Livy and Florus give different versions: in the latter, to which Titus refers, she has been dishonoured by Appius Claudius. Virginius is the theme of Webster's *Appius and Virginia* (1625–30), and many subsequent plays.
  38 enforced raped, overcome by violence.
  40 Because So that.
  43 lively striking, vivid.
  65 meed for meed measure for measure.

[He kills Saturninus]

MARCUS You sad-faced men, people and sons of Rome,
By uproars severed, as a flight of fowl
Scattered by winds and high tempestuous gusts,
O let me teach you how to knit again
This scattered corn into one mutual sheaf,   70
These broken limbs again into one body.
AEMILIUS Let Rome herself be bane unto herself,
And she whom mighty kingdoms curtsy to,
Like a forlorn and desperate castaway,
Do shameful execution on herself,   75
But if my frosty signs and chaps of age,
Grave witnesses of true experience,
Cannot induce you to attend my words.
Speak, Rome's dear friend, as erst our ancestor,
When with his solemn tongue he did discourse   80
To lovesick Dido's sad-attending ear
The story of that baleful burning night
When subtle Greeks surprised King Priam's Troy.
Tell us what Sinon hath bewitched our ears,
Or who hath brought the fatal engine in   85
That gives our Troy, our Rome, the civil wound.
My heart is not compact of flint nor steel,
Nor can I utter all our bitter grief,
But floods of tears will drown my oratory
And break my utt'rance, even in the time   90
When it should move ye to attend me most
And force you to commiseration.

---

65 SD] *Rowe (subst.); not in* Qq, F   67 as] Q, Q2; like Q3, F   *72 SH AEMILIUS] *Sisson; Romane Lord* Qq; *Goth* F; *Marcus continued, Capell, Wilson*   72 Let] Qq, F; *Lest Capell*   90 my] Q, Q2; *my very* Q3, F   91 ye] Q; *you* Q2–3, F   92 And force you to] Q; *Lending your kind* Q2–3; *Lending your kind hand* F

*66 It is altogether fitting that Marcus should appear 'aloft' here, as in Act 1. At 129–32 he and Lucius seem to be standing on a high place, but there is no convenient point in the text at which they could ascend. The 'sad-faced men' may include the audience, as in Act 1: few others are left on their feet.

70 **mutual** unified.

*72 **Let** Q begins 'Let' and assigns 72–94 to a 'Romane Lord'. Most editors find this speech better suited to the aged, magisterial Marcus, and substitute 'Lest', altering the meaning. I have assigned this and 175–7 to Aemilius because he might be present at the 'parley' he has called, as ambassador

(5.1.156–61). He is the only noble Roman available, without introducing a new character.

76 **But if** if, unless; not used thus elsewhere in the play.

76 **chaps** wrinkles, cracks; more usually, cheeks or jaws.

79 **erst** once.

79 **our ancestor** Aeneas.

84 **Sinon** The Greek who persuaded the Trojans to move the wooden horse inside their walls (Virgil, II). His name was proverbial for treachery.

86 **civil wound** i.e. wound from civil war.

87 **compact** composed.

Here's Rome's young captain; let him tell the tale
While I stand by and weep to hear him speak.

LUCIUS Then, gracious auditory, be it known to you   95
That Chiron and the damned Demetrius
Were they that murdered our emperor's brother,
And they it were that ravishèd our sister.
For their fell faults our brothers were beheaded,
Our father's tears despised, and basely cozened   100
Of that true hand that fought Rome's quarrel out
And sent her enemies unto the grave.
Lastly myself unkindly banishèd,
The gates shut on me and turned weeping out
To beg relief among Rome's enemies,   105
Who drowned their enmity in my true tears
And oped their arms to embrace me as a friend.
I am the turned forth, be it known to you,
That have preserved her welfare in my blood,
And from her bosom took the enemy's point,   110
Sheathing the steel in my advent'rous body.
Alas, you know I am no vaunter, I;
My scars can witness, dumb although they are,
That my report is just and full of truth.
But soft, methinks I do digress too much,   115
Citing my worthless praise. O pardon me,
For when no friends are by, men praise themselves.

MARCUS Now is my turn to speak. Behold the child;
Of this was Tamora deliverèd,
The issue of an irreligious Moor,   120
Chief architect and plotter of these woes.
The villain is alive in Titus' house,
And as he is to witness this is true,
Now judge what cause had Titus to revenge
These wrongs unspeakable, past patience,   125

93 Here's Rome's young] Q; Here is a Q2–3, F   94 While . . . by] Q; Your hearts will throb Q2–3, F   95 Then, gracious]
. Q; Then, noble Q2–3; This Noble F   96 Chiron and the dammed] Q; cursed Chiron and Q2–3, F   108 I am the] Q, Q2;
And I am Q3, F   118 the] Q, Q2; this Q3, F   123 And . . . is to witness . . . true,] Qq; And . . . is, to witness . . . true.
F; And . . . is to witness . . ., true. *Maxwell;* Damn'd . . . is, to witness . . . true. *Theobald*   124 cause] F4; course Qq, F

99 **fell** cruel, savage.
100 **cozened** cheated.
101 **out** to a finish.
114 **report** reputation; or perhaps the account
of himself which he has just given.
117 **For . . . themselves** Proverbial: Tilley
N117, *ODEP,* p. 560.

123 The punctuation here is uncertain, and variations make a considerable difference in meaning.
Actors and readers should feel free to experiment.
124 **cause** The Q reading does not make
sense unless it is interpreted as a contraction of
'recourse', which seems unlikely in the context.

Or more than any living man could bear.
Now have you heard the truth; what say you, Romans?
Have we done aught amiss? Show us wherein,
And from the place where you behold us pleading,
The poor remainder of Andronici   130
Will hand in hand all headlong hurl ourselves,
And on the ragged stones beat forth our souls,
And make a mutual closure of our house.
Speak, Romans, speak, and if you say we shall,
Lo, hand in hand, Lucius and I will fall.   135
AEMILIUS Come, come, thou reverent man of Rome,
And bring our emperor gently in thy hand,
Lucius, our emperor; for well I know
The common voice do cry it shall be so.
MARCUS Lucius all hail, Rome's royal emperor!   140
[*To Attendants*] Go, go into Titus' sorrowful house
And hither hale that misbelieving Moor
To be adjudged some direful slaught'ring death
As punishment for his most wicked life.

                                    [*Exeunt Attendants*]

Lucius all hail, Rome's gracious governor!   145
LUCIUS Thanks, gentle Romans. May I govern so,
To heal Rome's harms and wipe away her woe.
But gentle people, give me aim a while,
For nature puts me to a heavy task.
Stand aloof, but uncle, draw you near   150
To shed obsequious tears upon this trunk.

---

129 pleading] Q; *now* Q2–3, F   131 hurl ourselves] Q; *cast us downe* Q2–3, F   132 souls] Q; *braines* Q2–3, F   136 reverent] Qq, F, *Maxwell;* reverend F4, *Wilson and most editors; see 2.3.296, 3.1.23*   *140 SH MARCUS] Qq, F; *Rom.* / *Capell; Romans / Waith; All / Cam.; also at 145*   141 SD] *Capell; not in* Qq, F   144 SD] *Cam.; not in* Qq, F

129–32 from . . . souls These lines seem to be spoken 'aloft'; see, however, Richard Hosley, 'Shakespeare's use of a gallery over the stage', *S.Sur.* 10 (1957), 86.

130–1 Marcus speaks for a number of Andronici here: perhaps Publius and the rest stand with him.

132 ragged rugged.

133 mutual closure common end.

***140, 145** Only Barnet agrees with me that these lines may both be attributed to Marcus, as in Qq and F. Compare the similar patterned, framed speech at 1.1.150–6.

141–2 Go . . . Moor A verbal SD addressed to anonymous attendants, to Aaron's Gothic captors, or even to Titus's kinsmen; see 15 and 174 nn.

142 hale drag.

148 give me aim An image from archery: he who 'gave aim' stood near the target and informed the archer where his arrow had struck (Onions).

149 puts me to imposes on me; see Tourneur, *Revenger's Tragedy* 4.2.2: 'How that great villain puts me to my shifts.'

151 obsequious dutiful; i.e. appropriate to obsequies.

O take this warm kiss on thy pale cold lips,
These sorrowful drops upon thy bloodstained face,
The last true duties of thy noble son.

MARCUS Tear for tear and loving kiss for kiss   155
Thy brother Marcus tenders on thy lips.
O were the sum of these that I should pay
Countless and infinite, yet would I pay them.

LUCIUS Come hither, boy, come, come, and learn of us
To melt in showers. Thy grandsire loved thee well;   160
Many a time he danced thee on his knee,
Sung thee asleep, his loving breast thy pillow;
Many a story hath he told to thee
And bid thee bear his pretty tales in mind,
And talk of them when he was dead and gone.   165

MARCUS How many thousand times hath these poor lips,
When they were living, warmed themselves on thine.
O now, sweet boy, give them their latest kiss;
Bid him farewell; commit him to the grave;
Do them that kindness, and take leave of them.   170

YOUNG LUCIUS O grandsire, grandsire, ev'n with all my heart
Would I were dead, so you did live again!
O Lord, I cannot speak to him for weeping;
My tears will choke me if I ope my mouth.

[*Enter some with* AARON]

AEMILIUS You sad Andronici, have done with woes.   175
Give sentence on this execrable wretch
That hath been breeder of these dire events.

LUCIUS Set him breast-deep in earth and famish him;
There let him stand and rave and cry for food.
If anyone relieves or pities him,   180
For the offence he dies; this is our doom.
Some stay to see him fastened in the earth.

153 bloodstained] F3 *(subst.)*; blood slaine Q, Q2; bloud-slaine Q3, F   163 story] Q; matter Q2–3, F   *164–8] Q; Meete, and agreeing with thine Infancie: / In that respect then, like a louing Childe, / Shed yet some small drops from thy tender Spring, / Because kinde Nature doth require it so: / Friends, should associate Friends, in Greefe and Wo. Q2–3, F   170 them . . . them] Qq; him . . . him F   174 SD] *This edn; Romans with Aaron / Rowe; not in* Qq, F   *175 SH AEMILIUS] *Conj. Dyce; Romane.* Qq; *Romans.* F

*152 **take . . . lips** The verbal SD shows that Lucius, and no doubt Marcus as well, have descended from 'aloft' since 129–30. Some point between 139 and 146 is likely.
*164–8 See 199 n.
168 **latest** last.
170 **them** i.e. Titus's lips.

*174 SD Whoever took Aaron away at 15 should fetch him at 144 and return with him here. Most editors give 'Attendants' here, while following Capell's 'Goths' at 15: this makes little sense. The exact point of his return is conjectural.
178 **famish** starve.

AARON Ah, why should wrath be mute and fury dumb?
      I am no baby, I, that with base prayers
      I should repent the evils I have done;   185
      Ten thousand worse than ever yet I did
      Would I perform, if I might have my will.
      If one good deed in all my life I did,
      I do repent it from my very soul.
LUCIUS Some loving friends convey the emperor hence   190
      And give him burial in his fathers' grave.
      My father and Lavinia shall forthwith
      Be closèd in our household's monument.
      As for that ravenous tiger, Tamora,
      No funeral rite, nor man in mourning weed,   195
      No mournful bell shall ring her burial;
      But throw her forth to beasts and birds to prey.
      Her life was beastly and devoid of pity,
      And being dead, let birds on her take pity.

                                       Exeunt

        Finis the Tragedy of Titus Andronicus.

---

183 Ah] Qq; O F   194 ravenous] Q; hainous Q2–3, F   195 weed] Q; weedes Q2–3   197 to prey] Qq; of prey F   198 beastly] Qq; beast-like F   *199 dead . . . take] Q; so, shall haue like want of Q2–3, F; *after 199* Q2–3, F *add*: See Iustice done on *Aaron* that damn'd Moore, / From [By Q2–3] whom, our heauy happes had their beginning: / Then afterwards, to Order well the State,/ That like Euents, may ne're it Ruinate.   199 SD *Exeunt*] Q; *Exeunt omnes* F; *not in* Q2–3   Finis . . . Andronicus.] Q; *not in* Q2–3; Finis. F

191 fathers' Neither Q nor F indicates where the apostrophe should be, but the distinction cannot be made in the theatre. In this context, Saturninus's dynastic role might prevail, and make an audience hear 'fathers'', i.e. 'ancestors''.

197 prey i.e. prey upon.
*199 For a discussion of the state of the text here and at 164–8, see the Textual Analysis, pp. 162–3 below. The corrupt text is given here as it appears in F.

TEXTUAL ANALYSIS

We have four different early texts of *Titus Andronicus*; three are quartos, and it is amongst the thirty-six plays collected in the First Folio (1623). Discovered in Sweden in 1904, the only known copy of Q (1954) was sold to Henry Clay Folger and is held in the Folger Shakespeare Library. The two extant copies of Q2 (1600) are in the Library of the University of Edinburgh and the Huntington Library in California. Confusion about the number of extant copies of Q3 (1611) seems to have been settled by G. Harold Metz, who enumerates seventeen.[1]

Both Q and F are authoritative in their exclusive spheres. The former is a 'good' quarto, usually thought to have been prepared from some form of 'foul papers'.[2] This was probably Shakespeare's working manuscript, and while he did not correct it meticulously, and the printing was less careful than we could wish, it is as close to his intentions as we can get: thus Q must be our copy-text for dialogue. It is likely, however, that the dramatist finished correcting his manuscript before the first known performance, by Sussex's Men at the Rose; thus, while the stage directions may show what he imagined happening on the stage, they do not necessarily represent what was actually done there.

Since Q2 was printed from Q, and Q3 from Q2, they can have no independent authority, particularly as the copy of Q which the Q2 printers used seems to have been defective. The Folio, however, introduces new material. There is a new scene (3.2) which is manifestly authentic; there is a full line (1.1.398) which is found in none of the quartos; some speech headings are regularised; and many stage directions are augmented and altered. Thus F must be copy-text for 3.2, for which it is our only source. But the stage directions present us with a more difficult choice. F was printed from a copy of Q3, collated to some extent with some other text which contained 3.2 and different stage directions. Since this was probably a prompt-book belonging to Shakespeare's company, the stage directions may not always be Shakespeare's own words; on the other hand, they may well represent what was done in the playhouse with his sanction, perhaps quite late in his career. Stanley Wells has argued persuasively that, in these circumstances, 'the basic editorial procedure to be followed in a fully edited version for the general reader should be to accept the evidence offered by the Folio that supplements or substantially replaces that offered by the quarto'.[3] I have taken Q as copy-text for stage directions, but have added those from F wherever they give a fuller sense of what is going on in the playhouse.

---

[1] G. Harold Metz, 'How many copies of *Titus Andronicus* Q3 are extant?', *The Library*, 6th ser., 3 (1981), 336–40.

[2] Paul Werstine, 'Narratives about printed Shakespeare texts: "foul papers" and "bad" quartos', *SQ* 41 (1990), 65–86, questions both of these terms. He shows that different scholars have defined foul papers differently, and points out that none are known to be extant.

[3] Wells, p. 112.

Q (1594)

Title page: THE / MOST LA-/ mentable Romaine / Tragedie of Titus Andronicus: / As it was Plaide by the Right Ho- / nourable the Earle of *Darbie*, Earle of *Pembrooke*, / and Earle of *Sussex* their Seruants. / [Device: McKerrow 281[1]] / LONDON, / Printed by Iohn Danter, and are / to be sold by *Edward White & Thomas Millington*, / at the little North doore of Paules at the / signe of the Gunne. / 1594.

Danter entered 'a booke intituled a Noble Roman Historye of Tytus Andronicus' and 'the ballad thereof' in the Stationers' Register on 6 February 1594. While he may have meant to publish a chapbook, Danter evidently used the entry to print Q.[2] There is some disagreement over the number of compositors employed,[3] but not over the quality of the printing; while Q appears to be an accurate text, and is our only source for a number of lines, it contains many misprints and the punctuation is weak.

There is evidence that it was printed from an imperfectly corrected manuscript rather than a playhouse copy. Speech headings are irregular. In the debate over the burial of Mutius (1.1.341 ff.) Q does not specify which lines are to be spoken by which of Titus's sons; Saturninus is sometimes designated as 'King' or 'Emperor', Tamora is sometimes 'Queene' and Aaron is frequently 'Moore'. It is unlikely that such inconsistencies would long stand uncorrected in the playhouse, where some of them could be a source of confusion. Greg characterised some of the stage directions as 'descriptive and literary, very much what we should expect from an author not connected with the theatre',[4] but these explicit stage directions are not so much literary as detailed. Perhaps the author, hoping to sell his play, wanted to persuade a manager that *Titus Andronicus* would be cheap and easy to stage, or to ensure that the players clearly understood how he wished it performed.[5]

The clearest evidence of revision is the sacrifice of Alarbus. In 1.1, Marcus says Titus has returned,

> Bleeding to Rome, bearing his valiant sons
> In coffins from the field, *and at this day*,
> *To the Monument of that Andronicy*
> *Done sacrifice of expiation*
> *And slaine the Noblest prisoner of the Gothes.*[6]

Despite Bolton's spirited plea for their retention, emending 'that *Andronicy*' to read 'the Andronici' and 'at this day' as 'at this door',[7] these lines are generally thought to have been superseded by revision; after writing them, Shakespeare decided to stage the sacrifice, presumably to emphasise Tamora's motive for her hatred of Titus. The

---

[1] A 'device' is an emblematic figure which printers used on title pages. They are catalogued in R. B. McKerrow, *Printers' and Publishers' Devices in England and Scotland 1485–1640*, 1949.

[2] See pp. 9–10 above.

[3] See Stanley Wells and Gary Taylor, with John Jowett and William Montgomery, *William Shakespeare: A Textual Companion*, 1987, p. 209.

[4] Greg, *Problem*, p. 117.

[5] See Appendix 1, pp. 167–8 below; also Wilson, p. 91.

[6] See 1.1.35 n.

[7] Joseph S. G. Bolton, 'A plea for 3 ½ rejected Shakespearian lines', *SQ* 23 (1972), 261–3.

incident interrupts the funeral; without it, line 150 would smoothly follow line 95. The revisions were careless: Shakespeare neglected to strike out the redundant lines (italicised above) and to add Alarbus to the stage direction which describes Titus's entrance with his prisoners (1.1.69 SD).

There are other signs of second thoughts. Wells develops a suggestion of Dover Wilson's that the killing of Mutius is an addition: if the episode were omitted, there would be a smooth transition from 1.1.286 to 1.1.299, retaining only Titus's line, 'Follow, my lord, and I'll soon bring her back' (289). And since, as Wells points out, 'people are usually dead before they are buried', the burial of Mutius might also be an afterthought.[1]

Maxwell and Dover Wilson have noted apparent repetitions of phrasing between 1.1.294, 343, 300 and 344, suggesting careless revision; but these are only echoes. More convincing is a duplication in 4.3, when Titus twice asks the Clown whether he can deliver a supplication to the emperor with a grace;[2] Waith's Oxford edition goes so far as to omit lines 102b–109. According to Greg, the 'typographical arrangement' at 89–91 suggests that the gag, 'From heaven? Alas, sir, I never came there. God forbid I should be so bold to press to heaven in my young days', was a marginal addition to the Clown's speech,[3] quite probably by Shakespeare. Maxwell further suggests that 5.2.44–59 may be an addition; Titus recognises 'Rape' and 'Murder' here, yet appears to have forgotten their identities at 5.2.61. This is not unassailable evidence, however: after all, Titus is mad at this point in the play. Nevertheless, there is enough solid evidence of revision to show that Q was in all probability set from foul papers; we need not emulate the disintegrators and find revisions everywhere.

Q2 (1600)

Title page: The most lamenta- / ble Romaine Tragedie of *Titus* / *Andronicus*. / As it hath sundry times beene playde by the / Right Honourable the Earle of Pembrooke, the / Earle of Darbie, the Earle of Sussex, and the / Lorde Chamberlaine theyr / Seruants. / [Ornaments] / AT LONDON, / Printed by I.R. for Edward White / and are to bee solde at his shoppe, at the little / North doore of Paules, at the signe of / the Gun. 1600.

Q2 was set from Q by an alert compositor who noted, and cut, the redundant lines about the sacrifice of Alarbus (following 1.1.35). Joseph S. G. Bolton says that he corrected five of Q's misprints, made thirteen new errors, and initiated twenty-eight minor variations.[4] These are of several types. Where Q is corrupt, an emendation is offered: the substitution of 'embrewed heere' for the meaningless 'bereaud in blood' appears to be an unfounded guess, but he had enough classical education to see that Q 'Tytus Raies' should read 'Tytans raies' (1.1.226) and 'Priamus' is 'Piramus' misprinted (2.3.231). Sometimes the compositor corrected Shakespeare's grammar: 'thy wits wants

---

[1] Wells, pp. 99–102.
[2] See commentary on 4.3.95–114.
[3] Greg, *Folio*, p. 204.
[4] Bolton, p. 766.

edge' becomes 'thy wit wants edge' (2.1.26) and 'thy annoy' is emended 'thine annoy' (4.1.49). He was right, but his aims differed from ours: he wanted a correct text, we want an authentic one.

Many variations are deliberate; they make sense, but are unnecessary: 'you Gothes' for 'your Gothes' (1.1.122), 'our' for 'your' (1.1.224), 'I doe' for 'doo I' (1.1.477). Some change the meaning: 'thou'lt do thy message' for 'my message' (4.1.117), for example; Lavinia's plea, 'Do thou entreat her show a woman's pity' (2.3.147), is altered to read 'show a woman pity'.

This was no ordinary compositor. Even in 1600, copies of Q cannot have been as plentiful as blackberries, since the only one available appears to have sustained some damage to the last two or three leaves of sig. K, where the end of the play was printed.[1] The last six lines of sig. K4 ʳ seem to have been partially or completely illegible, obliging the compositor to guess. One word of 5.3.163 was defaced; Q2 substitutes 'matter' for 'story'. The remaining five lines were sufficiently obscured to prevent him from reading any part of them, or even detecting the speech heading for Marcus at 166. Someone, presumably in the printer's shop, saw that five lines were needed and proceeded to write them, attributing them all to Lucius:

> Meete, and agreeing with thine Infancie:
> In that respect then, like a louing Childe,
> Shed yet some small drops from thy tender Spring,
> Because kinde Nature doth require it so:
> Friends, should associate Friends, in Greefe and Wo.

On the verso of the same leaf, he was unable to read the beginning of the word 'ravenous' (194) and substituted 'hainous'. Five lines later, at the end of the text in Q, only the beginning and the last word were legible, so he composed a new middle:

> And being dead let birds on her take pittie (199)

becomes

> And being so, shall haue like want of pitty.

On this side of the leaf, he was unable to see that this was the end, and consequently went on to compose four more lines:

> See Iustice done on *Aron* that damn'd Moore,
> By whom our heauie haps had their beginning:
> Than afterwards to order well the state,
> That like events may nere it ruinate.

He was no Bard, this compositor or editor; but Shakespeare was not at his brightest and best at the end of Act 5. Greg suggests that even if the editor of the Folio was aware that the lines were spurious, he might have preferred them: 'The editor of Q2 did

---

[1] Bolton (pp. 776–80) suggested this theory; see also R. B. McKerrow, 'A note on *Titus Andronicus*', *The Library*, 4th ser., 15 (1934), 49–53.

his work skilfully and his reconstruction is in no obvious way inferior to the original. Particularly at the end it might be thought that lines had been deliberately added to provide for Aaron.'[1]

The extent of these changes suggests that the worst damage to Q was sustained by leaf κ4, but leaves κ2 and κ3 may have been mutilated as well. The stage direction at 5.2.25, where Q reads *Trumpets sounding*, is altered to *Sound trumpets* in Q2, which also has *placing the meate on the table* instead of Q *placing the dishes*. Overleaf, in Q Titus says, 'Why there they are, both bakèd in this pie', which Q2 changes to 'that pie' (59). Both alterations, however, can be easily explained as the sort of editorial emendations the Q2 compositor liked to make; the substitution of 'that' for 'this' is in line with his penchant for correcting Shakespeare's grammar. Here, Q's leaf κ2 may not have been damaged, but κ3 was probably effaced in the bottom inner corner where lines 92–6 are printed on the recto and lines 129–32 on the verso. On the former, the beginnings of lines were affected, and on the latter, the endings; here again, the Q2 editor supplied the deficiencies.[2]

Maxwell identifies another sector of possible damage at the top of Q, sig. 14, which 'involves only one word in each of the two lines concerned, but since the two words are in precisely the same position on recto and verso, there must have been an injury here too'.[3] Here, Q refers to Titus's 'brain-sick humours' while Q2 has 'brain-sick fits' (5.2.71). On the verso Q reads, 'Well shalt thou know her', and Q2, 'Well maist thou know her' (5.2.106).

Q3 (1611)

Title page: [Ornament] / THE / MOST LAMEN- / TABLE TRAGEDIE / *of Titus Andronicus*. / *AS IT HATH SVNDRY* / *times beene plaide by the Kings* / Maiesties Seruants. / [Device, McKerrow 284] LONDON, / Printed for Eedward White, and are to be solde / at his shoppe, nere the little North dore of / Pauls, at the signe of the / Gun. 1611.

The third quarto has no authority. It was set up from Q2 by a compositor who was careless enough to omit two whole lines (3.1.35, 4.4.102). Most of his deviations from the Q2 text are obvious typographical errors, but a few correct Q2's mistakes: he substitutes 'brothers' for 'bothers' (4.2.36), 'Thou' for 'Thon' (5.2.19), 'trenches' for 'trenchers' (5.2.23). There are a few attempted emendations: both Q and Q2 render 'fair-faced' as 'fairefest', which Q3 emends as 'fairest' (4.2.68). 'Lauicious' (Q, Q2) he emends as 'Lasciuious', which is correct, but probably not what Shakespeare wrote.[4] Deliberate emendations are few, prosaic, and frequently wrong: 'Good' for 'God' (4.2.51) robs the Nurse of a touch of homely dialect, and 'But' for Aaron's 'Tut' (5.2.150) is flat and uninteresting.

---

[1] Greg, *Folio*, p. 209.
[2] See collation of 5.3.92–6 and 129–32.
[3] Maxwell, p. xiii.
[4] See commentary on 2.3.110.

F (1623)

The First Folio appears to have been set from Q3, but there are three major variations. Act divisions have been introduced; the text contains an entirely new scene (3.2); and the stage directions vary considerably from those in the quartos.

Since none of the quartos has act or scene divisions, the division of the F text into acts (but not scenes) is likely to be the result either of a 'classicising' policy on the part of the F editor or a change in playhouse practice. The division between Acts 1 and 2 does not seem to have been part of Shakespeare's original scheme. When everyone else leaves the stage, the Q stage direction is *Exeunt. Sound trumpets, manet Moore*. Aaron remains behind for his soliloquy, 'Now climbeth Tamora Olympus' top . . .' After *Exeunt*, the F editors have inserted the division, *Actus Secunda*, followed by *Flourish. Enter Aaron alone*. Evidently Shakespeare meant the action to be continuous, which suggests that at the time of the play's composition, audiences were not necessarily given frequent intervals.

The new scene (3.2) illustrates the madness of Titus without advancing the dramatic action. Stylistically it seems maturer than the rest of the play, and the fact that speech headings give *An*. throughout, instead of *Titus*, is slight but objective evidence that it was written at a different, presumably later, time. While the action flows smoothly from 3.1 into 4.1, the insertion of 3.2 creates an awkward transition between 3.2 and 4.1 unless the former is followed by an interval.[1] This suggests that the scene may have been added after the interval custom was established.

Since 3.2 is not in Q, it cannot have been included in Shakespeare's manuscript. It was probably written after Q went to press, in order to exploit a vogue for mad scenes in the theatre. If its source is the theatre, it is likely to have come to the editors of F in a prompt-book belonging to the King's Men. But since the rest of the F text was primarily set from a copy of Q3, it follows that the editors collated Q3 with the prompt-book.

The Folio includes a line attributed to Marcus, 'Yes, and will Nobly him remunerate' (1.1.398), which appears in none of the quartos. There is also a short line after 4.1.36, 'What booke?', which makes no contextual sense. Waith explains the latter as a compositor's error, 'caused by glancing ahead to l. 41'.[2] The former, however, may be an authentic line which was in the original manuscript but was carelessly omitted by the Q compositor, as 3.1.35 and 4.4.102 were omitted by the Q3 compositor. It can only have come to F by way of the prompt-book.

Collation with a playhouse text is also suggested by the Folio's tendency to normalise speech headings. Bolton finds twenty-seven altered without change of speaker: thus, at several points, *Moore* becomes *Aron; Queene* is emended as *Tamora, King* as *Sat.* and *Puer* as *Boy*.[3] Many stage directions also appear to have been taken from a prompt-book. The first in the Folio text begins with a *Flourish* that is not in Q; it also adds the phrase *at the other* (door) and alters Q *Drums and Trumpets* to *Drums & Colours*. At 1.1.18 it adds the information that Marcus enters *aloft* with the crown, and specific business is

---

[1] See Appendix 1, p. 173 below.
[2] Waith, p. 40.
[3] Bolton, p. 771.

added at several other points: a table is to be brought in for the final banquet, an *Exeunt* and *Manet Lucius* are added, one speech is explicitly identified as an aside, and when Quintus falls into the pit after Martius, the Folio (inaccurately) adds *Boths fall in.*[1] There are many new or modified music cues. Seven flourishes are added,[2] the fourth to cover a stage wait (*A long Flourish till they come downe*). Another flourish and *Hoboyes* are substituted for trumpets at different points (4.2.48, 5.3.25). While the Q stage directions may represent Shakespeare's intentions, those in the Folio are probably taken from a prompt-book and therefore represent what was actually done in the playhouse, presumably with the author's sanction. In that case, the Folio directions may represent Shakespeare's second thoughts, and could therefore be taken as authoritative.

If we accept that the Folio text was printed from Q3 collated with a prompt-book, it would be helpful if we could know the nature of the latter. It could have been a scribal transcription of Shakespeare's manuscript, or a marked copy of any of the quartos. In any case, 3.2 would have been added in manuscript. Greg points out that an editor who was careful enough to collate additional stage directions from a manuscript prompt-book ought not to have allowed the Q2 corruptions to stand. 'The only conclusion seems to be, that in this instance, owing presumably to the loss of the original prompt-book, a copy of one of the later quartos had been used and annotated in the theatre, and that this was at the disposal of the printer of F.' In a note he adds, 'F was . . . printed from Q3, but if it was Q2 that was used by the prompter, his notes may have been transcribed into a copy of Q3 for use at press.'[3] Elsewhere he adds, 'there is no reason to suppose that in 1623 the company possessed any other prompt-book than a printed quarto in which one scene had been inserted in manuscript'.[4] The original manuscript prompt-book might have been lost in the Globe fire of 1613.

Dover Wilson takes issue with Greg, arguing that the presence of Q2 and Q3 errors in the Folio text is not inconsistent with the use of a manuscript prompt-book. The editor would know, of course, that 3.2 had to be set from the prompt-book, but his only other serious concern would be the stage directions 'which, to judge from the treatment of the other F texts, he felt it incumbent upon him to bring up to date; and this he could easily do by running his finger down the margins and copying into the quarto the prompter's additions to the original s.D.'s'.[5] He did not read the prompt-book text, so he would overlook discrepancies. This view of the editor's practice appears to be confirmed by the Folio stage direction at 2.2.10, which reads, *Wind Hornes. Heere a cry of houndes, and winde hornes in a peale* . . . Greg and Wilson agree that the duplication might result from collation. The editor may have read the prompter's music cue in the margin of the prompt-book, and then appended the Q3 stage direction to it.[6] It might be argued that if this was the editor's procedure, he would not have noticed and restored 1.1.398, which is missing from the quartos. Wilson counters: 'I claim that as

---

[1] 5.3.25, 2.4.10, 3.1.286, 4.4.34, 2.3.245.
[2] 1.1.1, 1.1.63, 1.1.149, 1.1.233, 1.1.398, 5.1.165, 5.3.15.
[3] Greg, *Problem*, p. 120.
[4] Greg, *Folio*, p. 208.
[5] Wilson, p. 97.
[6] Greg, *Problem*, p. 176; Wilson, p. 96.

the exception which proves the rule. For stage-directions are thick on the page at that point, while the line in question is followed by a particularly elaborate direction at the head of which he has copied in a "Flourish" taken from the prompt-book. He could hardly have missed the presence of an additional line at that point.'[1]

Hinman attributes the printing of the whole Folio text of the play except the first page, which is printed on sig. cc4, to Compositor E, the least accurate of the F compositors.[2] But Greg identifies only two compositors working on the entire First Folio,[3] while T. H. Howard-Hill disputes some of Hinman's analysis[4] and A. C. Partridge effectively questions the validity of compositor analysis based on spelling habits.[5] It is difficult, therefore, to guess whether the miscellaneous differences between Q3 and the Folio are attributable to editorial policy, compositor error or playhouse practice. For example, F omits five lines found in Qq. While no loss of sense results from the omission of 2.1.101 or 5.3.52, there is no obvious reason to cut them, either. Aaron's 'Villain, I have done thy mother' (4.2.76) might have been censored, but its omission makes nonsense of Demetrius's reply. At 4.2.8 the Folio omits the speech heading and first line of an aside by Young Lucius: thus his speech is attributed to Demetrius, and makes no sense. And the omission of the last line of a speech by Titus (5.2.161) erodes the sense of Publius's subsequent line.

Most changes from Q3 are obvious typographical errors, but a few appear to be deliberate corrections of errors like 'mournining', 'gooly Lady' and 'ingratude' (1.1.70, 261, 447). A few others may be well-meant but unsuccessful attempts at correction: 'yelping' for 'yellowing', 'scowle' for 'scrowl' (2.3.20, 2.4.5). Like Maxwell, I have accepted an emendation at 5.2.18, where the Folio substitutes 'Wanting a hand to give it action' for 'give that accord' in the quartos; but I cannot accept the substitution, no doubt equally deliberate, of 'things' for Q3 'Armes', which at least makes sense of a sort. At 5.2.150 the Folio restores Aaron's 'Tut', emended in Q3 as 'But', which also makes sense in the context; this may be a minor example of the editor collating from a prompt-book.

---

[1] Wilson, p. 97.

[2] Charlton K. Hinman, *The Printing and Proof-reading of the First Folio of Shakespeare*, 2 vols., 1963, 11, 157.

[3] Greg, *Folio*, p. 457.

[4] T. H. Howard-Hill, *A Reassessment of Compositors B and E in the First Folio Tragedies*, 1977.

[5] A. C. Partridge, *Orthography in Shakespeare and Elizabethan Drama*, 1964.

APPENDIX 1
TITUS ANDRONICUS AT THE ROSE

Titus Andronicus is a young man's play. The young poet's hand is equally evident in lush Ovidian conceits and pedestrian dialogue. The young playwright is uneven in his characterisation, passionate about Lavinia's pathos, alternately frigid and inspired in Titus's suffering, and melodramatically exuberant as Aaron wallows in evil. In the process, Shakespeare plainly enjoys himself. And when an actor carries the audience with him as he plays Aaron to the hilt, or a crunching-bone effect fells the stalls like ten-pins, a modern theatre company shares the young dramatist's zest. *Titus Andronicus* is great fun to play.

In the later twentieth century, Shakespeare's first tragedy has returned to the living repertoire and proved that it can be effective theatre. The secret, I think, is that a company must believe in the play. To do that, they must concentrate on what is best in it. While we occasionally glimpse young Shakespeare's promise as a dramatic poet or a creator of believable characters, it is his stagecraft that is consistently brilliant. He is frequently perceived as a poet by nature, reluctantly compelled to earn his bread in the playhouse. *Titus Andronicus* challenges that view. The author is no word-drunk young poet wrestling ineptly with the complicated technicalities of the theatre. Indeed, he seems more like an accomplished theatrical craftsman struggling with verse. This struggle is most conspicuous in Act 1, which may be Shakespeare's earliest writing to survive. The quality of its verse has cast doubt upon its authorship even amongst some who accept the authenticity of the rest of the play. But the stagecraft of Act 1 is beyond the capacity of Peele or Marlowe. Its mastery of space, movement and grouping is characteristic of Shakespeare, resembling his mature use of these devices as dramatic metaphors for theme and meaning. Perhaps Shakespeare was a dramatist by nature, who subsequently learned to be a poet.

The question of stagecraft can tell us something about the playhouse for which Shakespeare wrote *Titus Andronicus*. This has become a matter of particular interest because it was part of the short season Philip Henslowe presented in June 1594. The playhouse was probably the Rose, which has recently been excavated. *Titus Andronicus* is thus the only play by Shakespeare to have been performed in a playhouse of which parts, at least, survive. While a section of the foundations of the second Globe (1614) has also come to light, there is little to see, pending further excavation.

Titus Andronicus is an ambitious attempt by a young dramatist who wants to achieve a lot, but knows he must make do with a little. As a new writer hoping to sell his tragedy, he shrewdly asks for the minimum and makes the most of what is already there. If we read it from Henslowe's point of view, *Titus Andronicus* plainly says, 'This play will be cheap to mount; it uses everything in the Rose, but it asks for nothing you don't already have.'

Before the first line of Act 1 is spoken, Shakespeare uses all the manpower and space at his disposal to establish dramatic conflict between ceremony and violence. Senators and tribunes 'aloft' (0 SD.1) represent the accumulated dignity of *Senatus populusque Romanus*. Below, symmetrical entrances balance tension between the rivals, reinforced by ceremonious processions of their factions with drums and trumpets.[1] Ironically, their formal rhetoric prompts a conflict that shatters the decorum; swords are out when Marcus enters with the crown (17 SD). Instantly, the uproar ceases and the audience is aware that this man has authority. The effect anticipates Othello's line to Brabantio, Roderigo and the Officers: 'Keep up your bright swords, for the dew will rust them' (1.2.59). Marcus's line is reinforced by a strong entrance aloft, between the dignitaries, while everyone below must turn upstage and look up at him.

Shakespeare has little to learn about the use of contrast for dramatic effect. The crowd trickles away, to enter again *as many as can be* in a Roman triumph designed to support the dignity of Titus. Two funerals, a coronation and a royal wedding follow, alternating with Bassianus's 'rape' of Lavinia, the violent death of Mutius, and the ironically ceremonious violence of a human sacrifice. Roman pomp thinly disguises a barbarism rivalling the Goths'. For all its ritual and custom, the sacrifice of Alarbus is primitive, like the man who orders it. While Rome's new emperor has the cruelty of a degenerate, Titus is like some austere *paterfamilias* of the early Republic. His gruff but dignified rejection of the symbolic 'palliament' foreshadows the Republican hero Coriolanus. In both plays, Rome is at war with herself, but while Marcius's antagonist is a mob with character, the crowds in *Titus Andronicus* have none: they are animated dummies in a pageant of civilisation that lends irony to the clash between primitive and degenerate cruelties.

When Shakespeare wrote *Coriolanus* the King's Men were numerous enough to let him allocate actors to small speaking roles in the mob. But *Titus Andronicus* was probably designed to be performed by as few as fourteen men and boys,[2] either on a tour or at the Rose, where excavation has revealed an unexpectedly small stage. A cast of fourteen would have looked like a crowd there; it was a playhouse built for small companies. The anonymity of the crowds allowed an actor to double repeatedly, appearing as a supporter of Bassianus, leaving the stage to swell Titus's triumph, and returning later in a speaking role such as Lavinia. It is likely that Shakespeare meant the 'Romans' and the 'people and sons of Rome' addressed in Acts 1 and 5 (1.1.203; 5.3.66, 127, 134, 146) to be represented by the audience. No one else is available. This economical stagecraft first draws us into the conflict and at length allows us to participate in a stern restoration of order that foreshadows the conclusions of such later plays as *Romeo and Juliet*.

---

[1] In this edition it is assumed that Q SDs give Shakespeare's original intentions, and that those in F come from his company's prompt-book, and hence represent what was actually done in the playhouse, probably with his sanction.

[2] See Appendix 2, pp. 174–5 below.

The quarto text contains more explicit stage directions (*He cuts off Titus' hand*)[1] than most subsequent works, possibly because Shakespeare was not a leading member of a company of players. If he could not count on directly influencing rehearsals, he may have used stage directions to tell the players how he wanted his tragedy staged. Thus he has left us useful information about the form and conventions of the playhouse at a comparatively early stage of its development. *Titus Andronicus* serves as a dramatic inventory of the resources at the disposal of an Elizabethan theatre company: their manpower, playhouse, properties, costumes, music and stage conventions.

The quarto and Folio texts are designed for a playhouse with playing areas on three levels. The play begins with tribunes and senators entering 'aloft', where Marcus soon joins them with the crown.[2] Marcus and Lucius address the Romans from here in Act 5 (5.3.66–144), visually recapitulating the first image to 'frame' the play. Here Lucius is crowned, and order is restored in Rome. Ironically, Saturninus scuttles aloft when drawn swords shatter the ceremonies of Act 1 (1.1.299); an emperor who dares to taunt Titus only from a safe height will be too weak to govern.

Verbal stage directions are dialogue words that require actions or objects on stage ('Get me a ladder'). One of these shows that Titus's 'study' is 'aloft'. Like Lear, who retreats to prison with Cordelia after 'the great rage ... is killed in him', he withdraws to this lofty cell when his madness has been spent in futile arrows. But, just as Edmund's henchmen breach Lear's cell to drag him back to suffering, Tamora and her sons tempt Titus with revenge. Her speech as he descends (5.2.70–80) is not meant for his ears; apparently the main stage level was accessible from 'aloft' by stairs within the tiring-house that took eleven lines (perhaps thirty seconds) to negotiate.

The space 'aloft' could accommodate at least five actors: Marcus, plus several senators and tribunes.[3] But the text neither calls for them to move nor to address each other: they relate only to players on the stage below. This is how the shallow, dark, railed gallery depicted in the 'de Witt drawing' would have to be used (see illustration 10). This drawing is a copy of a Dutch tourist's sketch of the interior of the Swan (*c.* 1596). Since it is our only picture of a playhouse interior in Shakespeare's time, it has been the subject of much discussion;[4] but in the absence of other visual evidence, we cannot reject its testimony. The shallow gallery would be worthless as an 'upper stage' where real scenes could be played; actors could only line the rail and look down.

The sketch gives no indication whatever that there was an 'inner stage' between the two doors in the tiring-house façade at the Swan, which was built in 1595. The Rose was built in 1587–8 and enlarged in 1592. There is little reason to suppose that its facilities were more advanced than those of the later playhouse. The excavated foundations tell us nothing about stage entrances, but the wording of stage directions may be significant.

---

[1] The Q SD; 6F adds 'left'.
[2] The F SD specifies that Marcus enters 'aloft', but Q does not say where he enters.
[3] The plural implies at least two senators and two tribunes: see Appendix 2, pp. 174–5 below.
[4] See Allardyce Nicoll, 'Studies in the Elizabethan stage since 1900', *S.Sur.* 1 (1948), 1–15; C. Walter Hodges, *The Globe Restored*, 1953; Leslie Hotson, *Shakespeare's Wooden 'O'*, 1960; Andrew Gurr, 'The Shakespearian stages, forty years on', *S.Sur.* 41 (1989), 1–2.

12 The de Witt sketch of the Swan playhouse

In the quarto, the first reads '*enter* Saturninus *and his followers at one dore, and* Bassianus *and his followers*' (1.1.0 SD.1–3); the Folio adds *at the other*. Later in Act 1, a quarto stage direction tends to confirm the evidence of the first; printed in two columns, it reads:

Enter the Emperour, Tamora	*Enter at the other doore*
and her two sonnes, with the	*Bascianus and Lauinia,*
Moore at one doore.	*with others.*

(1.1.398 SD.2–4)

More evidence comes from a quarto direction in Act 4: '*Enter* Aron, Chiron *and* Demetrius *at one doore, and at the other doore young Lucius, and another with a bundle of weapons, with verses writ upon them*'. If a discovery space or third door *had* been available, the stage directions would have read *another doore*, not *the other doore*. Nowhere does the action require either an inner stage or a third entrance, unless one was used as the tomb in Act 1.

Even assuming that a third entrance existed, had Shakespeare used it for the tomb he would have failed to take advantage of an opportunity to exploit space for thematic effect. The 'detested, dark, blood-drinking pit' into which two of Titus's sons fall in Act 2 can only be a trap; they can hardly fall into an inner stage. Since this lowest acting level was evidently available at the Rose, it surely doubled as the tomb where two other sons of Titus are buried in Act 1. The ironic visual link between the honourable grave of the Andronici and the base snare manufactured by Aaron would function like Shakespeare's use of the level 'aloft'. It is hard to believe that he would have overlooked this opportunity and blocked one of his main entrances to boot.

In *Titus Andronicus* the main stage is a neutral space transformed, in the spectator's imagination, into a forest (2.3) or the interior of Titus's house (5.3) as dialogue or action suggests. In Shakespeare's later plays these 'scene changes' normally occur only when the stage is cleared, but here the convention is more flexible. Early in Act 1 the tiring-house represents the Capitol, with the tomb before its gates; at line 333, however, the tiring-house has become the Pantheon, yet the tomb is still there (349ff.). In the quarto there are no act divisions; Aaron remains on the stage to rebuke Tamora's sons for brawling 'So near the emperor's palace' (2.1.46). Dialogue has changed the scene once more.

Shakespeare experiments with this convention. Dialogue paints the scene, then alters it. Tamora describes an idyllic forest:

> The birds chant melody on every bush,
> The snakes lies rollèd in the cheerful sun,
> The green leaves quiver with the cooling wind
> And make a chequered shadow on the ground . . .   (2.3.12–15)

A few lines later the aspect of the place has changed:

> A barren detested vale you see it is;
> The trees, though summer, yet forlorn and lean,
> Overcome with moss and baleful mistletoe;
> Here never shines the sun, here nothing breeds
> Unless the nightly owl or fatal raven . . .   (2.3.93–7)

Conventional flexibility had limits. Dialogue cannot paint a scene in thin air. Some of Shakespeare's later plays require special set-pieces which must have been carried on for certain scenes. Olivia's garden in *Twelfth Night* (2.5, 3.4) needs a box-tree; *The Merchant of Venice* cannot be performed without three caskets that answer specific descriptions in the dialogue; and something approximating a 'bank' is required for Jessica and Lorenzo to sit upon (5.1.54–8), or for Lysander and Hermia in *A Midsummer Night's Dream* (2.2.40). In *Titus Andronicus*, however, Shakespeare asked for nothing special to be built; he relied upon words to transform the physical features of the playhouse into the scenery he needed. Perhaps when Saturninus called on the tribunes and senators to 'open *the gates* and let me in' (1.1.62, my italics), double doors like those illustrated by de Witt swung open. Aaron could say he was burying gold 'under a tree' (2.3.2) because there was something concrete that could *become* a tree: de Witt shows columns on-stage at the Swan, and columns seem to have been installed at the Rose when it was reconstructed, probably in 1592.[1] Whether these were an innovation or were already standard features of the playhouse, the young dramatist turned them to good effect.

Properties are few and commonplace: a table, stools and dishes for the banquets, a basket and pigeons for the Clown (4.3.76 SD), a ladder for Aaron (5.1.53). These and the tools, bows and arrows used by Titus's kinsmen in 4.3 could be found in any yeoman's cottage. Their archery, awkward and dangerous in today's theatre, might have been simpler at the Rose, where the players could aim 'a mile beyond the moon' and shoot their arrows right out of the unroofed playhouse, to the surprise of passersby (see illustration 1, p. 2 above). It is to be hoped that no sharp arrowheads were used.

Shakespeare takes care to have his 'props' set and 'cleared' from the stage by actors. Lucius orders his Goths to fetch the ladder, and Titus himself carries on the 'dishes' containing the fatal pie (5.3.25 SD.2). Corpses are carried off. Verbal stage directions require Chiron and Demetrius to remove the body of the Nurse (4.2.163–5). The human bits and pieces that litter the stage at the end of 3.1 are all borne away by actors:

> Come, brother, take a head,
> And in this hand the other will I bear;
> And Lavinia, thou shalt be employed in these arms;
> Bear thou my hand, sweet wench, between thy teeth.   (3.1.278–81)

Ingenuity could scarcely go farther.

In a play which calls for so little in other respects, violence appears to make considerable demands on the special effects department. Realistic violence is the bloodstream of *Titus Andronicus*: six people are stabbed to death on-stage, Lavinia bleeds from her stumps and mouth, Tamora's sons have their throats cut and Lavinia collects the blood in a bowl. It is possible that in an Elizabethan playhouse these effects were regarded as routine, any 'prop shop' would have severed heads in stock, and the on-stage lopping of Titus's hand was all in a day's work. Plays of the period, from *Cambyses* to *'Tis Pity She's a Whore*, are full of gruesome stage business.

The Longleat drawing (illustration 2, p. 15 above) suggests that the costume inventory would include Roman dress, but historical consistency was considered

[1] See pp. 5–6 above.

unnecessary. Armour and weapons are Elizabethan, and while Tamora dresses roy-
ally, there is nothing Gothic in her attire. Everything could be 'pulled from stock'.
Even the costumes worn by Tamora and her sons as Revenge, Rape and Murder (5.2)
might have been available; allegory could still be seen in the public playhouse. Faustus has his Seven Deadly Sins and his Good and Evil Angel, and Revenge appears as
Chorus, with Andrea's ghost, in *The Spanish Tragedy*.

Music plays a significant part in *Titus Andronicus*. Stage directions in the texts
call for a variety of instruments: drums, trumpets, horns and 'hoboyes'. Ceremony is
underscored by music, which falls silent as savagery prevails. Early in the play, rivalry
for the crown, the triumph, funeral, coronation and hunt all require musical effects. In
contrast, the central scenes are devoid of music, except for the trumpets that ironically
announce the birth of Tamora's bastard (4.2.48 SD). Music resumes with the coming of
Lucius and the Goths, and emphasises ceremony at the final banquet.[1] But the tragedy
ends without a note: Lucius is acclaimed only with shouts. Flourishes have proven
empty.

Titus Andronicus may contain a clue to a change in stage practice. The fact that 3.2
was printed for the first time in the Folio, as well as its relatively sophisticated verse,
suggests that it is a later addition, perhaps to exploit a vogue for mad scenes. The
transition to 4.1 is awkward. Titus and Young Lucius exit with Lavinia to read in
her closet, which implies that Marcus leaves by the other door. Next Young Lucius
runs on, pursued by Lavinia; they meet Marcus and Titus, who evidently enter by
the other door. Shakespeare avoids bringing actors on for another scene immediately
after an exit. This re-entry requires a clumsy backstage regrouping, aggravated by the
attendants who would have to 'strike' the properties used in the 'banquet' and rush
into the tiring-house with their burdens just in time to collide with actors regrouping
for their entrance in 4.1.

This is decidedly odd. The journeyman Shakespeare contrived smooth transitions
between acts, but as an experienced craftsman adding a scene years later, he seems to
have forgotten his skill. Perhaps playhouse customs had changed; where action had
flowed continuously when *Titus Andronicus* was new, an interval was now inserted
between Acts 3 and 4, precisely where a modern audience would expect it.

---

[1] The F SD replaces the bastard's trumpets with a flourish, and adds a flourish for the exit of Lucius and the
Goths.

APPENDIX 2
PERFORMANCE BY A SMALL COMPANY

This scheme shows how *Titus Andronicus* could be performed by a company of fourteen men and boys. I do not suggest that the characters were ever allocated in precisely this way, either in Shakespeare's time or any other. As a spectacle it would not have been impressive. However, it is possible without eliminating any characters called for by the text.

The scheme is based on two practical principles. First, when the text calls for plural senators and tribunes, there is no absolute requirement that the players furnish more than two of each. Second, the conventions of Shakespeare's theatre did not call for perfect illusion: actors could double parts, so long as they were able to leave the stage

	ACT 1			ACT 2			
Scene	1.1–69	Triumph	70–end	1	2	3	4
Actor							
1	—	Titus	Titus	—	Titus	—	—
2	—	Aaron	Aaron	Aaron	—	Aaron	—
3	Marcus	Marcus	Marcus	—	Marcus	—	Marcus
4	Saturninus	Saturninus	Saturninus	—	Saturninus	Saturninus	—
5	Bassianus	Bassianus	Bassianus	—	Bassianus	Bassianus	—
6	Saturninus's follower	Mutius	Mutius	—	Attendant	Attendant	—
7	Saturninus's follower	Lucius	Lucius	—	Lucius	—	—
8	Bassianus's follower	Martius	Martius	—	Martius	Martius	—
9	Bassianus's follower	Quintus	Quintus	—	Quintus	Quintus	—
10	Senator	Tamora	Tamora	—	Tamora	Tamora	—
11	Senator	Alarbus	Lavinia	—	Lavinia	Lavinia	Lavinia
12	Tribune	Chiron	Chiron	Chiron	Chiron	Chiron	Chiron
13	Tribune	Demetrius	Demetrius	Demetrius	Demetrius	Demetrius	Demetrius
14	Captain	Captain	—	—	Attendant	Attendant	—

long enough to change costumes. Contemporary audiences cheerfully accept as much: I have seen the same man play Polonius and the First Grave-digger.

A player who appears as a senator or a follower of Bassianus early in Act 1 can return as Lavinia or Martius, and can swell the triumph without straining convention. In the same way, an actor who plays a character who dies early in the play need not sit in the tiring-house for the rest of the performance, but can return in another part later in the play. Sempronius and Valentine are doubled because it is possible that Shakespeare changed the name of a character.

On the other hand, Titus can hardly double, because he is central, and appears in almost every scene; and Aaron's make-up prevents him from appearing in any other part.

The fourteen actors are represented by numbers in the left-hand column. Remaining columns represent the scenes of the play. 1.1.1–69 and the triumph are counted as separate scenes for this purpose. The part an actor plays in each scene is named. If he does not appear, a name is replaced with a dash.

ACT 3		ACT 4				ACT 5		
1	2	1	2	3	4	1	2	3
Titus	Titus	Titus	—	Titus	—	—	Titus	Titus
Aaron	—	—	Aaron	—	—	Aaron	—	Aaron
Marcus	Marcus	Marcus	—	Marcus	Marcus	Marcus	Marcus	Marcus
—	—	—	—	—	Saturninus	—	—	Saturninus
Judge	—	—	—	Publius	Aemilius	Aemilius	Publius	Aemilius
Judge	—	—	—	Sempronius	—	Goth	Valentine	Goth
Lucius	—	—	—	—	Attendant	Lucius	—	Lucius
Martius	—	—	—	Caius	—	Goth	Caius	Goth
Quintus	Young Lucius	Young Lucius	Young Lucius	Young Lucius	—	Goth	—	Young Lucius
Senator	—	—	—	—	Tamora	—	Tamora	Tamora
Lavinia	Lavinia	Lavinia	—	—	—	Goth	Goth	Lavinia
Tribune	—	—	Chiron	—	Chiron	—	Chiron	Tribune
Tribune	—	—	Demetrius	—	Demetrius	—	Demetrius	Tribune
Senator	—	—	Nurse/ Clown	—	Clown	Goth	—	Attendant

READING LIST

This list comprises books and articles which the editor has found useful in preparing the Introduction. The reader may wish to use it as a guide to further study of *Titus Andronicus*.

Aebischer, Pascale. *Shakespeare's Violated Bodies: Stage and Screen Performance*, 2004
Barker, Francis. *The Culture of Violence: Essays on Tragedy and History*, 1993
Bate, Jonathan. *Shakespeare and Ovid*, 1993
Bennett, Susan. *Theatre Audiences: A Theory of Production and Reception*, 1997
Bevington, David. *Action Is Eloquence: Shakespeare's Language of Gesture*, 1984
Blumenthal, Eileen, and Julie Taymor. *Playing with Fire*, 1999
Bolton, Joseph S. G. 'The authentic text of *Titus Andronicus*', *PMLA* 44 (1929), 765–88
Bradbrook, M. C. *Themes and Conventions of Elizabethan Tragedy*, 1933
Braunmuller, A. R. 'Early Shakespearian tragedy and its contemporary context: cause and emotion in *Titus Andronicus, Richard III* and *The Rape of Lucrece*', in *Shakespearian Tragedy* (*Stratford-upon-Avon Studies* 20), 1984, pp. 97–128
Brooke, Nicholas. 'Marlowe as provocative agent in Shakespeare's early plays', *S.Sur.* 14 (1961), 34–44
    Shakespeare's Early Tragedies, 1968
Broude, Ronald. 'Roman and Goth in *Titus Andronicus*', *S.St.* 6 (1970), 27–34
Brown, John Russell. *New Sites for Shakespeare: Theatre, the Audience and Asia*, 1999
Brucher, Richard T. ' "Tragedy, laugh on": comic violence in *Titus Andronicus*', *Renaissance Drama*, ns, 10 (1979), 71–91
Buhler, Stephen M. *Shakespeare in the Cinema: Ocular Proof*, 2002
Bulman, James C. (ed.). *Shakespeare, Theory and Performance*, 1996
Bulman, J. C., and H. R. Coursen (eds.). *Shakespeare on Television. An Anthology of Essays and Reviews*, 1988
Burt, Richard (ed.). *Shakespeare after Mass Media*, 2002
Calderwood, James L. *Shakespearean Metadrama: The Argument of the Play in 'Titus Andronicus', 'Love's Labour's Lost', 'Romeo and Juliet', 'A Midsummer Night's Dream' and 'Richard II'*, 1971
Cartmell, Deborah. *Interpreting Shakespeare on Screen*, 2000
Danson, Lawrence. *Tragic Alphabet: Shakespeare's Drama of Language*, 1974
David, Richard. 'Drams of eale', *S.Sur.* 10 (1957), 126–34
Davidson, Clifford. 'A reading of *Titus Andronicus*', *Susquehanna University Studies* 11 (1976), 93–100
Davies, Anthony, and Stanley Wells (eds.). *Shakespeare and the Moving Image: The Plays on Film and Television*, 1994

Delgado, Maria M., and Paul Heritage (eds.). *In Contact with the Gods? Directors Talk Theatre*, 1996

De Sousa, Geraldo U. *Shakespeare's Cross-Cultural Encounters*, 1999

Dessen, Alan C. *Rescripting Shakespeare: The Text, the Director and Modern Productions*, 2002

Shakespeare in Performance: 'Titus Andronicus', 1989

'Two falls and a trap: Shakespeare and the spectacles of realism', *ELR* 5 (1975), 291–307

Eliot, T. S. 'Seneca in English translation', *Selected Essays*, 2nd edn, 1934

Engle, Ron, Felicia Hardison Londré and Daniel J. Watermeier (eds.). *Shakespeare Companies and Festivals: An International Guide*, 1995

Enterline, Lynn. *The Rhetoric of the Body from Ovid to Shakespeare. Cambridge Studies in Renaissance Literature and Culture*, 35, 2000

Ettin, Andrew V. 'Shakespeare's first Roman tragedy', *ELH* 37 (1970), 325–41

Evans, Bertrand. *Shakespeare's Tragic Practice*, 1979

Fawcett, Mary Laughlin. 'Arms/words/tears: language and the body in *Titus Andronicus*', *ELH* 50 (1983), 261–77

George, David. 'Shakespeare and Pembroke's Men', *SQ* 32 (1981), 305–23

Hamilton, A. C. '*Titus Andronicus*: the form of Shakespearean tragedy', *SQ* 14 (1963), 201–13

Hansen, Iorgen Wildt. '*Titus Andronicus* and logos', *Orbis Litterarum* 31 (1976), 110–24

Hatchuel, Sarah. *Shakespeare: From Stage to Screen*, 2004

Hattaway, Michael, Boika Sokolova and Derek Roper (eds.). *Shakespeare in the New Europe*, 1994

Hazlitt, William. 'Doubtful plays of Shakespeare', *Characters of Shakespeare's Plays*, 1817

Hill, R. F. 'The composition of *Titus Andronicus*', *S.Sur.* 10 (1957), 60–70

Hoenselaars, Ton (ed.). *Folio: Shakespeare – Genootschap van Nederland en Vlaanderen*, Jaargang 4, Nummer 2, 1997

Hogan, Charles Beecher. *Shakespeare in the Theatre 1701–1800: Volume 1: A Record of Performances in London 1701–1750*, 1952

Hulse, S. Clark. 'Wresting the alphabet: oratory and action in *Titus Andronicus*', *Criticism* 21 (1979), 106–18

Hunter, G. K. 'Shakespeare's earliest tragedies: *Titus Andronicus* and *Romeo and Juliet*', *S. Sur.* 27 (1974), 1–9

James, Heather. 'Cultural disintegration in *Titus Andronicus*: mutilating Titus, Virgil and Rome', in *Violence in Drama, Themes in Drama*, James Redmond (ed.), 13 (1991), pp. 123–40

Shakespeare's Troy: Drama, Politics, and Translation of Empire, Cambridge Studies in Renaissance Literature and Culture, 22, 1997

Johnson, Samuel. *Johnson on Shakespeare*, ed. Walter Raleigh, 1908

Jones, Eldred D. 'Aaron and melancholy in *Titus Andronicus*', *SQ* 14 (1963), 178–9

Kahn, Coppélia. *Roman Shakespeare: Warriors, Wounds and Women*, 1997

Karr, Judith M. 'The pleas in *Titus Andronicus*', *SQ* 14 (1963), 278–9

Kennedy, Dennis. *Looking at Shakespeare: A Visual History of Twentieth Century Performance*, 1993

(ed.). *Foreign Shakespeare: Contemporary Performance*, 1993

Kolin, Philip C. (ed.). *Titus Andronicus: Critical Essays*, 1995

Kott, Jan. *Shakespeare Our Contemporary*, 1965

Leggatt, Alexander. *Shakespeare's Tragedies. Violation and Identity*, 2005

Lehmann, Courtney. 'Crouching tiger, hidden agenda: how Shakespeare and the Renaissance are taking the rage out of feminism', *SQ* 53 (2002), 260–79

Loomba, Ania. ' "Delicious traffick": alterity and exchange on early modern stages', *S. Sur.* 52 (1999), 201–14

Gender, Race, Renaissance Drama, 1989

Shakespeare, Race and Colonialism, 2002

Marshall, Herbert, and Mildred Stock. *Ira Aldridge, the Negro Tragedian*, 1968

McCandless, David. 'A tale of two *Titus*es: Julie Taymor's vision on stage and screen', *SQ* 53 (2002), 487–511

Metz, G. Harold. 'The date of composition of *Titus Andronicus*', *N&Q* 223 (1978), 112–17

'A stylometric comparison of Shakespeare's *Titus Andronicus*, *Pericles*, and *Julius Caesar*', *SNL* 29 (1979), 42

'Stage history of *Titus Andronicus*', *SQ* 28 (1977), 154–69

Shakespeare's Earliest Tragedy: Studies in 'Titus Andronicus', 1996

Miola, Robert S. 'An alien people clutching their Gods'? Shakespeare's ancient religions', *S.Sur.* 54 (2001), 31–45

Muir, Kenneth. *Shakespeare's Tragic Sequence*, 1972

Murray Kendall, Gillian. ' "Lend me thy hand": metaphor and mayhem in *Titus Andronicus*', *SQ* 40 (1989), 299–316

Nevo, Ruth. 'Tragic form in *Titus Andronicus*', in A. A. Mendilow (ed.), *Further Studies in English Language and Literature*, Jerusalem, 1973, pp. 1–18 (Scripta Hierosolymitana 25)

Palmer, D. J. 'The unspeakable in pursuit of the uneatable: language and action in *Titus Andronicus*', *The Critical Quarterly* 14 (1972), 320–9

Parrott, T. M. 'Shakespeare's revision of *Titus Andronicus*', *MLR* 14 (1919), 16–37

Price, H. T. 'The authorship of *Titus Andronicus*', *JEGP* 42 (1943), 55–81

Pughe, Thomas, 'Loyal to Shakespeare? Friedrich Dürrenmatt's and Heiner Müller's adaptations of *Titus Andronicus*', *Shakespeare Worldwide: Translation and Adaptation 13* (Yushodo Shoten Ltd, Tokyo, 1991)

Reese, Jack E. 'A formalization of horror in *Titus Andronicus*', *SQ* 21 (1970), 77–84

Ribner, Irving. *Patterns in Shakespearian Tragedy*, 1960

Rosenthal, Daniel. *Shakespeare on Screen*, 2000

Rothwell, Kenneth S. *A History of Shakespeare on Screen. A Century of Film and Television*, 2nd edn, 2004

Rothwell, Kenneth S., and Annabelle Henkin Melzer. *Shakespeare on Screen: An International Filmography and Videography*, 1990

Rowe, Katherine A. *Dead Hands: Fictions of Agency, Renaissance to Modern*, 1999
  'Dismembering and forgetting in *Titus Andronicus*', *SQ* 45 (1994), 297–303
Rutter, Carol Chillington. 'Looking like a child – or – *Titus*: the comedy', *S.Sur.* 56
  (2003), 1–26
Schafer, Elizabeth. *MsDirecting Shakespeare. Women Direct Shakespeare*, 1998
Schlegel, Augustus William. *Lectures on Dramatic Art and Literature*, trans. John Black,
  1879
Scuro, Daniel. '*Titus Andronicus*: a crimson-flushed stage!', *Ohio State University The-*
  atre Collection Bulletin 17 (1970), 40–8
Sher, Antony, and Gregory Doran. *Woza Shakespeare! 'Titus Andronicus' in South Africa*,
  1996
Simmons, J. L. 'Shakespearean rhetoric and realism', *The Georgia Review* 24 (1970),
  453–71
Sommers, Alan. ' "Wilderness of tigers": structure and symbolism in *Titus Andronicus*',
  EIC 10 (1960), 275–89
Spencer, T. J. B. 'Shakespeare and the Elizabethan Romans', *S.Sur.* 10 (1957), 27–38
Starks, Lisa S., and Courtney Lehmann (eds.). *The Reel Shakespeare. Alternative Cinema*
  and Theory, 2002
Střibrný, Zdeněk. *Shakespeare and Eastern Europe*, 2000
Taymor, Julie. *'Titus': The Illustrated Screenplay*, 2000
Tempera, Mariangela. *Feasting with Centaurs: 'Titus Andronicus' from Stage to Text*,
  1999
Thompson, Ann. 'Philomel in *Titus Andronicus* and *Cymbeline*', *S.Sur.* 31 (1978), 23–32
Thomson, J. A. K. *Shakespeare and the Classics*, 1952
Traversi, Derek. *An Approach to Shakespeare I: 'Henry VI' to 'Twelfth Night'*, 3rd edn,
  1969
Tricomi, Albert H. 'The mutilated garden in *Titus Andronicus*', *S.St.* 9 (1976), 89–105
Ungerer, Gustav. 'An unrecorded Elizabethan performance of *Titus Andronicus*', *S.Sur.*
  14 (1961), 102–9
Velz, John W. 'The ancient world in Shakespeare: authenticity or anachronism? A
  retrospect', *S.Sur.* 31 (1978), 1–12
Vickers, Brain. *Shakespeare, Co-Author: A Historical Study of Five Collaborative Plays*,
  2002
Vickers, Nancy J. 'Diana described: scattered woman and scattered rhyme', *Critical*
  Inquiry 8 (1981–2), 265–79
  ' "The blazon of sweet beauty's best": Shakespeare's *Lucrece*', in Patricia Parker
    and Geoffrey Hartman (eds.), *Shakespeare and the Question of Theory* (1985),
    pp. 95–115
Waith, Eugene. 'The metamorphosis of violence in *Titus Andronicus*', *S.Sur.* 10 (1957),
  39–49
Wells, Stanley. 'Shakespeare performances in London and Stratford-upon-Avon, 1986–
  87', *S.Sur.* 41 (1988), 159–81
Werstine, Paul. 'Narratives about printed Shakespeare texts: "foul papers" and "bad"
  quartos', *SQ* 41 (1990), 65–86

West, Grace Starry. 'Going by the book: classical allusions in Shakespeare's *Titus Andronicus*', *SP* 79 (1982), 62–77

White, Jeannette S. ' "Is black so base a hue?": Shakespeare's Aaron and the politics of race', *CLA Journal* 40 (1997), 336–66

White, Martin. *Renaissance Drama in Action: An Introduction to Aspects of Theatre Practice and Performance*, 1998

White, R. S. *Innocent Victims: Poetic Injustice in Shakespearean Tragedy*, 2nd edn, 1986

Wilbern, David. 'Rape and revenge in *Titus Andronicus*', *ELR* 8 (1978), 158–82

Willis, Susan. *The BBC Shakespeare Plays: Making the Televised Canon*, 1991

Willis, Deborah. ' "The gnawing vulture": revenge, trauma theory, and *Titus Andronicus*', *SQ* 53 (2002), 21–52

Wilson, J. Dover. '*Titus Andronicus* on the stage in 1595', *S.Sur.* 1 (1948), 17–22

Wynne-Davis, Marion. ' "The swallowing womb": consumed and consuming women in *Titus Andronicus*', in Valerie Wayne (ed.), *The Matter of Difference: Materialist Feminist Criticism of Shakespeare*, 1991, pp. 129–53